1767931

WITHDRAWN

Soviet Ideologies in the Period of Glasnost

SOVIET IDEOLOGIES IN THE PERIOD OF GLASNOST

Responses to Brezhnev's Stagnation

VLADIMIR SHLAPENTOKH

with the participation of
DMITRY SHLAPENTOKH

PRAEGER

New York
Westport, Connecticut
London

Library of Congress Cataloging-in-Publication Data

Shlapentokh, Vladimir.
  Soviet ideologies in the period of glasnost : responses to Brezhnev's stagnation / Vladimir Shlapentokh with the participation of Dmitry Shlapentokh.
      p. cm.
      Bibliography: p.
      Includes index.
      ISBN 0-275-92671-0 (alk. paper)
          1. Soviet Union—Politics and government—1953-1982.   2. Soviet Union—Politics and government—1982-   3. Soviet Union—Social conditions—1970-   4. Soviet Union—Economic conditions—1976-
I. Shlapentokh, Dmitry.   II. Title.
DK274.S414   1988
947.085—dc19   88-5878

Copyright ©1988 by Vladimir Shlapentokh

All rights reserved. No portion of this book may
be reproduced, by any process or technique, without
the express written consent of the publisher.

Library of Congress Catalog Card Number: 88-5878
ISBN: 0-275-92671-0

First published in 1988

Praeger Publishers, One Madison Avenue, New York, NY 10010
A division of Greenwood Press, Inc.

Printed in the United States of America

The paper used in this book complies with the
Permanent Paper Standard issued by the National
Information Standards Organization (Z39.48-1984).

10 9 8 7 6 5 4 3 2 1

To my dear friends
Zhenia and Aron Katsenelinboigen

Contents

Acknowledgments		ix
Introduction		xi
Chapter 1	The Role of the Consumer: The Main Problem of Soviet Society	1
Chapter 2	Privatization: The Response to the Poor Evaluation of Performance	31
Chapter 3	Soviet Society in the Early 1980s	61
Chapter 4	The Political and Ideological Situation before 1985: The Search for a Solution	75
Chapter 5	Conservative Ideology	87
Chapter 6	Neo-Stalinist Ideology	105
Chapter 7	The History of Liberal Ideology	125
Chapter 8	Gorbachev's Ideology: A Version of Liberal Authoritative Ideology	145
Conclusion		185
Selected Bibliography		189
Index		205

Acknowledgments

I would like to express my gratitude to Aron Katsenelinboigen, Vladimir Kontorovich, and Robert Solo for regular discussions of the ideas that make up the core of this book.

I am very thankful to Mr. Andrew Marshall for support of this project as well as to the Department of Community Health Science of MSU which was very benevolent to my research.

I am deeply grateful to Alison Bricken, acquisition editor at Praeger, for her endorsement of the project and her patience when dealing with me. My special gratitude to Noreen Norton, senior project editor, and Charles Naylor, copy editor, for their editing of my manuscript.

Without their permission, I also want to give my thanks to the brilliant Soviet sociologists Iurii Levada and Boris Grushin, whose ideas influenced my work.

Introduction

In the mid-70s Soviet society entered a period of stagnation and decline in practically all spheres. The depth of the decline of Soviet economy, culture, science, as well as morals, was by all accounts well known already at the end of the 70s to the political elite, with its secret sources of information, as became clear to the intelligentsia and the masses in 1983–1987 when, after Brezhnev's death, the Soviet mass media gradually began to disclose the more interesting data on the state of Soviet society.

In fact, what Soviet society experienced in the 70s and 80s was typical, practically, for all the socialist countries, which in one way or another were also plunged into deep economic and social troubles subsequent to the relatively short period after the revolution or liberation from German occupation. By the mid-80s the crisis of socialism as a social system, at least as it functioned in the USSR, China, Eastern Europe, Cuba, and Vietnam, especially as that of a centrally planned economy, became a fact not to be denied by even those who were in the past its admirers. The bettering of the reputation of market economies in Third World countries, like Mozambique and Tanzania, among others, who considered themselves to be socialist societies, is only one indicator of this radical change in world mentality.

The internal economic, social, and moral crisis in the USSR unavoidably generated various ideologies that offered their own programs for transforming society and coping with existing problems. These ideologies came into fierce conflict with each other, and the outcome of these conflicts would have tremendous impact on the evolution of Soviet society, as we here understand the ideology, along with the established traditions—the more or less cohesive set of values and beliefs that determine the goals of human activities at various levels (individual, group, societal) and the moral standards for human behavior (see Kluckhohn 1951, Geertz 1973; see also Shlapentokh 1986). Regarding ideology as a set of directives for activity as well as the means for rationalizing human behavior, the author of course does not share the views that ideology can be in fashion or obsolete simply because social life is impossible without it. Certainly, this fact becomes especially evident in a period of sharp political and social conflicts when the participants have to reveal their social goals as well as criteria for evaluating human behavior, as was the case in Moscow in the mid-80s.

The author makes a distinction between public and internal (inner party) ideologies as well as between official ones, that is, those endorsed by the ruling political elite, and unofficial ideologies. This distinction is very helpful in analyzing the convoluted ideological developments in the USSR where the political leaders publicized only a part of their goals and motives, and where official Marxist ideology is faced with various other visions of the present and future.

The author sees as his task in this book to delineate the character of the processes in the USSR that led to the stagnation of the Soviet economy and the lowering of morals, and to analyze various ideological responses to these developments.

The author attempts to approach developments in the Soviet Union, both at the level of "objective reality" and of the "subjective world" of the Soviet people on the basis of a concept that puts the evaluation and rewarding of human performance at the center of social analysis. In the author's opinion, the main problems of a Soviet-type society stem from its failure to evaluate and reward human work on its merits and from its tendency to stimulate bad performance and conformism.

Not only did the founders of so-called "scientific communism" (Marx and Engels) not consider this problem to be important when they compared capitalism and socialism, but also the founders of the Soviet state and its subsequent leaders paid no great attention to it. This issue has been largely neglected by students of socialist society in the West. Only recently have Soviet intellectuals begun to push this problem to the foreground in their analysis of their society. It was supposed that administrative control over human performance, based on hierarchical principle and ideological fervor, would be efficient enough to mobilize human energy and intellect for the creation of a new society. It saw the strong belief in the capacity of the state not only skillfully to allocate resources and determine what should be produced but also to control human performance from top to the bottom. However, it turned out that a command society—socialism of the Soviet type—can not solve this task without the active participation of consumers: consumers of all sorts, including those served by politicians, judges, or journalists. Russia, like any other country, has no chance to escape this.

In analyzing the response of a society of the Soviet type to its failure to evaluate and reward human performance in accordance with official goals, the author focuses on the process of privatization. In his view, the diminishing of participation in activity controlled by the state together with the growing role of informal groups and private business (along with the growing trend of exploitation of rank for private interests at the expense of the state), is the most important process taking place in Soviet society in the post-Stalin era. This process has significantly aggravated crucial problems in Soviet society and put its survival in jeopardy (the concept of privatization is also discussed in the author's book *Public and Private Life of the Soviet People* 1988).

The author considers three major ideological alternatives offered by the political elite as ways out of the stagnation and illegal privatization of society: one conservative (Brezhnevian) and two dynamic (neo-Stalinist and liberal-Marxist). The ideology espoused by Gorbachev's regime is scrutinized with special attention. This ideology started as neo-Stalinist and evolved in a short period of time into a liberal-Marxist one.

This book is based on various sources of information on ideologies in the USSR: Soviet official materials; mass media—including Soviet TV (which became accessible to the author in 1987), sociological studies, literature and movies, as well as foreign sources, including the Western press; emigrant publications; and others.

The first two chapters of the book are devoted to the analysis of the "objective" processes which led Soviet society to its critical situation toward the middle of the 80s, when Gorbachev offered his program for solving the major Soviet problems. In Chapter 1 the author analyzes the role of the consumer in Soviet history as a key to many of the society's peculiarities, whereas in Chapter 2 he dwells on the privatization of this society in the post-Stalin era. Chapters 3 and 4 deal with the economic, political, and ideological situation in the country in the early 80s.

Chapters 5 and 6 are devoted to conservative ideology, with its justification of the last two decades' stagnation and to neo-Stalinist ideology as the first program offered by a faction of the political elite for overcoming this crisis, while Gorbachev's ideological revolution is discussed in Chapters 7 and 8 and in the conclusion.

Soviet Ideologies in the Period of Glasnost

Chapter 1

The Role of the Consumer: The Main Problem of Soviet Society

Socialist society of the Soviet type, that is, based on the Stalinist model, manifests its strength in the first decades after its installation. Only in this period can the political elite manage to fulfill many of its proclaimed goals and radically change society.

The emergence of the new order—through a genuine revolution or in another way—creates a unique situation that can last only a limited period of time. In this period the political elite can mobilize the most active part of the population and submit its energy to the needs of the state, bringing about the coordination of social and individual goals in a way extremely favorable to the state.

At this point, something broke in the Soviet system, and it entered the process of gradual privatization, the withdrawal of the energy and interests of the active part of the population from public to private pursuits. People started to attain their personal goals not through conscientious service to the state and leadership but through means that could only damage the interests of society. The privatization of the bureaucracy, of the party and state apparatus, was certainly a leading element in this process. The central power for a number of reasons turned out to be unable to halt or even slow this process, which had broad repercussions for all segments of society.

Then, unavoidably, the system entered a period of rapid economic, technological, and intellectual stagnation, when the gap between the socialist countries and the West started to grow, bringing many consequences which include the growing gap between human aspirations and the state's resources, the ossification of the bureaucracy, the spread of corruption, the decline of labor ethics, and the growth of cynicism.

What are the causes of the degeneration of the Soviet system which looked so vigorous and strong at the beginning? Ultimately, the weakness of this system manifested itself in the first place in a floundering, inefficient and technologically backward economy. Indeed, if with all its other flaws—the disregard of human needs, even mass repression—the Soviet economy were technologically advanced and prosperous, the question of the backwardness of Soviet society would not have emerged; it would have arisen neither for the Soviet political elite nor for the supporters of the idea of socialism and social equality.

Certainly, inefficiency became the illness not only of the economy but of all other spheres of social life—science, culture, medical service, even propaganda. In other words, the Soviet people at all levels of the hierarchy, from minister to rank and file, turned into bad workers whatever their area of professional activity.

An analysis of the inefficiency of Soviet society and of the myriad of various problems generated by it is necessary for understanding the character of various ideologies, which in the 80s have offered programs for overcoming the economic, social, and moral crisis in the USSR.

THE EVALUATION OF PERFORMANCE (EP)—THE CENTRAL ECONOMIC AND SOCIAL ISSUE

Our analysis of the problem in Soviet society will be based on four elements of a model of human action: the decision of the character of the action, the action itself, the evaluation of its performance, and the reward for it. In the author's opinion, it is the third element which plays the leading role in determining the efficiency of human performance. This element explains the major differences in the efficiency of different social systems.

From this perspective it is fruitful to consider human social processes as the interaction between producers and consumers, using these terms very broadly. It is assumed that the individual functions as a producer of various goods and services—from material goods to cultural work to political services. Indeed, his actions as a member of society, based on the division of labor, can be regarded as oriented to the satisfaction of the needs of "others."

The major concept that underlies this book suggests that the paradigm "producer-consumer" is applicable to all spheres of human activity and that EP in political, cultural, economic and other subsystems ultimately depends on the consumer's influence on the production of goods and services, including those which are provided by politicians, journalists, the military, scholars, writers, and, of course, those who produce "consumer goods" in the narrower sense of the term.

The crucial characteristic of society (as well as any other organization) is the mechanism for evaluating producers' performance, which includes as an important component the reward, negative or positive, for the performance. It is the organization of the negative reward—the sanctions for bad performance—which exerts a special impact on the efficiency of producers.

The evaluation of performance offers a seminal perspective for the analysis of societies because it allows discussion of their efficiency in all (not only in economic) spheres within the same theoretical framework. In fact, the EP approach demonstrates that the flaws in all segments of the Soviet system stem from the same source: the almost complete autonomy of producers from consumers, whether we take the party and state apparatus, health service, or industry. In no way do I want to suggest that the mechanism of EP is the sole independent variable responsible for the differences in efficiency of societies in their activities for the achievement of their own specific, proclaimed goals, whatever they may be (military might, high standard of living, social equality or another). Political order, economic structure, and cultural traditions are only the most important variables which directly, and not only through the EP mechanism, influence the efficacy of a system in the attainment of its goals.

The critical (and not secondary) role of consumers in the evaluation and reward of performance has been until now almost completely ignored by students of Soviet society belonging to various schools of thought (see, for instance, Bialer 1986, Byrnes 1983, Colton 1987, Hill 1985, Hoffman and Laird 1985, Kelley 1986, Lane 1985, Pipes 1983).

Even experts on the Soviet economy do not put the role of consumers in the fore of their analyses of Soviet economic malaise, mentioning them at best among many other factors accountable for it (see, for instance, Gregory and Stewart 1974).

Janos Kornai (1986) (and to some degree Alex Nove, 1980) represents the outstanding exception in this respect. Unlike others he puts in the center of his analysis of socialist economics the relationship between producers and consumers, defining capitalism as a "demand-constrained system" and socialism as a "resources-constrained system." According to his theory, the reason for low quality in production lies in the competition between enterprises—consumers of investment goods and raw materials, which are moved by the desire for expansion and of possessing a practically unlimited amount of money (the "soft budget constraint"), and grab everything the producers can give them.

However, in an economy of the Soviet type the bulk of the investment goods are distributed by planning agencies, and the freedom of enterprises to obtain resources is limited, even if one takes into account the role of various informal and even illegal methods for their procurement (especially concerning the time spent getting needed raw materials or semifinished goods). Therefore, the role of the competition between consumers of investment goods and consequently of the "soft budget constraint" is not very high.

Against the application of Kornai's theory explaining the low quality of the Soviet economic performance, there is also the fundamental fact of the existence and growth of stocks of unsold goods in the Soviet economy. Meanwhile, the stocks of unsold goods, in both retail and wholesale trade, as well as in industry, in 1985 amounted to almost one-third of the value of retail sales in the country. This represents a significant increase since 1940, when the figure was less than 20 percent (TSU 1986, p. 474).

What is more, all the other sectors of Soviet society besides the economy—science, health service, and culture—also produce products of low quality which is impossible to attribute to the competition between consumers and all the more to a "soft budget constraint."

Agreeing with Kornai about the lack of consumer control in a society of the Soviet type, I try to link the low efficiency of Soviet society, not to excessive financial possibilities of consumers, but to the political nature of this society, which can only exert administrative control over human performance.

I try to suggest here that major problems of Soviet society, in particular, the relatively low standard of living and technological retardation, should not be accountable to the fact that the political elite devoted too much attention to political and military goals. Of course, the militarization of the Soviet economy bears significant responsibility for the many problems of Soviet society, and all other things being equal, a decrease in military expenditures would have serious positive effects on the Soviet quality of life.

However, as Nikolai Shmelev aptly remarked in his famous article in 1987, "The causes of our difficulties are not only and even so much the heavy burden of military expenditures and the very expensive global responsibility of the country. Reasonable use of the remaining material and human resources could be enough for maintenance of a balanced economy oriented to technological progress and the satisfaction of the traditionally modest social needs of our population" (Shmelev 1987, p. 144).

The low efficiency of Soviet industry and agriculture, science, and health service is mostly the direct result of a defective mechanism of EP: the incorrect assessment of human work and improper public reaction to bad performance.

The analysis of the differences in economic organizations in most cases revolved, until recent times—both in the West and in socialist countries—around two issues: the stimulation of work and the advantages or disadvantages of central planning versus the market in decision-making processes, that is, around the autonomy of the producer.

However, both these issues with all their importance can be considered, as will be shown later, as the variables (along with some others) the importance of which depends mostly upon their level of influence on the mechanism of EP.

It happened that the best mechanism of EP could be created by a system in which the consumer, and not the superior of the producer, calls the shots and passes final judgment on his work. It turned out that the consumer can get such possibilities only in a society based on the principles of democracy. These principles are important not only for the political subsystem of a society—political freedom, election of government and direct participation in the political decision-making process through voting, referendums, polls—but also for all other spheres of society guaranteeing the ordinary individual the ability to influence, mostly as a consumer, the activity of producers of goods and all sorts of services. In other words, the major merit of democracy from this perspective lies in its capacity to involve the whole population, even if in a very unequal way, in the control of human performance in all spheres of social life.

Analyzing the causes of the numberless crimes and errors in Soviet politics after the revolution, Sergei Zalygin, a prominent Soviet writer, directly relates them to the absence of public opinion which in the context of 1987 was a synonym for democracy. "No," he exclaims, "we have not achieved that genuine democracy where public opinion directs the activity of any institution, and if it determines, also controls it and appoints and removes the leaders of an institution. . . . Perhaps, almost all the disasters of Soviet society," he continues, "all the transformations of villages into agrocities, and the appearance of 'the queen of the fields'—corn" (an allusion to Khrushchev's infatuation with corn after his trip to America), "and impotent heroes of labor five times awarded medals—all this stems from the violation of rational, open relationships between state, institution and society" (Zalygin, 1987, pp. 233–34).

CENTRAL PLANNING AND THE EVALUATION OF THE QUALITY OF DECISIONS

Indeed, central planning and in general the central administration of a command society can theoretically guarantee the reasonable, if not optimal, allocation of resources, and theoretically probably even better than the market. The computerization of management and the use of mathematical methods can only perfect the mechanism of central planning. In fact, if good decisions can be taken by the directors of big corporations, why can it not be the case with such a gigantic corporation as Soviet society? The theories which propose approaching Soviet society as a big corporation are not groundless (see Meyer, 1965).

The argument against central planning that the planning body cannot systematically obtain information concerning consumers' demands (this argument was actively used by Soviet "market economists" in the 60s against the advocates of optimal planning) as well as concerning the potential of producers is not convincing, especially now that it is possible to use computers for this purpose. It is also theoretically invalid to insist that central planning bodies are incapable of knowing the "internal reserves" of single enterprises. Such information is absent not because of the planning as such but because consumers do not play any serious role in a society controlled by the political elite.

The minuses of central planning are certainly not found in its ability to take decisions which affect the whole society and the economy in particular (such decisions, for instance about the interest rate are made as well in a "pure" capitalist economy), but in the absence of a mechanism that can publicly evaluate the quality of decisions and punish the authors of bad ones. Being the direct instrument of the political elite which holds a monopoly on power, central planners are exempt, as are their bosses, from any criticism.

Theoretically speaking, if it were possible to make central planning "democratic," as has been presented in Soviet textbooks (see, for instance, Fedoseev, 1985), and if the central planning bodies were not controlled by organs like the Politburo, but by consumers (if it were possible), then it would be possible to mitigate or even eliminate the major flaws of a command society and the discussion of the comparative merits of planning and market would acquire a new perspective—the position of planning would not have been as hopeless as it is now.

Meanwhile, as the history of socialist society suggests, planning mistakes have been discovered and recognized publicly only at best after the damage to the economy was already done. Soviet history is full of planning blunders, miscalculations, and negligence of various sorts and of a total impunity of those who commit them.

Planning mistakes of a great scale have usually been divulged by the succeeding regime. Khrushchev denounced a number of the economic decisions made by Stalin's administration. Brezhnev's regime blamed most of Khrushchev's economic decisions as "voluntaristic," in particular in agriculture. Gorbachev did not spare criticism for Brezhnev's planning decisions and rejected many of them, for instance, the project to reroute Siberian rivers to the south—despite the tremendous expenditures already made for the implementation of the project.

There were also cases when mistakes in planning were admitted by the same regime as committed them, but again the critique took place when the damage had already been done.

Of no less importance is the fact that very rarely have those responsible for planning mistakes been seriously punished. Most chairmen of Gosplan have held their positions for many years, whatever have been the results of their activity. Nikolai Baibakov, for instance, served as the chairman of this body twenty years in a row (1965–1985) in addition to an earlier stint of two years (1955–1957). Cases of the removal of any high official for planning mistakes are practically unknown.

No one was punished, for instance, for the adventurous projects carried out by the Ministry of Water Supply with the support of the Academy of Sciences in the 70s and early 80s which were responsible for significant damage to the ecology and economy. However, in 1986–1987 it became obvious that in pursuing its own particular interests—the expansion of its activity—the Ministry had conspicuously disregarded the interests of society.

As Sergei Zalygin wrote, the Ministry of Water Supply "performed the role of consumer-client and producer at the same time. The Ministry chose the objects for building, prepared the projects, carried them out and approved them after completion" (*Novyi Mir* 7 (1987): 225). The same shameless collusion between designers, builders, and consumers, all part of the same Ministry, is underscored by other participants in discussions on ecological issues of 1986–1987, for instance, N. Glazovskii, a professor at Moscow University (see the materials of these discussions in *Nash Sovremennik* 1 (1987): 112–69; *Novyi Mir* 1 (1987): 3–18, and *ibid.* 7 (1987):181–235; see also Leonid Pleshakov's interview with Ivan Silaev, deputy chairman of the Council of Ministers, who recognized the lack of consumer control over the machine-building industry in *Ogoniok* 48 (1987): 2–5).

The same is true in other spheres of Soviet society. Those who have made incorrect decisions in culture or in science were only very rarely punished by the regime that had appointed them for their mistakes in directing their branches. If they had troubles with the leadership it was almost always because of political intrigues. Only the next regime took them to task for their real mistakes. Even in the period of *glasnost*, when Brezhnev's regime was being strongly castigated in the mass media, none of those who were responsible for the wrong decisions were taken to task.

The question of the responsibility of those who directed culture, in particular, the movie industry, in the 70s and early 80s was raised many times during 1985–1987, however, even the most brave heralds of *perestroika* did not even dare to give the names of the officials who shelved good movies. Alexander Lipkov, the author of a very valiant article in *Novyi Mir*, in his analysis of the fate of Aleksei German's films (*Checks at Road Blocks* and *My Friend Lapshin*), could put his finger practically only on those officials in the State Committee of Movie Production who had already been dismissed from their positions (Lipkov 1987). Even Rolan Bykov, the most valorous speaker at the unusually critical Congress of Soviet Film Makers in 1986 (it was the consensus in Moscow that this was the peak of civic courage among intellectuals in the early period of *glasnost*), took to task only one, and a not very high official (the director of the children's film studio) (*Iskusstvo kino* 10 (1986): 35–38).

Gorbachev's regime as well as Khrushchev's fired many apparatchiks appointed by the previous rulers, however both leaders—reformers—did not publicly have anybody punished for a concrete wrong decision.

It is curious that even the harshest critics of socialist economics did not single out the incapacity of a command society to create controls over the performance of producers as a special problem, which at best was only implicitly included in discussions on the role of competition. It is true even of such profound analysts of planned economies as Friedrich von Hayek and Ludvig von Mises, who did not pay serious attention to the evaluation of performance in socialist society nor to the lack of consumer control as a major cause of the inefficiency of such a society.

Speaking about the individual whom planned economy ignores, Hayek had in mind practically only the fact that people could not have any influence on shaping the goals of economic activity, which are set by the omnipotent state. He dismissed the possibility of elaborating the national goals on a democratic basis, through a parliament, for instance, because the government would always be free to implement its own policy. He also pointed out the impossibility of combining central planning with freedoms; he even spoke about the negative consequences of the replacement of monetary rewards with reward in kind—"in the form of public distinctions or privileges, positions of power over other men, or better housing or better food, opportunities for travel or education"—but again he regarded this practice as bad because it narrowed human choice and again did not touch on the effects on the productivity of the recipients of such rewards (Hayek 1944, pp. 56–87, 88–91).

Ludvig von Mises was closer to understanding the role of EP. With his emphasis on the idea that calculating economic activity under socialism to the full scale is impossible, he almost approached the discussion of EP in both types of economies, socialist and capitalist. Yet, on the surface, Mises was wrong when he denied any correlation in socialism between "the magnitude of the share which is assigned for the use of each citizen" and "the value of the service he renders" (Mises 1936, p. 154). As historical experience has shown, socialism managed to introduce a mechanism that could remunerate somewhat people according to their work. However, Mises was in substance right because so far socialism has not been able to make this mechanism effective enough, which is what accounted for the failures of the economy and many other sectors of socialist society. What is more, Mises also realized, unlike many of his contemporaries, that it was impossible to choose people able to evaluate "objectively" the merits of workers and in this way supplant the function of consumers as judges (p. 157).

MATERIAL STIMULATION AND EP

The evaluation of the performance of an individual worker in any organization is carried out by administrators (and not directly by consumers), and in any society the estimates of productivity are far from being ideal. However, in the West, especially in private businesses, managers evaluate the performance of their subordinates having in mind more or less the reaction of consumers. This is not mostly the case in Soviet society where managers are concerned with the attitudes of their superiors and with the formal observations of plan directives. The lack of consumer pressure is the ultimate reason why, as was admitted in the USSR, the existing schemes are mostly ineffective and even counterproductive.

This statement does not imply that Soviet managers (in all those cases where they want to force people to work) cannot find a way to stimulate them. But in many cases (though certainly not in all) when Soviet managers do this, the incentives—from big bonuses to bottles of vodka offered to workers after the completion of a job—are used for the achievement of goals that have little in common with state interests: the formal fulfillment of the plan with total ignorance regarding the quality of the product.

Anatolii Azol'skii's novel *Stepan Sergeievich* (having been rejected for publication in 1969, it came out in 1987) describes the mechanism of stimulation in an experimental electronics plant in Moscow. Anatolii Trufanov, the director, as well as his managers, were able to work miracles in the accomplishment of their official assignments, generously paying workers overtime for jobs (some of the workers could stay in the plant three days in a row), however, in most cases consumers received apparatus of very bad quality, a fact known by all the workers actively participating in the rat race during the last days of any month when completion of the plan is at stake (Azol'skii 1987).

It is only natural that being aware of these weaknesses in their system, Soviet leaders and ideologues have always cherished the idea of the old utopians as well as Marx that for the ideal member of a new society, work for the common cause has to become a primary need, a source of satisfaction in and of itself, which will remove all the complicated problems of stimulating workers. Just because of this, in the period of the Brezhnev stagnation, ideologues with growing energy insisted that the bulk of the working class had already entered the stage of holding a communist attitude toward work (see, for instance, Changli 1978, Ivanova 1983, Blinov 1979, Shkaratan 1978, Klopov 1985).[1]

As has been said, the cause of the failure of material stimulation in the USSR is the lack of control on the part of the consumers over the quality of goods and services produced by any given unit. Since the status of the director of the unit depends on its work only in a minimal way (we will discuss this subject in detail later), his relationship with his subordinates is also determined by various factors among which efficiency often plays only a modest role.

The manager of any Soviet institution and its subunits tends to fill positions with people loyal to him and ready to serve his private interests and who can be trusted to perform semilegal or illegal acts. Trufanov, in Azol'skii's novel, intentionally selects people for managerial positions in his enterprise who have sullied pasts: drunkards or people with a propensity for criminal activity. "With such people Trufanov worked more willingly than with those whose reputations were good." Relying on such people he could even risk deceiving a high military commander who had to accept their products (Azol'skii 1987, v. 1, pp. 52, 69–76).

Being involved in such a coalition with subordinates, the manager is deprived of the possibility of being demanding toward them, toward the quality of their work in the first place. A sort of social contract between the director and his workers is concluded.

The existing incentives did not work even in those cases where managers were really devoted to their work. Very often the evaluation of performance is based on the assessment of intermediary products. This practice was especially strong in agriculture where a tractor driver's performance was measured by the number of acres he processed (plowing or sowing), whatever the harvest later turned out to be, an issue of many decades' discussion in Soviet economic literature (see, for instance, Venzher 1966).

No less detrimental to stimulation was the almost total disregard for the quality of the accomplished work, with quantitative indicators being the main yardstick. Without the direct pressure of consumers, managers in all spheres of society—in industry, health service, mass media, culture, science—are prone to assess the work of the people below them only on the basis of quantitative estimates. The director of a plant producing tractors condones his engineers' and workers' production of machines of such bad quality that collective and state farmers have to repair brand-new vehicles, whereas the director of a publishing house winks at the quality of work when he endorses an evidently mediocre manuscript written by his friend, subordinate, or superior (for more on the tolerance of Soviet publishing houses of authors whose books almost nobody buys, see the materials of the Congress of Writers in the Russian Republic and of the Congress of Writers of the USSR in 1985, *Literaturnaia Gazeta*, December 18, 1985 and June 25, 1986).

The same absence of market pressure makes even honest Soviet managers indifferent to technological progress, to the production of really new models. With the emphasis on the fulfillment of the current plan in quantitative terms, Soviet managers are only reluctantly ready to divert their resources to innovative activity, a subject of perennial complaint to all Soviet leaders in the post-Stalin period (Brezhnev 1971 and 1976, Andropov 1983, Gorbachev 1985, 1986).

PROPERTY, THE RESPONSIBILITY FOR BAD PERFORMANCE

Theoretically it is possible to plan out the economy and other spheres of a society in which enterprises and other units are owned by the state (or by "society") but which are run as autonomous entities with complete dependence on consumers. Some attempts in this direction were made in Hungary and Yugoslavia, but in fact they were only very moderately successful.

Property is the key issue for efficacy of EP because it determines the character of the responsibility for bad performance. A command society relieves officials and managers from the responsibility for losses ensuing from bad decisions and bad work. The numerous attempts of leaders in socialist countries to introduce various forms of accountability into individual enterprises always bumps into property relations, into the fundamental fact that the enterprise belongs to the state and by definition cannot suffer any results for bad performance. The accountability of enterprises to consumers can only be effective if it is combined with the accountability of enterprises to owners.

It is the real owners, and not the state, which have to pay for bad work and bad decisions, and the lack of a mechanism of punishment (this mechanism is more important than the mechanism of positive reward) is in fact the ultimate reason why the deregulation of a planned economy cannot go too far. Even the installation of bankruptcy as an institution of a socialist economy—this idea was vividly discussed in various socialist countries, Hungary and Yugoslavia being pioneers—cannot be an effective response to this problem if it is not combined with the privatization of enterprises, for instance, through the sale of stocks—an idea which is also included in the agenda of reformers in socialist countries. The consistent implementation of both ideas would certainly radically modify a socialist society of the Soviet type as it exists now.[2]

The command societies have tried to use the collective of workers as a surrogate for property owners. The presentation of workers as the masters of their enterprises has always been one of the most important tasks of Soviet ideology (on the official description of the collective see Fedoseev 1985, pp. 214–16, Il'ichev et al. 1983, pp. 264–65, Rumiantsev 1983, pp. 97–101). This myth held out even through the storms of *glasnost* and was supported by Gorbachev himself even if only as a rather desirable idea (see Gorbachev 1986, 1987a, 1987b).

However, even sociological surveys conducted by ideologically committed social scientists found that only a minority of the workers (no more than one-third) even at the verbal level accepted the idea that they were the masters of their factories or state or "collective" farms (see Volkov and

Mukhachev 1976, p. 80, Svininnikov 1985, pp. 109, 123, Plaskii 1982, p. 97, Klopov 1985, pp. 209, 220, Blinov 1979, p. 65).

Describing the Stalinist model which underlies present Soviet society as an "administrative-bureaucratic state power ... not accountable to the people" and speaking about "state property which was represented as belonging to the people," Anatolii Butenko, a prominent Soviet philosopher, writes that "beneath the husk of the powerful centralized directorship of this property its meaninglessness is manifested very clearly: through the lack of real human interests in its control, efficient use, and augmentation" (*Moskovskiie Novosti* 43, 1987, pp. 8–9). Butenko is seconded by I. Korol'kov, a journalist, who wrote about Soviet "bureaucratic centralism," the base of which became "impersonalized—the so-called property of all the people was in fact state property" (*Komsomol'skaia Pravda*, October 23, 1987).

For the same reason, other attempts to sidestep the property constraint, for instance, to set up competition between state enterprises or to make the organs of quality control independent of the administration of the enterprise (so-called "state inspection of finished goods," *gospriemka*, introduced by Gorbachev in 1987), only beg the question because, in all such cases, again it is the state in the person of its representatives, and not consumers, who makes the final decisions on the quality of performance. Nikolai Shmelev reasonably refused immediately to regard "state inspection of finished goods" as a device capable "of revolutionizing industry," as the high Soviet official assigned to this mission, the chairman of the Committee of Standards, emphatically proclaimed (Shmelev 1987, p. 153; about the bureaucratic character of *gospriemka*, see *Literaturnaia Gazeta*, August 5, 1987). In fact, this body again does not directly represent consumers and by definition cannot substitute for them.

For the same reason, competition between Soviet enterprises can have only a limited positive effect on the economy. Like the notorious socialist emulation, it supposes again some state agencies as arbiters in making final decisions on who is better.

The absence of direct and harsh responsibility for performance in a socialist society accounts for the gigantic waste of resources and pilfering of raw materials and goods. As Gorbachev said himself, "State property means in the eyes of many people 'no man's property at all'" (Gorbachev 1987a). According to Soviet official data, the losses of agricultural products in the USSR are no less than one-third of the harvest.

The beneficial effect of private activity in a socialist country is ultimately to be attributed not directly to the rise of the productivity of the workers, but to their real accountability to consumers, which includes the risk of financial losses. At the same time, as soon as the owners of private businesses acquire some monopoly on the market, for instance, through collusion among private enterprises (restaurants or repair shops), or go into cahoots with the state sector (for instance, through the resale of goods made in the state sector), the quality of their work will almost immediately drop to the level of state production.

Kornai, a great expert on the Hungarian economy, ascribes some achievements of the economy in his country mainly to the expansion of the private sector and not to the decentralization of state management. It is the private sector, with its unstifled competition, that injected some stamina into the Hungarian economy (see Kornai 1986).[3]

"PRIVATE INSTINCT" IN SOVIET LITERATURE NOW AND THEN

It is now useful to look back, along with many Soviet authors of 1985–1987, to the 20s and see how painstakingly and methodically the Soviet order destroyed the "property instinct" of peasants and other categories of the population. With what hubris and arrogance the agents of the state suggested in that period how absurd, obsolete, reactionary, and irrational private property was and how obscure and conservative are the people who cherished this instinct.

It is interesting to read now the novels of orthodox Soviet authors written in the 20s and the 30s and to learn how they all spurned private property and the attachment of peasants to their own land, and did not see any advantages in these for society and the economy in particular (see, for instance, Panferov's *Bruski* 1986, Gladkov's *Cement*, 1964, Malyshkin's *People from a Remote Place*, 1957).

It is especially curious to compare these novels with the writings of Soviet authors of the 60s (for instance, Belov's *On the Eve*, Zalygin's *On Irtysh*), and in the first place of course with works published in 1985–1987 when Soviet intellectuals could almost freely lament the destruction of private property and the "private property instinct" during the 20s (see Ananiev, 1987, Streliannyi, 1986, the debates between Tikhonov and Kozhevnikova in *Literaturnaia Gazeta*, April 8, 1987; see also the Soviet TV series "People in a Swamp" [1988], in which the attachment of Belorussian peasants to their property and their resistance to collectivization was depicted with great empathy and compassion).

We find the case to be the same if we compare the attitudes of the authors of the 20s and 30s with those of the 80s toward the roles of the market, money, and consumers in society. It is remarkable how far were those who sincerely believed in the ideals or at least in the triumph of the new social order from understanding the role of consumer control over human performance in the 20s and early 30s. This error was revealed with special clarity in their belief in the superiority of the coordination of human activity by the state, inspired by lofty goals, over the primitive regulation through the market.

Intellectuals who joined the ruling elite in this period by all accounts sincerely believed that the rejection of money, of mercantilist stimuli, would be in and of itself extremely beneficial for society. The idea of control over human performance did not occur to anyone among them.

Fedor Panferov in his novel *Bruski* (it was written between 1928–1937) describes the dialogue between a former red soldier and a bolshevik activist. The first tries to present his idea for becoming a good farmer ("I want to enter communism through an individual, cultural farm") in the aftermath of the civil war as being very useful for the state but stumbles on the crass rejection of this idea as "that of a petty tradesman," as indecent to communism (Panferov 1986, p. 47). Panferov's positive heroes as well as those of Mikhail Sholokhov's *Virgin Soil Upturned* (1932–1960) had no doubt that the collective farm would manage to stimulate in the most efficient way the work of their members.

At the same time, these and other authors greeted the decline of money as the basis for the distribution of consumer goods and hailed social status as the major factor determining access to them. Even to such popular satirical writers as Ilia Il'f and Evgenii Petrov (see their *Twelve Chairs* [1928/1975] and *Golden Calf* [1931/1975]) as aptly noted Benedict Sarnov (1987), this process seemed very progressive and they had no premonition that with money would also disappear relatively effective methods of control over human performance.

THE CONSUMER IN SOVIET DEBATES

The public discussions on the efficiency of the Soviet economic system started after 1953 with debates on material stimulation, an issue politically less controversial than any other.

It was rather the consensus among intellectuals and officials that it was necessary to enhance material incentives. However, already by the middle of the 60s it had become clear that an increase in material reward for performance by itself had been unable to produce a significant rise in productivity and especially in the quality of goods and services. Agriculture demonstrated this first in the most obvious way. The spurt in the monetary income of collective farmers was not accompanied by an adequate increase in productivity (see Shlapentokh 1982c).

With the failure of material stimulation to increase the efficiency of the Soviet system, in particular, of the economy, Soviet sociologists and economists started to look for other factors which could enhance productivity. They advanced various theories on this issue. The theory about the decisive role of the content of the work was the most prominent of them (see Iadov et al. 1967).

Since the late 70s the discussion of the role of material stimulation was renewed, this time concentrating on the upper limit for earnings. Whereas the liberal economists, sociologists, and writers insisted on the removal of any ceilings for honest earnings, conservatives, especially in the party apparatus, wanted to preclude the rise of salaries beyond a very limited level.

It is remarkable that in the discussions since the late 70s we observe growing, if limited, interest in the evaluation of work, which should be stimulated, a subject which was almost completely ignored in the 60s. The praise of the autonomy of small production units in particular, of a team working with its own contract, was linked also to the possibility to better check the quality of the work of each of the team's members. However, the consumer as the major judge of work was still very far off on the horizon.

By the middle of the 60s, with some liberalization in society it had become possible to move to other issues—to the comparative advantages of central planning and market mechanisms.

Both those who insisted on the computerization of management and on the wide application of optimal programming (Aron Katsenelinboigen, Victor Volkonskii, Victor Glushkov, Nikolai Fedorenko, and Abel Aganebegian) as well as the representatives of "market socialism" who advanced the autonomy of the enterprise as the major response to economic problems (Gennadii Lisichkin, Nikolai Petrakov), argued almost exclusively over the quality of economic decisions made by the central planning body or by the individual producer. In the center of this discussion was economic information—the capacity of the planner to collect and process it in time, in particular information about consumer behavior and the rights of managers to make decisions in their enterprises.

Still, in 1987 Igor Moiseev, a prominent Soviet mathematician who since the 60s has been strongly involved in the application of mathematics in economics and sociology, in defiance of the growing prestige of democratic principles contended that for economic success one needs not "private initiative, market, or free trade," but only "the autonomy of managers" (*Nash Sovremennik*, 1, 1987, p. 164).

After Brezhnev, with the renewal of economic discussion, the comparative advantages of decision-making mechanisms were again at the center of attention. However, in 1986–1987 the public discussion still concentrated on both issues mentioned before, gradually beginning to include a new, and separate element—the mechanism of the evaluation of human performance, in particular in the decision-making process, which was discussed in the past only in passing.

The growing role of this new dimension in economic debates was the direct result of the understanding in the 70s that the major problems in the Soviet economy are the low quality of goods and low rate of technological progress, phenomena which can hardly be ascribed only and even mostly to flaws in the decision-making process and even in the incentive mechanism.

The public discussions on this issue revealed that low efficiency in work was easily tolerated in all spheres of society mostly because the consumer had no possibility of influencing producers. However, the scholars and the public were moved to an understanding of the genuine role of control over product quality and service rather slowly. Still, in 1986–1987, the evaluation of human performance yielded strongly in the public perception to the old traditional issue—the autonomy of economic units.

It is curious that the quality of performance and the ways it is evaluated emerged as the main issue in 1985–1987 in the discussion on cultural activity. Exactly in the articles and speeches about the state of affairs in this domain it became clear that the conflict between various types of controls over performance is the main cause of the degradation of culture in Brezhnev's period.

In 1985 the figures of theaters who started to take stock of their problems and to show that not the viewers but people indifferent to the quality of their work make all the crucial decisions in their field (see the articles of the leading Soviet theater directors and actors Mark Zakharov, *Sovietskaia Kul'tura*, November 29, 1980, Oleg Efremov, *Pravda*, February 21, 1986, and Georgii Tovstonogov, *Literaturnaia Gazeta*, December 25, 1985).

The theater figures were joined then by movie people who in their turn denounced the multi-level system of censorship which killed many outstanding movies that, having been released after delays of years, were acclaimed by the public. Criticism of the administrative methods of control reached its height during the congress of movie figures (1986), where the speakers openly attacked the state bodies directing the movie industry (see *Iskusstvo kino* 10 [1986]).

In the 70s mediocrity was prevalent in literature and theater and cinema as well, where accusations of nepotism and corruption were leveled against the administrative control for the flood of gray works which filled the market (see the materials of the Congress of Russian Writers, *Literaturnaia Gazeta*, December 18, 1985).

Social scientists, even the most critical of them, like Zaslavskaia, joined actors and writers in understanding the role of consumers one or two years later, if one takes into account the dynamics of the first years of Gorbachev's regime.

Tatiana Zaslavskaia in her articles (Zaslavskaia 1984, 1986, 1987) paid practically no attention to performance control on the part of the Soviet people, emphasizing in her sociological analysis of Soviet problems the human factor almost exclusively—the necessity to improve radically the stimuli to work and to take into account in this connection the interests of various groups in the population, a theme which Gorbachev made a leading one in his speech on economic reforms in 1987 (*Pravda*, June 27, 1987).

Naming three conditions which will stimulate people to work "using their full capacities," Zaslavskaia lists "the levelling of the opportunities at the start of life of people belonging to different social groups. . . .the distribution of jobs according to the personal labor potential of the people" and "the creation of the conditions for efficient work" (normal supply of raw materials, independence, and the opportunities for creativity). Zaslavskaia ignores the importance of the objective evaluation of human performance as the major flaw of the Soviet system (Zaslavskaia 1986, p. 68).

Gavriil Popov, an economist who emerged in 1987 as a leading intellectual of *perestroika*, was among such scholars when he suggested in his superb article, inspired by Alexander Bek's novel *The Appointment* (see Bek 1971), that "the concentration of decisions only on the highest floor of management and the volitional character of these decisions" and the fear which was "an obligatory element of any more or less rigid administrative mechanism" made each official a conformist and unable to fend off his superiors' incorrect directives (Popov 1987a, pp. 61, 62).

He, however, did not explain why a decision taken by the head of the administrative system can be nefarious. In fact, those who control big corporations also often impose their will on their subordinates and promote conformism among them. The point is that even the most despotic manager must, with a short lag, face the consequences of his misdeeds, as was not the case for Stalin and his myrmidons in the national economy as they were described in Bek's novel and analyzed by Popov. The author eloquently describes how the administrative system in its various forms (not only in the Stalin-Beria version) generates submissive people, but seemingly does not want to recognize that such a tendency is typical for all organizations (including those which function in the Western countries), and that it shows the sole remedy to countervail this tendency (and only from outside): the impact of consumers on the goods and services produced by an organization through punishment of the leaders for incorrect decisions.

Leonid Butenko, who started the social critique of the Brezhnev period even earlier than Zaslavskaia (see Butenko's articles on the contradictions in socialist society, 1982 and 1984), also saw the major obstacle to progress in Soviet society in the dominance of the bureaucracy, which monopolized power in the country, but did not single out the role of consumers as a major problem in a society of the Soviet type (*Sovietskaia Kul'tura*, June 23, 1987). He was much closer to this issue in his incisive article on the essence of the Soviet system published a few months later (*Moskovskiie Novosti* 43 [1987]: 8–9).

The participants in the extremely brave discussion in *Literaturnaia Gazeta*, who did not mince words in condemning socialism in its present form, did not raise the question of consumers. Even Gennadii Lisichkin, a prominent economist and consistent defender of market socialism, inveighed against bureaucratism, the remnant of feudalism in Soviet society in this discussion, but ignored the consumer issue (*Literaturnaia Gazeta*, June 8, 1987). The same is true about Abel Aganbegian, who, describing the economic reforms in the country, emphasized only the autonomy of the enterprise, almost also avoiding the role of consumers (see *Ogoniok* 3 [1987]: 15).

It was the logic of the denunciation of bureaucrats as the major culprits for all Soviet evils—the official doctrine of Gorbachev's regime—which gradually pushed Soviet intellectuals and even politicians to the analysis of the role of consumers in Soviet society.

Nikolai Shmelev was one of the first authors who being moved by this logic elevated the issue to the forefront of discussion. In his article "Advances and Debts" (Shmelev 1987) he inveighs against "administrative economics" and "religious belief in organization." However he is somewhat ahead of other authors in his analysis of the Soviet malaise, approaching the major direct causes of Soviet failures in the economy and in technology—the lack of competition, the dominance of producers and the helplessness of consumers—and even the condition which alone can make the consumers' voice be heard—the responsibility of managers for their decisions—even if he does not take the final step in his analysis and does not openly discuss property relations, and even if he discusses the various flaws of the Soviet economy, such as the irrational price system, as being treatable separately.

Shmelev writes, "Choice, competition, is an objective condition which has to be observed if the economy wants to be vital or at least effective enough" (Shmelev 1987, p. 154). Underscoring the role of the consumer he said that "only the market, and not simply administrative innovations, can submit the whole chain—from research to service after the sale—to the demands of consumers" (p. 155). In the same line, he regards the responsibility of a manager only to his superiors to be an organic defect in the Soviet economic system (p. 156). Shmelev rejects also, as was mentioned, the "state control over quality" introduced by Gorbachev's regime in 1986, as being a panacea for improvement in the quality of goods and points out that this state control again ignores the consumer—whether an enterprise or an individual in a shopping center (Shmelev 1987, p. 154).

Therefore, Shmelev is close to an idea far alien to the mentality of many liberal thinkers, that the autonomy of an enterprise by itself—if consumers do not evaluate its performance and if workers do not check themselves for errors and bad work—is no cure for the Soviet economy.

In 1987 a growing number of authors began to espouse the idea that the role of the consumer, of democratic control over human performance, lies at the bottom of the Soviet problem. Trying to understand what is the main cause of inefficiency in all spheres of Soviet society A. Makarov, a leading journalist in *Sovietskaia Kul'tura*, sadly notes that "nobody depends on anybody—a physician does not depend on his patients, a salesgirl on customers, writers on readers" (*Sovietskaia Kul'tura*, July 28, 1987). Leonid Pleshakov, an *Ogoniok* journalist, was also one of few authors on economic issues who advanced to the foreground of discussions on economic reform the role of consumers in the economic process (see *Ogoniok* 48 [1987]: 2–6). In a discussion about Soviet health service, a physicist, rejecting various administrative measures—from above—as inefficient, demanded the installation of patient control over hospitals as the only way to positive change.

It is interesting to note with what bewilderment the Soviet people learned from the mass media that not only the food sector and light industry but also the communication, health service, transport and other sectors of the economy were exempted from any control from the consumers and were concerned only with the assessment of their activity from "above."

The dependence of technological progress on the consumer came to the surface of the public conscience in the USSR later and in an even less distinctive way. Now the slowness of technological progress more and more often is linked with the lack of competition in Soviet science and industry, which is not far short of the recognition of the role of the consumer and the incapacity of the administrative bodies to run this sphere successfully as well.

EVALUATION OF PERFORMANCE IN CLASSIC SOCIALIST SOCIETY

Whereas in the West human performance is mostly evaluated by a horizontal mechanism with the participation of millions of people, the same mechanism in a society of the Soviet type is based on an administrative, hierarchical, mechanism. This mechanism supposes that each level of the hierarchy brings together the assignment of a task to the lower level, the evaluation of the quality of performance, and often the character of any reward.

The combination of the function of decisionmaker and controller is deeply ingrained in management in general. The chief of any unit in the United States or France not only issues orders to subordinates and endorses their decisions, but also checks how well these orders and approved decisions have been carried out. Such a fusion of two different tasks in management is tolerable insofar as the efficiency of a given unit is checked by the market, be it economic, political, cultural or otherwise. In any organization that is in one way or another protected from those who consume or use its products or services, the same processes develop as have in Soviet society.

Some fundamental circumstances that shape the very special attitudes of a manager toward the decisions of his subordinates and their fulfillment ensue from the lack of consumer control over producers.

First, any member of the hierarchical structure tends to be lenient toward the activity of his subordinates—both in the sphere of the decision-making process as well as in the practical one. With a lack of consumer control, in a non–zero sum situation, the official leans toward collusion with his subordinates at the lower level, which allows him to get more benefits from their activity in comparison to the case where he would be preoccupied with the interests of consumers.

The practice of "correcting the plan" which was almost universal in Brezhnev's period and which was strongly criticized by Andropov and Gorbachev (see Andropov 1983, Gorbachev 1985, 1986, 1987a) can illustrate this phenomenon. By the middle of the current year or even later, the director of a Soviet enterprise would realize that he had no chance to fulfill the state plan of production. Instead of mobilizing all his resources to do it he would ask his superiors in the Ministry to "correct the plan," in other words, to diminish the plan figures and thereby to gain the possibility of reporting by the end of the year on the great achievements of his enterprise—which would also allow the Ministry to so report to the government, which had also permitted the correction of the plan.

As many other economists could say after Brezhnev the idea of "correcting the plan," that is, the adaptation of the plan to the bad work of producers, destroys the idea of planning all by itself and makes it ludicrous. It is only amazing how George Orwell could predict, in *1984*, the prominent role of the adaptation of the plan to the "achieved level of production" in order to have successes and praise.

The collusion between enterprises and ministries takes many other forms. Azol'skii's novel describes in detail the mechanism of the cooperation between a parent ministry and its enterprise. One episode in this novel is especially interesting. The director of a research institute suddenly discovered that two of his laboratories had been assigned by error to the same task. Millions of rubles and two years had been wasted. The fact would sooner or later be known by the Ministry. The resourceful director found the way out: He asked one of his subordinates with criminal propensity and a tainted past to make a tour of all the research institutes under the auspices of his Ministry in order to find other parallel examples of work on identical issues. As was expected, such facts were found, and when the Ministry tried to remonstrate with our director, he displayed to the officials the information he possessed about them, and the conflict was immediately settled (Azol'skii 1987).

Another, even more important, consequence of the collusion of the officials at adjacent hierarchical levels was the disregard for the quality of performance and technological progress. Since the quantitative indicators of the plan are easier to check and special formal decisions are necessary to diminish them, the quality of products and services are the main arena of the fraternization between various categories of officials as well as between them and workers. The quality of work is discounted in all spheres of a society of the Soviet type—from agriculture to literature and the cinema.

Again, Brezhnev's period managed to reach the extreme in its lack of concern for the quality of human performance. The low quality of Soviet consumer goods became notorious throughout the whole world.

It is enough to mention that no less than one-third of the color TV sets produced in the 80s turned out to be defective and were returned by buyers. In the last five years the breakdown of color TV sets caused 18,400 fires in the country and 2,000 in Moscow alone in which 912 people died and 512 were injured—events unimaginable in any other country in the world (*Ogoniok* 25, pp. 20, 29, and 51).

The yearning of the Soviet people for foreign goods attained almost ridiculous proportions. The USSR, like a country of the Third World, could export almost only raw materials (the proportion of finished goods in Soviet export to countries with convertible currency was less than 10 percent).

In the 70s cultural activity also reached its nadir because the country was inundated with extremely mediocre or bad novels, movies, and plays, a fact that was fully recognized in 1985–1987, when figures in literature and the arts began to denounce vehemently the extremely low quality of their output, demonstrating that it was the direct product of the coalition between officials directing culture, editors, and mediocre authors.

Certainly, the neglect of the quality of products and services also demanded the falsification of data. The fulfillment of the plan by means of the production of goods, material or cultural, which were unable to satisfy the most moderate needs of the consumers had become a fixture in Soviet life. What is more, superiors often instigated, covered up, or ignored the falsification of statistical reports on the results of the activity of their subordinates. Such prevarication reached a peak in Brezhnev's time, when the majority of the apparatchiks in one way or another distorted data about the activities of their units with the approval of the next level of the hierarchy. The case of Uzbekistan as well as Turkmenistan and Tadzhikistan, where the real production of cotton was significantly lower (in Uzbekistan by more than one-quarter) than was said in the official report, is typical for this period (the deception was widespread in practically all branches of the Soviet economy).

Soviet planning and statistical bodies strongly favored the distortion of data through allowing enterprises to claim a rise in price for goods and services which they presented as new but in fact in no way differed from the old ones. This trick permitted significant increases in the reported rate of growth of Soviet industry (see Seliunin and Khanin 1987).

The distortion of information started almost immediately at the time of the emergence of socialist society and the first area was the political police (Cheka and GPU), where accusations against political adversaries were concocted at all levels of the hierarchy with the approval of the next. The official morality, which, rejecting universal values, preached the expediency of any means if they serve the goals of the socialist state, was excellent justification for this practice.

The coalition of superiors and subordinates against consumers is also based on the principles of appointment in the Soviet system. Formally quiet, often the official is endorsed ultimately not by his own superior but by the superior of his superior (a Deputy Minister, for instance, is formally endorsed by the council of Ministers whereas the correspondent of a central newspaper like *Pravda* is formally endorsed not by the editor in chief but by the secretariat of the Central Committee).

However, it is the immediate superior who selects the cadre and who makes the final decision about his appointment. Having made his choice the official lays his authority on the line and from the moment his protegé enters his office he tries to support him, expecting, certainly, complete conformism on his part. I will later show how this regularity was at the bottom of the process of feudalization which embraced Brezhnev's society in the 70s. I do not want to say that the average Soviet official does not fire his subordinates or does not reprimand them for poor accomplishment of his orders. I speak only about the tendency to regard those who were chosen by him as "his people" whose good standing is for him of the greatest importance.

MEASUREMENT OF PERFORMANCE

Market control over political or economic activity supposes that the burden of the measurement of producers' performance lies with the ordinary people who with their votes or money express their attitudes toward the value of officials, books, movies, TV sets, and so on. The administrative control over human performance requires the use of a special technique of measurement, a technique which is of some importance to management in Western society (mostly for the evaluation of work inside a company or corporation) but which is of crucial significance to a command society. It is evident that a superior has to have a special instrument in order to gauge the performance of his subordinates.

The problem of measurement of performance plays an extremely important role in the history of the Soviet economy, ideology, culture, health service, and other spheres of social activity. The discussions on these issues in the USSR over the last five decades have no equivalent in the West in terms of intensity and social consequences. The passion with which Soviet scholars and managers debate indicators is easily explained in terms of our paradigm of the two types of EP. For administrators it is extremely important to have a set of indicators that can grade the performance of their people for determining their reward as well as promotion. With the disregard for consumers these voluntarily established indicators acquire a role in socialist society incomprehensible in a market society where the ultimate grades are assigned by the mass consumer.

The history of Soviet society is replete with cases in which the introduction of a new indicator affected in the most striking way economic activity, diminishing or increasing the production of various kinds of goods or services. So, in Khrushchev's times the new indicators in agriculture which became the basis for EP of the party apparatchiks and managers in the countryside were able to force collective and state farms to expand corn growing even in areas not favorable to it, decrease the sowing areas for traditional crops, and violate common sense in husbandry (since the number of cows became a very important indicator, farms were compelled to keep even cows that did not produce milk, and so on) (regarding this, see Shlapentokh 1970).

Despite the tremendous efforts of scholars, the Soviet system has failed to elaborate indicators that can satisfactorily measure performance and serve as a reliable basis for reward.

The failure of these efforts is especially evident in economics. Over five decades the debates could not find an indicator that would be recognized by the majority of the experts as satisfactory. The main indicator—the gross output (the value of finished and unfinished goods at the current or "base" prices)—has been criticized over the years as stimulating enterprises to produce only expensive and material-consuming goods, and was, as the major indicator, opposed to many others, such as "commodity output," "normative output," "profit," and some others; however, each rival of the first indicator revealed its own weaknesses and flaws (regarding the economic indicators, see the recent works of Abalkin 1981, Aganbegian and Moskvin 1984, Radaiev 1984, Cherniavskii 1985, and Gvozdev 1985).

No more successful were Soviet attempts to obtain a set of indicators for the evaluation of scientific work. In the Soviet context, even those indicators such as the number of publications, which have some meaning in the West, failed. The proliferation of ghostwriters, the mass exploitation of junior scholars by their chiefs and by scholars with administrative positions, made this indicator void of any significance (see Zvorykin 1976 and 1977, Kelle 1978, Shcherbakov 1975, Gvishiani 1973, and Moskalenko et al. 1979).

The Soviet system tried also to elaborate indicators for EP in other spheres. Many efforts were devoted, especially in the 60s, to the creation of indicators for culture and ideology. Hundreds of books and articles discussed how to appraise the activities of writers, painters, movie directors, and especially people who work on the ideological apparatus and the institutions involved—the mass media, propaganda corps, political schools, and so on (see, for instance, on the measurement of ideological work Zhuravlev 1980, Bikkenin 1983, and Iakovlev 1984).

The absurdity of many Soviet indicators was manifested especially blatantly in so ludicrous a phenomenon as socialist emulation. Socialist emulation developed as a substitute for real competition and for treating the real consumers as appraisers of performance. The determination of the "victors" required the creation of dozens and dozens of indicators for each branch of society including science and culture. Many of them are so ridiculous that they have long since become the target of satirists (see Changli 1973 and 1979).

THE SELECTION OF CADRES

The isolation of judgment of performance from the consumer and the application of unreliable indicators for EP make the manager free to choose and promote his subordinates with total disregard for the merits of the individual necessary for "real work." Certainly, the subjective factor is very significant also in the cadre policy of a big U.S. or Japanese corporation. However, the fear of the ultimate judgment of consumers mostly (of course, not always) forces managers to stifle their personal tastes as well as their egotistical interests in making appointments and promotions. Deviation from the objective process of selecting cadres is one of the most obvious forms of evidence of a sickness for any institution.

The criterion of professional competence and devotion to work in the selection of cadres in the Soviet system was sacrificed from the very beginning to political considerations and to loyalty to the superior. It does not mean that Soviet rulers could not find in the pool of potential candidates those who combine both merits—political and professional. However, as will be shown later, gradually, with the movement far away from the revolution and its enthusiasm, despite the educational progress of cadres, the tendency to prefer people less capable but more conformist gradually has been gaining the upper hand. Analyzing Bek's novel *The Appointment*, Gavriil Popov demonstrates how "the system" cannot "reproduce the managers that it needs. It is doomed to behave in such a way that each new appointment will be worse than the previous one, even if only a little." The system unavoidably gears to the selection of more and more conformed people, rejecting individuals who will defend their professional decisions (Popov 1987a, p. 59).

The professional criterion, as shown over the course of Soviet history, not being protected by the interests of consumers, has been unremittingly losing its significance. It was almost completely disregarded in cadre policy in Brezhnev's period when the ruling elite ostentatiously encouraged its contempt for talented and hard-working people in all spheres of life, preferring to deal with colorless conformists whose low professional skills made them totally docile and obsequious.

As many materials published during Gorbachev's *glasnost* have demonstrated, in all domains of Soviet life the mediocre managers have appointed even more mediocre subordinates, and for ten years the whole country has been reined by mediocre people. As one scholar in *Pravda* explained, even in science the principle "I do not like him because he must be cleverer than I" became dominant in the selection and promotion of cadres (*Pravda*, July 6, 1987).

OUTSIDE CONTROL

The incapacity of a Soviet official and manager effectively to control the performance of his subordinates was realized in the very beginning of Soviet history. The special committee for monitoring the activity of the party and state apparatus from outside (beside the procurators) was created already in 1920. Since this period the system of outside control has grown incessantly up to Gorbachev's regime.

Almost all Soviet administrative units from the national level down to the regional, and often even to the district and city level, have a department of audit. Such departments, with dozens and dozens of workers, make up a part of the state and party apparatus, of ministries and directorates.

Along with these departments the command system created a number of central institutions the goals of which consist only in supervisory capacity. In most cases these institutions possess their own network of regional agencies which employ hundreds of thousands of people—full-time controllers. Among such institutions are the Ministry of Popular Control, the Party Committee of Control, the Ministry of Internal Affairs—with its special department (OBKhS) assigned to the fight against corruption, the Inspectorate of Quality of the Ministry of Trade, the State Bank, the Ministry of Finance, and many others.

However, the most remarkable feature of the command system is its determination to involve a great portion of the active population in the process of control on a so-called voluntary basis. According to official data in 1985, no less than ten million Soviet people (almost one-tenth of the employees in the economy) took part in auditing activity to perform their social obligations (TsSU 1985, p. 11). Some authors have suggested that the number of "voluntary controllers" has reached 10–15 percent of all employees. Among the party members this figure is even higher—25 percent (Bokarev 1979, p. 33).

In Moscow alone in the late 70s the number of activists in the audit realm reached 320,000, almost doubling since the 60s. In some auditing campaigns the number of participants reached 200,000–300,000 Muscovites, a considerable figure even for a city with 8 million residents of whom probably 6 million are adults (Ikonnikov 1984, pp. 101, 179, 212).

The gigantic system of outside administrative control created in Soviet society turned out to be completely helpless in preventing almost total disarray in the evaluation of human performance and the corruption of the whole society.

First of all, it itself slipped into collusion with those whom it had to audit, having elaborated rituals which brought no danger to the bureaucrats. What is more, the whole system of control could not avoid corruption itself and again the period of *glasnost* has provided us with numerous facts.

In all those cases where auditors really wanted to bring to light a violation of laws, they were mostly persecuted, themselves, by the mafia-like officials, both regional and central. One such example was brought to our attention by *Komsomol'skaia Pravda*. The events had already taken place in Gorbachev's period and it is easy to imagine what would have happened a few years earlier. A young and conscientious auditor in the Directorate of Poultry Production found terrible errors and even criminal misconduct in the activity of the Orenburg branch, which was then regarded as the "vanguard." Tatiana Bogdanova, the auditor, was effectively destroyed by the alliance between local party bodies and the leadership of her own organization whose interests she presumably represented. She was discredited, excluded from the party, and fired. At the same time, the chiefs of the Orenburg branch practically got away from the scandal scot-free. The article in the central newspaper could only, and probably again only temporarily, force the authorities to restore Tatiana to the party and at her job (*Komsomol'skaia Pravda*, July 8, 1987).

Discussing major flaws of the Soviet system of management, Gorbachev recognized that "the system of control is inefficient, too big, wastes labor time, diverts without effect a large amount of people and resources" (*Pravda*, June 25, 1987, p. 3). According to Philip Taubman, the chief of the New York *Times* bureau in Moscow, during a meeting Gorbachev, in reaction to a complaint by a manager about the cumbersome system of outside control which wastes the time of managers whom it supposedly audits, said "we should dismantle this system" (New York *Times Magazine*, July 19, 1987).

THE CONSUMER—WHO HE IS

Advancing the consumer as the major figure of the social process I should discuss him in detail. It is obvious that there are different categories of consumers and that each of them plays a different role in society.

In a socialist society it is reasonable to single out such types of consumers as the political leadership, the dominant class or *nomenclature* (i.e. people appointed by the party to commanding positions in society), the military, and the rest of the population—the masses including also the intelligentsia. From the perspective chosen by us the Soviet economy, ideology, culture, science and all other spheres of social activity produce goods and services for this array of consumers.

The strength of the consumers is different, and is revealed in their ability to influence producers. Evidently, the most powerful consumers are those from the political leadership, who possess unlimited control over society. Let us describe the preferences of this consumer group.

The political leadership as consumer prefers, evidently, power to all other needs. And as the strongest group of consumers they can implement this desire, being forced to neglect many other of their needs.

There is no doubt that the Soviet leaders always wanted the well-being of the population to be as high as possible. The prosperity of the population can only enhance the power and the prestige of the political elite. All other things being equal, not only post-Stalin rulers but Stalin himself would have been glad if the ordinary people had been happy.

The leadership naturally would be happy also with efficacy not only of the economy producing goods and services for the population but from all other sectors of society that have to serve their interests such as science, culture, ideology, health and others. However, the Soviet leadership could not make all these subsystems efficacious, mostly because they could not force apparatchiks at all levels to fulfill successfully their roles as evaluators of performance according to the requirements of the state and at the same time could not replace them in this capacity with consumers who alone are able to do this job well.

As a result, the leadership has to acquiesce to their permanent failure to achieve the goals which they proclaimed and which would have been beneficial both to society and for them, such as a higher standard of living, rapid scientific and technological progress, effective ideological work, and so on. With the existing mechanism of EP, they are compelled to satisfy themselves with the preservation of the given political order which in their opinion is necessary for the survival of the system.

The incapacity of the leadership to achieve its goals pushes it toward self-deception, to the encouragement of reports that distort reality, which can only accelerate the process of decay of the EP mechanism (see Shlapentokh 1988 regarding the attitudes of the political elite to information).

A radical change in the mechanism of EP would demand a radical change in the social fabric of Soviet society because the political elite would lose their role as the ultimate judge of the activity of the people in the country and at the same time, their monopoly on the appointment of managers in all spheres of life.

It is characteristic that the Soviet system never allowed the creation of really independent organizations for the protection of the interests of mass consumers. The numerous organizations, official or "voluntary," were completely under the control of party committees, could play only a very minor role, if any, and tended to go into cahoots with producers for some benefits.

In only one case has the leadership since Stalin endowed the consumers with great clout over the producers—this is the military, a fact which only underscores that the Soviet rulers have always been aware that only consumers, and not the superiors of producers, can be the real appraisers of performance. Military products in all research institutes and enterprises have been checked not by the department of quality control, which was a part of the factory administration and was always in collusion with the administration that appointed it, but by representatives of the army (*Voenpred*) who have the obligation and the full right to reject goods that do not satisfy their requirements (see Grekovs's *On the Test* 1971 regarding the work of military representatives).

What are the influences of the Soviet dominant class, the nomenclature, which with the members of their families make up nearly 5 percent of the population (Voslenskii 1980)? This group is big enough and important enough to the political elite that its consumer interests cannot be ignored by the ruling elite.

The solution was found in the creation of a special network of stores, hospitals, and vacation resorts, as well as in granting access to the West through travels, entrance to foreign movies in special theaters, and so on. Having isolated the nomenclature from mass consumption the ruling elite could maintain the Stalinist model of EP without antagonizing the party and state apparatus, and, moreover, to force them to appreciate their privileges especially strongly. Certainly, the members of the ruling elite itself were isolated from mass consumption to even a greater degree than their subordinates (about the consumption of the Soviet ruling class see Vishnevskaia 1984, Allivuieva 1969, Djilas 1970).

However, in spite of heavy pressure, the Soviet economy turned out to be unable to produce goods and services, even for its own privileged class—even for the top political elite. The consumption demands of the apparatchiks of even the highest level are satisfied by imports. They use only Western electronic goods, dress in Western clothes, and are served in hospitals with Western equipment and medicines and often by Western doctors. They are also entertained by Western movies and books. It is very likely that imported food is a very important part of their diet as well.

The Soviet nomenclature has been successful as a group of consumers only in terms of service. They visit their own special stores where they are treated no worse than customers in the West and their nurses in hospitals are perhaps even more amicable to them than medical personnel in the West are to their patients.

Besides the privileged customers—in all respects the major part of the Soviet population plays—a mostly insignificant role as consumers. The requirements of the mass consumer are mostly ignored by all branches of the economy, by health service, the educational system, the mass media, publishing houses, and the entertainment and vacation industries.

The wishes and expectations of the Soviet masses as consumers are also ignored by the gigantic administrative apparatus to which the Soviet individual is regularly forced to turn with hundreds of issues—from the bathroom repairs to permission to live in a given city. The Soviet individual as an electer of the members of governmental bodies, whose intervention he asks on his behalf, has zero clout, and none of the officials who rudely reject his requests concerns himself with the voting consequence of such a deed.

If the impact of the mass consumer on the Soviet machine—economic or political—has been generally the same over the decades, then in the last period, even before Gorbachev's regime, some changes took place in his favor. The primary satisfaction of some basic needs and the permanent flow of imported goods allows the Soviet consumer to reject many domestic goods, which creates some inconveniences for Soviet industry. The amount of unsold stock in Soviet retail trade has increased from 9 percent of the value of retail sales in 1940 to 21 percent in 1970, and 25 percent in 1985. If we take into account also the stocks of consumer goods in wholesale trade and industry, the percentage of unsold stock against retail value is now 32 percent, compared to 17 percent before the war (*TsSU* 1986, p. 474). The excessive stocks of finished goods have become a plague for many Soviet enterprises.

Since the commodity-money relationship plays a role of sorts in the Soviet economic system, a role which the government has been trying to increase in the whole post-Stalin era, the reluctance of consumers to buy creates problems for enterprises and the state, such as the postponement of the payment of workers, difficulties in relations between suppliers, and so on. The lack of a hunger for various goods in the country has introduced a sort of pressure on producers.

However, as was mentioned before, Soviet producers are saved from all their inconveniences by the state, and the growing amount of stock cannot significantly change things, especially with reference to the role of the Soviet individual as the consumer of services rendered by sectors that are not affected by such concerns as stock backlogs—here his position in the last two decades became rather worse. The movie industry and theaters did not react to the decline in patrons. The position of the consumer in health service, the vacation industry, and as petitioners in dealing with the bureaucracy became even worse in the 70s and the first half of the 80s, due to rampant corruption and the weakening of administrative control from above—the sole defender of the consumer.

NOTES

1. Ludvig von Mises noted that work for society's sake, being the driving stimulus, would have been the most consistent pattern of behavior, given the essence of socialist society which is unable to measure correctly the contribution of the individual in the economy (Mises 1936, p. 173).

2. An extraordinary event took place in the factory producing buses in Likido (Moscow region)—a three-day strike. The direct cause: the introduction of state inspection independent of the director, which drastically reduced the number of buses considered up to standard and curtailed significantly the workers' salaries. The reaction of the Ministry: subsidization of the salary fund. *Moscow News*, which reported this event, did not mention any sanction against the administration (*Moskovskiie Novosti*, October 18, 1987, pp. 8–9).

3. The revelation in the mid-80s of the fantastic spoilage of resources in Soviet society is interesting to compare with Karl Kautsky's ideas about socialism as a society which will perpetrate "economies of every description." He particularly mentioned economies of materials, transport charges, advertisements, and publicity costs (Kautsky, *Die soziale Revoluzione* II, p. 26).

Chapter 2

Privatization: The Response to the Poor Evaluation of Performance

PRIVATIZATION CONCEPTS

The inability of a system of the Soviet type to create an effective mechanism of evaluation of performance (EP) had tremendous consequences for the USSR. The most important of them was the disruption of the coordination between societal and individual goals. The Soviet system is based on almost total control by the state of the most vital areas of social life—from the economy to health service and culture. The gradual refusal of the members of the nomenclature to identify their personal interests with the goals of the state, even the long-term interests of their own class, and the ensuing deterioration of the mechanism of EP, were the immediate causes of the decline in the quality of management in Soviet society with many ramifications for economic, social, and political developments.

But before moving to the analysis of the processes engendered by the failure of the mechanism of EP we need to lay out briefly the theoretical concepts that we will find necessary here.

The paradigm "public-private" is important for the study of any society, but it is seminal for analyzing processes in a society of the Soviet type. The term *public* is used here as a characteristic of the activities and institutions that pursue social, mostly societal, national goals or that at least follow the standards of behavior endorsed by society. Since in modern society the interests of the whole nation are presumably represented by the state, "public" relates mostly to the central government and its agencies, to such a degree that the term *official* is often used in the same sense. This identification of "public" and "official" is made with respect to command societies like the Soviet one where the state controls all major spheres of life.

The term *private* as the antonym of "public" means activity that pursues the goals of single individuals or single organizations. This activity is beyond the systematic control of outside forces, the state in the first place, and presupposes wide initiative on the part of the subjects of this activity as well as their freedom to choose for the purposes of communication and cooperation only those whom they like.

However important the informational aspect of the definitions of "private" and "public" (the availability of and access to information about the activity of the individual or organization) may be, it is the "material" intrusion (or absence thereof) of the state into the activity of groups and individuals that makes the real distinction between "public" and "private" spheres of activity (regarding the "public-private" paradigm, see Benn and Gaus 1983, Moore 1984 and 1985, Rubin 1983, Sennett 1977, Slater 1970, and Young 1978).

For our analysis it is also important to make a distinction between the legal and illegal dimensions of public as well as private life. Again, this is of special significance for Soviet society with its omnipotent state defining what activity is lawful and what is not. The definition of what is legal or illegal has changed very significantly in Soviet history. Each regime introduced its own concepts on this issue in many spheres. However, the life of the Soviet people has always been strongly influenced by the current interpretation of what is regarded at the given moment to be legal or illegal in the public or private sphere.

The good Soviet citizen, according to the official Soviet model of life, expends most of his energy and emotions in the legal public sector, where he works professionally for the state and takes part in voluntary activity in social work. This means that as a worker or manager the Soviet individual satisfies most of his personal, private needs through activity devoted to the state, pursuing official goals with official means. His activity in the legal private sector—in family or interactions with friends—takes only a small portion of his time and attention.

The ideal model of Soviet society also presupposed the effective coordination of societal and individual goals as they were shaped in the 20s. If the political leadership did not expect that all Soviet people would follow these prescriptions in their life, they were certain that party activists, apparatchiks, managers—the core of the dominant class—would definitely be devoted servants of the new state.

The cult of the state and the necessity of submitting to it were the leading themes in the late 20s and the early 30s when Stalin molded the new society. It was suggested by all means that only by serving the state, obeying its orders without hesitation and always believing in its expediency and wisdom, could the individual achieve high status in society with all its perquisites. This ideology of the state and how it was planted in the minds of the Soviet people was vividly described in Vasilii Grossman's monumental novel *Life and Destiny* (1980) and to some degree also in Bek's *Appointment* (1971) and Anatolii Rybakov's *The Children of the Arbat* (1987).

The main thesis developed here is the contention that the authority of the state as employer, and in the first place of its capacity fairly to judge human performance, has drastically declined since 1953. This was the ultimate cause of the privatization of Soviet society. Only in the first period after the revolution with mass terror and authoritative ideology was the state regarded as more or less objective toward those who served it, and relatively efficiently able to coordinate social and individual goals. In the following periods individual goals more and more often gained the upper hand over the individual.

The corrosion of the EP mechanism is directly the result of the gradual movement of the Soviet apparatchiks from being representatives of the state to corrupted cynics who started to seek immediate benefits from their positions.

In fact, the efficacy of the EP mechanism directly depends on the activity of managers at various levels. They not only make decisions and issue orders but also, as was underscored, control the decisions made by their subordinates as well as their "material behavior." As soon as managers neglect their function as the controllers of the lower levels of an organization the efficacy of work immediately goes down, pushing workers to disregard their public duties and immerse themselves in activity that pursues only private goals, usually deleterious to public ones.

So, before moving to the core of the process of privatization, it is necessary to dwell briefly on the evolution of the party and state apparatus in the USSR after the revolution. We will use a number of indicators that will help to follow the process of the transformation: attitudes toward state and subordinates, the role of career, interest in the material comfort, the role of nepotism, and a few others.

THE FIRST GENERATION OF MANAGERS—STOCKHOLDERS

In the first decade of the existence of the Soviet state the mechanism of performance evaluation worked relatively well. There was a special combination of circumstances. The uniqueness of this period lay in the specific character of the Soviet officials of this period. Coming to power from the revolution most of them were people who deeply believed in communist ideals and saw their future in committed work for the party and the state—the main instrument for the implementation of these ideals. Quite often these people did not possess the necessary professional skills but they were eager to learn and compensated for insufficient competence with the strongest involvement in their tasks.

In their devotion to the cause they were radically different from the masses which, as was indicated above, were mostly consumed by the need for physical survival. Even the authors of cheerful novels of the 30s—Ehrenburg's *Second Day* or Kataiev's *Time Ahead*—without speaking of more sober works such as Malyshkin's *People from Remote Places*—could not conceal this radical difference. Nikolai Rzhanov, a little boss from *Second Day*, thus perceives the work of the rank and file during the construction of a metallurgical plant in Kuznetsk: "They worked despondently . . . twisted their hand-made cigarettes for a very long time, constantly squabbled with each other and tried to gain an additional five or ten minutes to not work . . . These people sometimes seemed to Nikolai to be criminals. He thought that it was necessary to try them, deprive them of their bread rations and send them to forced labor camps" (p. 31). What is more, we learn that among these workers are "former kulaks" and prisoners, people who can hardly be trusted.

Party activists such as Nikolai Rzhanov or especially Grigorii Shor, another character from the same novel, regarded themselves as the stockholders of a corporation who could really take part in the direction of the enterprise and who were responsible for all the negative phenomena in Soviet society. Shor, a party member from prerevolutionary times, revered the party as a sacred institution. "To Shor, the party seemed to be the whole world . . . The road of the party was long and this road was Shor's life" (p. 71).

The same image of a manager was portrayed by Anatolii Rybakov in his *Children of the Arbat* (1987). Mark Riasanov, director of a large Siberian plant, a strong willing person with a high devotion to the idea of industrialization, is able to take many risky decisions on his own initiative, even to ignore and isolate for a few days a team of controllers from Moscow, having realized that these people could hamper the implementation of his plan. With all his fear of Stalin in 1934 he nevertheless had the courage to argue with him and defend his ideas.

Many of the apparatchiks were extremely demanding of themselves and of their subordinates. Shor, as Ehrenburg wrote, absolutely did not spare his health while working at construction in Kuznetsk. At the same time they were ready to take initiative and to defend their views to their superiors, as was Gleb Chumalov in Fedor Gladkov's *Cement*, who decided to restore a plant destroyed during the civil war despite the opposition of local authorities (Gladkov 1925/1964), and the managers such as David Margulies and Korneev in Valentin Kataiev's *Time Forward* (1932/1956).

With all their suspicion of alien class elements, the first generation of Soviet managers tried to fill slots in the party and state apparatus with individuals really able to perform their functions and lent relatively minor importance to personal relations. They were all free from nationalistic feelings and ignored the national origin of people, choosing anyone for any job.

In no way is it necessary to consider them all to be fanatics (although there were quite a few of these). The majority of the apparatchiks and managers were as concerned with their personal interests as was the rest of the population. They liked material comfort and privileges and enjoyed them very much. They had, for instance, the use of cars for their personal interests, they had their own cafeterias, or even organized luxurious private binges for themselves, as was mentioned by Fedor Gladkov in *Cement* (pp. 188, 189–90) and by Ehrenburg in *Second Day* (p. 105) (see also the description of the lifestyle of apparatchiks in this period in Ginzburg's memoir 1985).

What is more, they almost all enjoyed power, the possibility of manipulating people. Many of them were ready to use this power and violence not solely in the struggle against their official enemies. "Among you there are many zealots, but there are also many horrible men who do not feel the damnation of blood," says a young woman belonging to the old intelligentsia to a party member in *Cement* (p. 186).

Lenin, as his works witness, was strongly concerned about this phenomenon, which was labeled "bureaucratism." The novels of this period (Gladkov's *Cement*, Il'f and Petrov's *The Twelve Chairs*, among others) were relatively honest in their portrayal of Soviet bureaucrats of this time. Addressing the local boss in the aftermath of the civil war, the chairman of the Soviet council, the hero of *Cement* says: "For a worker to meet you is as difficult as to take Perekop" (an allusion to one of the most bloody episodes of the war). Chibis, the head of the local branch of the Cheka (political police), speaks in this 1925 novel about bureaucratism almost in the same terms as in Gorbachev's times: "Bureaucratism is a system," he said, having in mind the party and state apparatus which had been born only eight years prior. "It," he continued, "is above the masses, above real life, and it destroyed creative thought" (Gladkov 1964, pp. 81, 88).

At the same time, the ideas of social equality were very dear to apparatchiks and many of them tried to be quite modest in their private life. They veered far away from the accumulation of any property and their comfort was based exclusively on the services provided by the state. Nepotism and the protection of family members or relatives was deeply alien to them, and they considered themselves to be very fair and honest in their relationship with others.

The genuine devotion of the first generation of Soviet managers to the state made them people who were really directed by the goals of the state as they understood them. Despite many predicaments, these apparatchiks were able to accomplish the many tasks posed by Stalin and the ruling elite, and on the whole this allowed the creation of a new type of society, which, as a model, could pass the most serious tests—the hostility of the majority of the population which often turned into riots, the starvation of millions of people, mass terror, the destruction of the officer corps of the army, the persecution of scholars and other intellectuals, and the extremely dangerous war.

Yes, the cost of all these successes was enormous—tens of millions perished during the collectivization, and in the Gulag, and the life of people in the "open zone," as Stalin's prisoners called the life outside their camps, was miserable.

THE SECOND GENERATION—THE SOLDIERS OF THE PARTY

The "stockholders," "old bolsheviks," the "Lenin Guard" were the major target of the purges that were necessary to Stalin to get rid of those who did not regard themselves to be the simple executors of the will of the state personified in him.

The "stockholders" were replaced by those who still held the true beliefs in the "cause," who spent all their energy and thoughts in the performance of their professional duties, but who at the same time regarded themselves to be only the servants of the state and obeyed the strong discipline of the hierarchy and abandoned the idea of internal party democracy.

Some of the apparatchiks of the new generation of managers were recruited from the previous cohort of managers. These survivors of the purges were ready to accept the new order in the country and were anxious to express their unlimited loyalty to Stalin and the people close to him.

Among the "survivors" were, for instance, Ivan Likhachev, who was appointed director of the Moscow automobile plant in 1926 and preserved his position after 1937, and Avramii Zaveniagin, who was appointed director of the Magnitogorsk metallurgical complex in 1933 and made a career later—as well as Ivan Tevosian, Stepan Akopov, Mikhail Pervukhin, and others (Vannikov 1988).

However, the second generation of managers consisted mostly of people who were brought up to managerial positions during the purges in order to replace those who were shot or sent to the Gulag. Such captains of Soviet industry in the 40s and 50s were Aleksei Kosygin, Boris Vannikov, Nikolai Voznesenskii, Maksim Saburov, and many others.

Still being hard workers, as their predecessors had been, the new cadres were probably even more demanding of their subordinates and regarded them less as their comrades in arms and expected from them absolute obedience. It was said that Zaltsman, director of a tank complex, ostensibly kept a gun on his desk as an argument for those whom he called on the carpet.

At the same time the managers of the new generation behaved extremely obediently with their own superiors. The author of the biography of Ivan

Likhachev recounts many episodes when Likhachev, a man of strong character, met with his superiors, in particular Serge Ordzhonikdze, in the 30s. In almost all cases, Likhachev without objections or hesitation expressed his consent. Likhachev tolerated Ordzhonikidze's wrath and lashings as his own subordinates usually did when he inveighed against them (Leontieva 1987, pp. 129, 131–2, 136–7).

With all this, however, the managers of the second generation encouraged the initiative of their subordinates and delegated to them wide power, and were in general rather objective in evaluating the performance of the people with whom they worked. They continued to promote talented and competent people even if personal feelings were already playing a growing role in their decisions (see in Daniil Granin's *Aurochs* 1987, how in 1945–1947 Zaveniagin, who understood the importance of genetic research, despite official condemnation, was active in the saving of Nikolai Timofeev-Riasovskii, a talented biologist, from the prison in which the scholar found himself after the Soviet army arrested him in Germany where he had stayed from the mid-30s when he refused to return to Moscow where the persecution of geneticists was at its height).

Still, they were mostly internationalists, no matter how much Russian chauvinism—gradually fomented by Stalin—found easy entrance into the consciousness of some, especially during and after the war. Ivan Likhachev worked with many Jews as his subordinates and strongly resisted the growing anti-Semitism in the country, and was finally dismissed when the KGB concocted "the Jewish plot" in his plant in the early 50s.

The majority of the new cadres, especially those who entered the party and state apparatus after 1937, were contemptuous of any egalitarianism in consumption and eagerly looked for any additional privileges they could grab. However, it was this generation of apparatchiks who could eat caviar in the besieged and starved Leningrad during the war, even if some of them, especially those who as old party members survived the purges, still tried to follow ascetic traditions. This generation of apparatchiks also was still cautious in using their positions to promote their children, but they had already made the first steps in this direction.

Alexander Bek describes a manager of this period, Alexander Onisimov (it is very likely that the protagonist of this character was Ivan Tevosian, a leading figure in industrialization) (Bek 1971). Gavriil Popov characterizes Bek's hero in this way: "It would be erroneous to say that business was the most important thing for Onisimov. It would be more correct to say that there was nothing in his life besides business" (Popov 1987b, p. 56). Old revolutionary, he was even rather ascetic in his private life, never using his privilege to full scale.

At the same time Onisimov was a perfect servant of the administrative system, "Stalin's soldier" as he used to call himself. His loyalty to Stalin was a blend of belief and fear. Only he survived in the directorate of the

Ministry during Stalin's purge which also devoured his beloved brother. Asked once by Stalin, who argued in his presence with Ordzhonikidze in Georgian, which Onisimov did not know, to say who was right—he, Stalin, or his opponent, with whom he sided, Onisimov after a few seconds of hesitation said "with you, Iosif Vissarionovich." He also, as an act of loyalty to the leader, never asked him about his brother, whose fate he removed from his head. As Popov observes, "fear is an obligatory element of the more or less rigid administrative mechanism." Without Beria and his camps the system would not have worked as effectively as it did (Popov 1987b, p. 62).

At the same time he was hated by Beria (with whom he had had a conflict during the civil war). Onisimov, despite Stalin's precarious protection, felt himself all the time on the verge of catastrophe. The fear never left him and could exacerbate his diligence and commitment to work.

Being very knowledgeable about the branch of industry under his command, he was an extremely demanding boss who checked the activity not only of the first level of his subordinates but also of the second and even the third and fourth. Having been named the new minister of Steel and Sheet Metal he called the director of Pipe Steel Production into his office and demanded information not only on the work of this branch in general but also of every single plant, then of all shops in each plant and even about the work of a single big furnace in each shop.

He went deep into the details of their work, and dealt with sloppy work with extreme severity. He could himself, using an abacus, check the figures in the papers that had to be submitted to Stalin. What is more, Onisimov nourished in himself a strong distrust of subordinates, liking to repeat, "If you trust somebody, you perish." He also used to enter the factory from a back door and tried to find the real state of affairs, whatever they were.

However, as Popov shrewdly observes, even such a seemingly impeccable servant of the Soviet state as Onisimov was far from being the perfect instrument of management. Imitating his boss, he did not tolerate the objection of subordinates and, what is even more important, he selected for promotion conformists, people personally devoted to him or dependent on him for instance, because they had been caught in petty crimes.

It is not accidental that even Onisimov, with all his dedication to "the cause," made a number of serious mistakes if one judges his behavior by state goals—he supported an adventurous project (Stalin demanded it) and refused to back real technological innovation because he trusted the expert of his Ministry who disliked the project.

Onisimov represents in some way not only the second but also the first generation of Soviet managers who came, as was mentioned, from the crucible of the underground struggle against tsarism, the revolution, and the civil war.

It was the single, the first and the last, impulse of the new socialist society which could produce the zealots, the enthusiastic servants of the state. It was a real constellation of favorable circumstances when the revolutionary fervor, a strong belief in the success of the official goals, and, certainly, the mortal fear of the leader could generate such people as Onisimov.

A pure representative of the second generation of apparatchiks who were promoted from the bottom to high positions after 1937 was Dementii Getmanov, the regional party secretary and commissar during the war in Vasilii Grossman's novel *Life and Destiny* (1980). With gigantic power in his region where he had to make final decisions from "the reorganization of the department of Biology in a university up to the location of a small shop," as a hard worker, he saw "the aim and the highest meaning of his work in the accomplishment of the tasks of the party and in the interests of the party." Getmanov, as a typical apparatchik of his times, was directed by "the spirit of the party which was above personal inclination and sympathies" (p. 60).

Vera Panova portrayed a somewhat similar type of director of a big enterprise in her novel *Kruzhilikha*. Alexander Listopad who was "blended with his job organically, almost physically," ran his plant with an iron hand. However, he was in most cases fair in the evaluation of the performance of people working for him. He could tolerate the whims of his talented and experienced main constructor. He did not hesitate for a second when asked if it was possible to pay a teenager a fantastically high amount of money which the boy had earned by inventing a device despite the policy of salary ceilings. Like the apparatchiks of the first generation he still could not get accustomed to the new emerging rule—that the place of a big official was in his office—and was bursting to go into shops and be in contact with ordinary workers (Panova 1947/1985).

THE BEGINNING OF PRIVATIZATION: THE THIRD GENERATION OF MANAGERS—CAREERISTS

With Stalin's death Soviet society entered a radically new period, leaving behind it almost everything that can be regarded as a product of the impulse of the revolution. The cessation of mass repression and the gradual decay of ideology led to the emergence of the new category of managers.

Having lost the mortal fear of their superiors and having growing suspicions about their wisdom, the new generation still believed in the strength of "the system" and continued to see in the service of the system the best way to personal success.

However, unlike the two previous generations of apparatchiks, for whom career was a product of their devoted activity for the benefit of the state, the new generation did not link their personal successes with the real achievements of the state and understood that their status depended in the first place on their personal relationships with their superiors, on the intrigues inside the party apparatus, and on other factors not related to "real work."

Believing sincerely, according to their mentality, in the mythological level of the progress of their country, enjoying very much the growth of its prestige and might (ultimately, all this favored them as members of the dominant class), these people in all cases when their career and personal prosperity were at odds with the interests of the state (as they understood it) without hesitation preferred to make decisions favorable to themselves, not to the state.

Possessed with careers, post-Stalin managers began to deceive their superiors, which the previous generation could not afford as Stalin did not tolerate lies if he himself did not suggest the necessity of the deception of the public. Cynicism crept into their minds, and their relationship with their subordinates began with growing speed to be influenced by private, and not public, considerations and to lose their identification with the state and the party.

Their attitudes toward subordinates became much milder in comparison with the past, and they were ready to overlook the violation of rules that did not endanger their own status. Many of them continued to work hard (party and state discipline even in the 70s was strong enough on the surface), much more often than their subordinates. However, staying in the office ten or even twelve hours often had little in common with work for the benefit of the state.

With all this, the labor activity of the new generation of apparatchiks, even in terms of hours in the office, was much less intensive than that of the previous generations and the apparatchiks of the post-Stalin era willingly indulged in various forms of entertainment and went with pleasure on long vacation trips inside the country and abroad with all the associated pleasures.

With some openness to the West after 1953, the apparatchiks of the third generation gradually acquired a taste for Western goods and comforts and began to pay growing attention to their apartments, clothes, and other appurtenances. They were also emboldened to protect their children, sending them to special schools and helping them to get good positions after graduation.

PRIVATIZATION AT ITS PEAK—THE CORRUPTED MANAGERS

Brezhnev's regime, with its open course toward stability and hostility to any serious change, opened the road to the emergence of the fourth generation of Soviet apparatchiks with a radically new mentality. Having completely relinquished, even at the mythological level of their consciences, the idea of building a communist society, they enthusiastically accepted the thesis of Brezhnev's regime that maintenance of the existing order is the highest state wisdom and all those who are against it are the real enemies of the country.

With even more enthusiasm they greeted Brezhnev's cadre policy which suggested lifelong tenure practically for all apparatchiks who did not challenge the General Secretary, paid homage to him, and did not interfere in foreign policy and domestic political security. The same rule was soon extended down through all levels of the hierarchy, and in such a way that each official got full confidence in his position if he demonstrated loyalty to his superior. For this price, an apparatchik got full control over his subordinates. A problem only existed for some people who showed too much initiative and were overly concerned with professional goals. In a few years almost all these people, if they did not change their style, were removed and replaced by placid, mediocre people who had to yield in all merits to those who appointed them.

The nationalistic factors in the selection of cadres grew in importance enormously even in non-Russian republics because, with the determination to have people loyal to them, Soviet apparatchiks chose people belonging to the same ethnic or even tribal groups.

What is more, apparatchiks not only grew benign to their subordinates but entered into collusion with them, shaping mafia-like relationships in practically all spheres of Soviet society. The glorification of the so-called Soviet collective was amply exploited by bureaucrats to their own advantage. Having corrupted a significant number of their subordinates and scared the rest, a manager could be sure that in the case of some conflict or threat from outside, the collective would unanimously support him or her and would cover all crimes committed in the enterprise or research institute.

With little control from above, many Soviet apparatchiks lost practically any serious concern for the interests of the state and made all their decisions based on their own private goals. Unlike the previous generation of managers, Brezhnev's people were not only careerists but also people who were strongly involved in the accumulation of goods and thinking about some sort of independence from the state. The stories about the enrichment of apparatchiks had started already in Khrushchev's time, but in the 70s they became a fixture of the whole period. From Brezhnev and his family collecting cars and diamonds to the last apparatchik—Soviet officials became nouveaux riches avidly collecting all valuable things.

The ostensible pursuit of private goals, the hunt for wealth and pleasures, led the majority of Soviet apparatchiks to the end of Brezhnev's rule into active corruption activity. Soviet officials established a close relationship with people who violated the law and practically collaborated with the second economy. Whole regions in the country, as it was formally acknowledged in 1985–1987 (Gorbachev 1985, 1986, 1987a), such as

Uzbekistan, Kazakhstan, Moldavia, the Rostov and Krasnodar regions, and the capital, became territories where corruption embraced almost all units: industrial, commercial, or scientific. Corruption and other violations of the law were so great that even in 1986, in the midst of Gorbachev's crusade against the party and state apparatus, 200,000 managers were censured by the office of the General Procurator (see the article of Alexander Rekunkov, the General Procurator, in *Pravda*, March 25, 1987).

In their consumerism the Brezhnev generation, of course, surpassed their predecessors many times over. They almost all became crazy about luxurious life, foreign goods, hunting lodges (which in most cases were ordinary bordellos), and other pleasures. Their nepotism became open and arrogant. All their children not only attended special high schools, but had the guarantee of being accepted by the best universities and institutes. The Institute of Foreign Relations, for instance, accepted practically only the children of the political elite (on the lifestyle of the nomenclature see Voslenskii 1980, and Neizvestnyi 1984).

THE CENTER AND THE REGION

The radical mutation in the behavior of the Soviet bureaucracy in Brezhnev's period manifested itself with special strength in the relationship between central and regional power.

Certainly, even at the peak of the totalitarian control over the country, not all bureaucrats behaved as Stalin wished. In many cases, regional as well as "central" apparatchiks simply could not accomplish what they were ordered to do and in a few cases tried to avoid directives—for instance, regarding the persecution of cadres. In any case, the resistance to Stalin's orders could be passive based on the hope that the leader would not learn about it. As soon as Stalin had even the slightest suspicion of disloyalty of any Soviet individual, of an apparatchik especially, his punishment was immediate and merciless, a fact substantiated by numberless sources. However, in general local bureaucrats were deprived of any serious autonomy and considered themselves the servants of the Center, implementing the most absurd of its orders (see, for instance, Fainsod 1958).

In order to keep local bureaucrats in permanent fear, Stalin executed the cruel "regional" purges exterminating apparatchiks en masse from time to time. In just the seven years after the war the terrible campaigns were carried out in Leningrad ("The Leningrad Affair" 1948), Georgia ("The Mingrel Affair" 1952), along with special ideological campaigns against "bourgeois" or "feudal" nationalism in Ukraine, Karelia, Kirgizia, and other places.

The concept of mass resistance of party apparatchiks to Stalin's policy, whatever the motivations attributed to them—democratic or totalitarian (for more on this see Getty 1986)—is a pure myth which became especially ludicrous when with *glasnost* many Soviet publications (see, for instance, Rybakov's *Children of the Arbat* 1987) started to depict the 30s in the same way as Conquest, Solzhenitsyn, and Vasilii Grossman (1980).

In fact, the total fear of the central power in regions did not disappear in Khrushchev's period. The new leader continued to remove local officials at his whim, and lambasted them publicly without sparing their dignity and status. The willingness of local apparatchiks to disobey Moscow's orders definitely increased, in particular in agriculture where Khrushchev invented one harebrained scheme after another. However, as under Stalin, the autonomy of the local bureaucrat was minimal, and, if perhaps to some degree less than in the past, complaints from ordinary people about the behavior of local apparatchiks could be dangerous for them. (On Khrushchev's rule see Crankshaw 1966, and Breslauer 1982.)

This situation radically changed under Brezhnev. The new leader endowed local bureaucrats with autonomy unmatched since the revolution and probably better compared with that current under the tsar. The majority of local apparatchiks held their positions during Brezhnev's whole period, fifteen to twenty years. They acquired the status of *gauleiter*, a tyrant with almost complete control over people living on his territory. Local bosses could lose their fief only under very special circumstances that might arouse Brezhnev's ire as was the case with Mzhavandze, the Georgian party secretary, or with Nasredinova, president of Uzbekistan.

The all-embracing collusion of the neighboring levels of the hierarchy led to the emergence of an extremely important phenomenon: practically all superiors were exempted from criticism of any kind, even the most mild. The point is that an attack against any official was treated by his superior as a personal insult and threat. Therefore, the head of a team in a collective farm could not be castigated for any crime because it would mean an attack against the chairman of this farm, who is a vassal of the district party secretary, who in turn is protected by the regional party secretary, who appointed him, and so on.

It is only natural that Brezhnev's regime forbade almost completely any public criticism of the local bureaucracy. It was impossible to censure the party secretary of a region or a republic (or even those at the district level as well as the directors of large plants or state farms). Even *Pravda* stopped publishing critical articles where some flaws were attributed to apparatchiks, a development that aroused the amazement and anger of the Soviet people at the end of the 60s who still remembered other periods when criticism of superiors was a given among the mass media (on the attitudes of the Soviet people to critical activity by newspapers see Shlapentokh 1969a, 1969b).

The central power interfered in the life of the region at a minimal level, allowing the local party secretary to be the absolute master of the police, courts, procurator, and to some degree even the KGB branch. These repressive bodies were actively used by the master of the region against anybody who dared to raise his voice about corruption or other violations of the law covered by the local bureaucracy. In 1983–1987 the mass media published many stories about the arrests and even killing of people unloyal to local bosses. What is more, the coalescence of local bureaucracy and organized crime reached its highest level at the end of the 70s, especially in Central Asia (see Likhanov's article "Clan" in *Strana i mir* 4, pp. 43–53), see also the articles about the corruption and the criminal activity of the party apparatus in Uzbekistan, Turkmenistan, Armenia in *Pravda*, January 18 and 23, and March 7, 1988, *Komsomol'skaia Pravda*, March 1 and 15, 1988.

It is remarkable that the autonomy of local party bosses was justified by the cult of the party as the leading force in society. Any attempt by the local branches of the police or procurators to investigate some crime against the will of the party secretary were treated as "an attempt against the party." The prosecutor who seemingly interrogated Medunov, the first party secretary of the Krasnodar region, wrote in an article in the period of *glasnost* that "even the fact of interrogation by prosecutors he perceived to be an absurdity, as an excess of their duties, almost as the subversion of the authority of the party" (*Sovietskaia Kul'tura*, January 17, 1987, p. 3).

In fact, the regions in the country became fiefs whose masters, observing some rules imposed by the central authorities, felt themselves mostly in full control of their domains. The practical autonomy from the center was able in only a short period to bring all regions of the country to corruption, partial or total. Local bosses much faster than apparatchiks in the capital came into close contact with all sorts of semi-legal and illegal criminal activity. Such was acknowledged the case in Krasnodar, Rostov, Uzbekistan, and other regions (on Krasnodar see Vaksberg 1987; on Uzbekistan see Ikramov 1987).

The corruption at the regional level was the basis for the creation of the special institutions that redistributed national income in the country on a high scale and that provided the central elite with additional income and services.

The new system under Brezhnev which took its most conspicuous forms supposed that each level of the hierarchy had to suborn the higher level using for this purpose the regular visits of apparatchiks to the territories—region, district, village—which are formally under his or her jurisdiction in one way or another. These visits were accompanied, according to the well elaborated rituals, by numerous binges in guest or hunting lodges which were kept mostly for the guest from above, with gifts and many other manifestations of gratitude for the sham inspection of local affairs or for ignoring complaints from ordinary people (on the lifestyle of the political elite in Uzbekistan, see Kamenskii and Alexandrova 1983).

If Moscow big shots were received mostly at the regional level, regional apparatchiks were treated in the same way by district authorities and the directors of large enterprises and finally, by directors of small enterprises and village or city bosses.

The visits of apparatchiks to the places of residence of their bosses were also an important part of the system that significantly increased the standard of living for the Soviet bureaucracy. These visits were also accompanied by revels in restaurants at the expense of those who were on "business trips," as well as by presents of various kinds—from cases of cognac to expensive rugs.

The process of feudalization that was going on in the 1970s was strongly reinforced by local nationalism as well as by tribal traditions. The hatred of Russians and Moscow only abetted the desires of the bosses in Central Asia and other regions to attain as much independence as possible from the center and ignore the interests of Russia. The national republics played the leading role in the process of privatization and corruption in the country. Already in the late 60s it was possible to speak in Moscow of the "Georgianization" of Soviet society.

THE PERSECUTED MANAGERS

There have been in all periods of Soviet history managers who, unlike the majority of their colleagues, tried to pursue the officially proclaimed goals and evaluate and reward the performance of subordinates on their real merits. Such managers in Brezhnev's period became the targets of harassment and finally persecution by their superiors, colleagues, and subordinates as individuals who were violating the rules of the game.

Soviet writers were the first to spot these strange figures along with inventors who, despite the evident hostile environment, tried to implement their ideas and be really beneficial to the state and society. Il'ia Dvoretskii opened a series of works on this issue with his famous play *The Man from Outside* (1972). He was joined by Alexander Gel'man with the plays *The Minutes of the Meeting* and especially *We Who Signed* (1979).

The period of *glasnost* allowed the unearthing of many stories about efficient managers who were persecuted with striking persistence and malice by party bosses, officials from ministries, and demoralized members of "the collective."

The fate of one of them, Ivan Khudenko, was very typical. Having become director of a state farm in Kazakhstan and using his own system of material stimulation, he was able to raise productivity by many times. His experience was strongly publicized in the country in the early 70s, in particular in *Literaturnaia Gazeta*. However, instead of support, the local authorities not only forbade his experiment and fired him but even excluded him from the party and sent him to jail on the basis of fabricated accusations. Only in 1987 was he posthumously (Khudenko died in prison) rehabilitated (see *Literaturnaia Gazeta,* January 21 and October 7 1987; see also Yanov 1978, and *Iskusstvo kino* 8 (1987): 25–27).

Igor Kirtbai is another brilliant manager who suffered for his willingness to raise the efficiency of the Soviet economy. As the director of a big building firm in Tiumen, a Siberian city, he tried to implement a new scheme in the organization of construction in the 70s. Again, as in the case of Khudenko, absurd accusations were concocted in order to discredit the talented engineer and manager who was ultimately fired and left unemployed for many years (see Ignatii Dvoretskii's article in *Isskustvo kino* 8 (1987):11–25).

Vitalii Surgutskii, the innovative director of a state farm in the Moscow region, followed the same pattern as Kirtbai, with the consequences of his activity for the benefit of the state almost as tragic as that of Khudenko. Having behind him one of the best state farms in the region, he was excluded from the party, put on trial, and spent two years in prison. Again, as in other cases, it was the authorities who could not tolerate a manager really devoted to his duties and who cooked up charges against him (see Dmitrii Kazutin's article in *Moskovskiie Novosti,* September 20, 1987).

THE PRIVATIZATION OF THE MASSES

The gradual degeneration of the Soviet bureaucrats and their refusal to serve the interests of the state, has thus far served only to encourage the alienation of the masses. However, before moving on to an analysis of this process, it is first necessary to discuss briefly the evolution of the public and private spheres in Soviet life after the revolution.

In the immediate aftermath of the civil war, the attention of the bulk of ordinary Soviet citizens was absorbed with concerns of private life, despite the existence of a militant and authoritative ideology which called for intense public commitment. Only the most committed party members and some zealous youths in the cities gave priority to public activities, conspicuously defying their families and regarding the family as an almost obsolete institution which in any case had secondary priority for true revolutionaries (Stites 1978).

Performing various social obligations, trying to be good workers, attending meetings, fulfilling social assignments, the average Soviet individual perceived the world from a personal perspective, evaluating various events and trends as influences first of all on their well-being, safety, and future.

Although there are very few sources of reliable information for reconstructing the life of the average Soviet citizen in the 20s, 30s, and 40s, it is possible to get some indication of how life was during this period from the plethora of Soviet literary works dealing with the plight of the individual. Among these are Ehrenburg's *Second Day* (1934), Ill'in's *Big Assembly*

Line (1934), Valentin Kataiev's *The Square of the Circle* (1928) and *Time Forward* (1932/1956), and Malyshkin's *People From a Remote Place* (1957). These works were concerned primarily with the description of enthusiastic supporters of the new order and do not really provide us with significant data on the mentality of the masses; however, even they can cast light on some aspects of human life in this period.

Perhaps a more reliable and informative source of information are the works of those who were opposed to the regime, especially those by Andrei Platonov (*The Pit*, 1987) and Mikhail Bulgakov (*Master and Margarita*, 1983). Except for *Master and Margarita*, these works were not published in the USSR not only under Stalin, but even under Khrushchev and Brezhnev, and became accessible to the Soviet public only in the period of *glasnost*. These novels, and here is the clue to explain their fate, displeased the leaders exactly because they "deheroize" Soviet reality of the 20s and 30s, making ordinary people immersed in their own private as well as public life their main heroes, without mentioning a satirical depiction of the new society with its ideology and practices. Lidiia Chukovskaia's novel *Deserted Home*, which was written in 1938 and has so far not been published in the USSR, also belongs to the category of works written by unfavored authors who were contemporaries of the events which they described.

Another source of information that may be tapped in order to get some picture of ordinary life in the thirty or so years after the revolution are those literary works and memoirs that have recently been published. In the former category are the works of Vasilii Grossman (*Life and Destiny*, 1980), Anatolii Rybakov (*Children of the Arbat*, 1987), Alexander Bek (*New Appointment*, 1987), Boris Vasiliev (*War Will Be Tomorrow*, 1985), and Sergei Antonov (*Vas'ka*, 1987). In the latter category are the memoirs of Soviet citizens, many of which have been published abroad (see Grigorenko 1982, Kopelev 1978, Vishnevskaia 1984, and Ulanovskii and Ulanovskii 1982).

To complement these literary and subjective accounts of life in the Soviet Union from the 20s to the 40s we can also turn to other sources for "hard" sociological data. Particular attention will be paid to the Inkeles and Bauer study "The Soviet Citizen: Daily Life in a Totalitarian State" (1959) derived from the Harvard interview project of Soviet displaced persons after World War II. Based upon the above sources, one can construct the interaction of the roles of the "public" and the "private" spheres in Soviet life during the interwar period.

In the interwar period, the percentage of people who strongly identified with the regime was relatively low, hardly more than 10 percent. Moreover, party members comprised only 3 percent of the adult population. The Young Communist League only embraced about 10 percent of Soviet youth as well.

Thus, the bulk of the population had not been significantly affected by the new order, at least in terms of their patterns of behavior. As was the case before the revolution, private concerns remained the center of individual life. Indeed the overriding concern was sheer physical survival, particularly during the "hard" years following the demise of the NEP.

Peasants (who comprised two-thirds of the population at this time) bore the brunt of the hardship. Mozhaiev, for example, portrays in *Alive* (1981) the tribulations of Fedor Kuzkin, a collective farmer who resorts to unbelievable tricks in order to prevent the starvation of his family. Other works, such as Fedor Abramov's *Two Winters, and Three Summers* (1968) and Viktor Astafiev's *Tsar-Fish* (1986) depict the hardships of peasants in Arkhangelsk and Irkutsk. I do not mention the life of peasants during the period of famine, especially in Ukraine, the northern Caucasus, and some other regions of the country (Conquest 1986; see also Vasilii Grossman's *All Flows*, 1971).

Although life in the cities during this period was not as bad as it was in the countryside, urban dwellers also had to deal with all sorts of discomforts and material needs. Millions of Soviet workers in the cities, most of whom were former peasants, lived under absolutely terrible conditions (for a description of life in labor barracks see Malyshkin's *People from a Remote Place*, 1957, pp. 112–20), while others were forced to live in overcrowded communal apartments with up to twenty families sharing one bathroom and one kitchen (about life in communal apartments see Chukovskaia 1981, Platonov 1987, and Rybakov 1987).

Fear of harassment at the hands of the authorities was also an everyday occurrence for most of the population. Indeed, Bulgakov's *Master and Margarita* paints a bleak picture of individual life, noting how arrests and the continual threat of arrest pervaded the daily lives of every character. Malyshkin also comments on the effect of the all-pervasive, iron authority of the state at this time. As one of the heroes of *People from a Remote Place* puts it, "the whole country is being combed with an iron hand." (pp. 76/193).

Andrei Platonov, in *The Pit* (1987), reconstructs the atmosphere of almost total arbitrariness of the state in dealing with the population, and the effects this had on people who could not understand why they were being harassed and tortured for no apparent reason. Out of desperation, as Platonov put it, the average Soviet citizens "decided to tolerate their life to the end," and to wait for "the time of the liquidation of everything" (pp. 65, 71).

Malyshkin, on the other hand, deals with a group of workers in the 30s who were assigned to build a new metallurgical plant. Indeed they were far less concerned with the goals of "socialist construction" and were far more concerned with their own private needs. Vasilii Podoprigora, for example, a party official and propagandist at the construction site, sadly recognized that his discussion with the workers "often deviated from the necessary direction because workers posed questions about their present life" (Malyshkin 1957, p. 190; see also pp. 112–205). Moreover, even those characters in the book who generally sided with the new order viewed the situation pessimistically. "Kolia," asks Olga the mistress of the journalist Soustin, "will we ever be happy?" His answer is not promising (pp. 22–23).

However, these difficulties only served to strengthen "private ties" with family and friends. Indeed reliance on private relations served to compensate for the hardships of life under the new order (see Grigorenko 1982, Orlova 1982). This argument is supported by data provided by the Harvard Study Group. To the question of how their relationships developed with their families during this time, about half of the respondents (58 percent for the intelligentsia, 42 percent of workers, and 45 percent of peasants) stated that "it grew closer"; only 18 percent (7 percent of the intelligentsia, 21 percent of the workers, and 30 percent of the peasants) replied that their families grew apart (Inkeles and Bauer 1959, p. 211).

Survey data on child-rearing practices also provides telling information on the effects of the new order on private lives. For example, the number of respondents who emphasized "personal values" in raising children increased from 18 percent in the prerevolutionary period to 22 percent in the postrevolutionary period, for nonmanual workers, and 11 to 23 percent respectively for manual workers. In contrast, the perceived role of "political values" in the same time period did not increase significantly—from 4 to 8 percent for nonmanual workers and from 7 to 9 percent for manual workers (p. 221).

The priority of private life for the Soviet masses was combined with the fact that the average Soviet individual looked at the state and its agencies with terror, awe, and even respect, and simply accepted as a fact of life that only by serving the new state machine well would it be possible to survive, let alone gain a comfortable life.

Therefore, even the most fierce enemies of the new order, swearing to themselves that they were bolsheviks, demonstrated their readiness to accomplish their duties as much as possible. The clash between the behavior and mentality of these people (and they probably made up a great part of the population—millions of people belonging to the persecuted classes of society such as the bourgeois, the landlord, kulaks, the old intelligentsia, former bureaucrats of the old regime, and later, the majority of the peasant class) was radically different from the hypocrisy of their descendants in the 60s and 70s. If the latter suggested to themselves and others that they liked the system while trying to deceive it as much as possible, the former hated the Soviet order with all their hearts, observing in most cases rules imposed on them by the authorities they so loathed.

The majority of those whose lives were destroyed by Soviet power in the

30s looked upon the state with consternation and panic. Terror had created a mass state of mind of utter helplessness. At the individual level, many people sought some type of rationalization for the atrocities they confronted. A people benumbed by the excesses of a monstrous leviathan during the period of the industrialization and collectivization was the picture painted by Platonov in *The Pit* (1987), which became available to Soviet readers only fifty years later.

Of course, even in this initial period many people, especially young ones, already rationalized their fealty to the regime by the use of lofty ideas that in no way were strongly internalized by them, as was demonstrated during the war with the Germans, when many Soviet activists, without batting an eye, changed sides. Vasilii Bykov depicted such cases vividly in his *Sign of Disaster* (1986).

The belief in the state as the employer, as the single source of all benefits, underlay the Stakhanov movement organized by the leadership for various reasons, mostly political, but also economic. Falsely depicted as "spontaneous," as initiated by the working class, as inspired by devotion to communist ideals, the campaign was able to recruit a large number of people who wanted to be singled out in their work in order to demonstrate political loyalty to their superiors, and gain more money and other benefits.

The role of the state as the single disburser of individual economic benefit and its ability instantaneously to destroy an individual reached its peak in the 30s and 40s. Indeed even previously self-sufficient peasants could not survive without the state. It was the state which controlled, through the person of the chairman of the collective farm, the distribution of lands for private plots, transport, and the disbursement of livestock forage without which life in the countryside would be almost impossible. Abramov and Mozhaiev vividly describe the almost absolute dependence of the peasants on the state during this time.

The situation in the cities was much the same. The state controlled the very means of subsistence for the urban dweller, not only through employment, but also as the principal provider of housing and medical services. The power of the Soviet leviathan over the individual is colorfully described in works such as Chukovskaia's *Deserted Home* (1940), and Bulgakov's *Master and Margarita* (written from 1929 to 1940, there is an episode in which on the day after the death of the writer Berlioz, thirty-two residents of his communal house lay claim to his room).

Despite this, some individual citizens still sought to better themselves, even through "extra-legal" means. Although a risky venture, since the power of the state to retaliate was great, there were a few, if modest, examples of efforts to beat the system. In Bulgakov's *Master and Margarita* the greatest crime was committed by Nikanor Bosoi, the real estate manager, who allowed a foreigner, Woland, to rent an apartment in return for a bribe provided in U.S. dollars. Other characters in the book attempt to circumscribe the requirement that they turn in their hard currency and jewels (Bulgakov 1983). Nonetheless, as was the case with the protagonists in Malyshkin's *People from a Remote Place*, Rybakov's *Children of the Arbat*, and Antonov's *Vas'ka*, people rarely resort to illegal means to obtain material goods.

Only those who enter the criminal world are ready to resort to any means or tricks for their own benefit. Ostap Bender, the "great operator" of Il'a Il'f and Evgenii Petrov's famous novel *The Golden Calf*, is a symbol of swindling and fraud, along with his best friend Ippolit Vorobianinov. They both are very far from the majority of Soviet citizens who in the 70s and 80s far surpassed Bender in deceptions of the system. However, the swindlers, crooks, speculators and defrauders of *The Twelve Chairs* and *The Golden Calf* (1928 and 1931, respectively), as well as those in the stories of another great satirist, Mikhail Zoshchenko, and of other Soviet writers (see, for instance, Valentin Kataiev's *Embezzlers* [1927]), all belonged to the 20s, before the hardening of the system with the remnants of NEP swept away by Stalin's iron hand.

THE GRADUAL SEPARATION OF THE SOVIET PEOPLE FROM THE SOVIET STATE

The disappearance of mass terror and the decline of ideology as a factor in Soviet life had a tremendous impact on the behavior and mentality of the average Soviet individual. Even more important was the gradual change in the behavior of superiors who, standing in front of the Soviet people, became more and more absorbed with their interests at the patent expense of the state, up to conspicuous corruptions and mafia-like activity.

With the acceleration of these processes, which had gone on since the late 50s, the state started to lose its authority in the eyes of the majority of the Soviet people, who began to find it unfair in the evaluation of human performance and in determining the rewards for good work. Soviet people gradually, but with growing speed, began to withdraw their energy, time, and emotions from public activity directed by the state, feeling increasing alienation from everything linked to it.

Labor Ethics

The post-Stalin era and the decompression of society has also led to fundamental changes in labor ethics. Since the 50s there has been a steady decline in labor ethics and discipline, stemming in part from the changing nature of official supervision. Moreover, other factors have also served to accelerate this process of the decline in labor ethics and discipline. These include the increase in individual aspirations resulting from the expansion of education and the mass media, the lack of material incentives in the form of the availability of material goods, and the growth of the so-called "second economy" with its easy way to gain much more than by working in the state sector.

As a result of this process of labor demoralization, there began to emerge a stratum within Soviet labor that became desensitized with regard to any form of material or moral incentives. The negative attitude towards work has developed into an underlying subculture in Soviet society, capable of replicating itself across generations. Another stratum, closely related to the above, is made up of those who refuse to be diligent in their state employment, but who work arduously when dealing in the private sector. It has been estimated that, together, these two groups will comprise about two-thirds of the Soviet labor force in the mid-1980s (see Zaslavskaia 1986, p. 63; Klopov 1985, pp. 229-30, 234; Kesel'man 1981, p. 149).

The principal group within Soviet society which has been most affected by labor demoralization is the youth of the country. One of the best Soviet studies in industrial sociology, for example, noted that in the late 70s the number of "violations in labor discipline" among workers below the age of thirty was more than twice that of workers over thirty (Iadov 1983, p. 56; see also Sonin 1986, pp. 143-44; Babosov, et al. 1985, p. 113; Plaskii 1982, pp. 53 and 56-57).

Resource Waste

With the subsidence of state terror in the post-Stalin era, there has emerged a growing problem with the waste of valuable resources through individual pilfering, indicative of the growing alienation of the individual from the state. According to official sources, for example, approximately one-third of the annual agricultural harvest does not reach the consumer. This is primarily due to resource waste. Along with agriculture there have been significant amounts of waste through mismanagement in the building industry, timber production, commerce, machine building, and many other sectors of the Soviet economy. Also, mismanagement in the production of capital goods has further contributed to the waste of valuable materials, capital, and labor (see Bunich 1986, p. 27; Gvozdev 1985, p. 88; Ageev 1984, p. 113). Indeed, part of the rationale for the widespread pilfering of "public property" is the popular notion that since it does not "belong" to anybody, it is therefore free to individuals to appropriate for their own use (see Gorbachev 1987a).

Ritualism in Public Life

The concept of a legal civil society (i.e. the social and political activity of people that does not fall within the purview of the state) has always been absent from Soviet society (although the official line has always asserted that it does exist). However, in the pre-war period, there did exist a considerable stratum of society (mainly party members and urban youths) that was genuinely dedicated to the cause of building socialism and did not simply mimic the party line in order to ensure its physical survival (Orlova 1982; Kopelev 1978; Grigorenko 1982). The exuberance of these Soviet activists is portrayed in several Soviet novels written during this period, as well as more recent works (see for example Antonov 1987).

Following the death of Stalin in 1953, factors similar to those which elicited a decline in labor ethics also contributed to increasing political cynicism and heightened ritualism in political life. For instance, by the middle of the 1980s, virtually all Soviet citizens regarded elections to governmental offices as nothing but a necessary but meaningless political ritual. "Activism" became a necessary evil to perform, and ideological and "voluntary" social work became devoid of any personal import. Party and trade union membership became vehicles to advance personal professional goals, rather than the result of spontaneous dedication to the goals or vision of socialism.

These attitudes of "passivity" and disinterest in the formal "mass" organizations is reflected in a number of works that have appeared during the period of *glasnost*. Indeed this mass "passivity" has been recognized by the Gorbachev regime as a central problem facing the reformist movement (see Gorbachev 1987a, 1987b, 1987c, 1987d; Iakovlev 1987). The memoirs of former Soviet citizens (Ashkenazy 1985; Vishnevskaia 1984) as well as Soviet novels (regarding Komsomol life see Poliakov 1985; regarding trade unions see Shtemler's novel *Supermarket*, 1984) and movies (*Fall in Love at My Own Desire* 1982; *Kind People* 1979; *My Dear Edison* 1986; *Office Romance* 1977) all treat this "passivity" as a central theme. Sociological studies conducted in the Brezhnev period also seem to confirm the deep alienation the Soviet people felt vis-à-vis official organizations (see for instance, Plaskii 1982, p. 89; Voinova and Petrov 1975, p. 163; Grushin and Onikov 1980; Voinova and Chernakova 1979, p. 82, 85, and 87–90).

THE GROWING ROLE OF PRIVATE LIFE

With the decline in the genuine involvement of the average Soviet citizen in officially sponsored organizational activity since 1953, there has emerged a corresponding increase in the emphasis on private life, the increasing role of illegal civil society (i.e. social activities that are not controlled by the state), and the expansion of illegal activity within the state itself. These three processes form the basis of current civil activity in the USSR.

The family, which had never really ceased to be the center of Russian life, despite the efforts of the state, has in recent years become the focal point of not only private activity, but public as well. Coupled with the increased reliance on the family as an alternative organizational unit of society, there has been an increased interest among Soviet citizens in the accumulation of personal property.

There are several reasons for this. First of all, since the late 1950s (unlike in the pre-war period) there has been an increasing abundance in the supply of consumer products, especially consumer durables. Because of this, the average Soviet citizen has been able to accumulate more personal property than ever before. Indeed, at present, almost all Soviet families possess television sets, refrigerators, and radios. Moreover 70 percent own washing machines, 37 percent possess vacuum cleaners, and 33 percent tape recorders and cameras (*TsSU* 1986). By the early 80s, up to one-third of the population had fancy furniture, and 14 percent of workers, 76 percent of peasants, and 25 percent of the intelligentsia owned "expensive jewelry" (Bigulov et al. 1984, p. 91). The mass appetite for conspicuous consumption was further whetted by the "automobilization" of the country in the 60s. By the middle 80s, 10 percent of Soviet families owned personal cars (Eko 1985, p. 103). The expansion in the number of privately owned condominiums and transformation of millions of citizens into private owners of housing has also contributed to the growth of the "privatization" of mass consciousness.

This spread of gross consumption and the spread of private property to city residents in the 70s (it was estimated that not less than half of all Soviet families own private plots; (see *Nedelia* 35 [1987]:17) has also served to increase the individual's involvement in his private affairs, at the expense of public activity. Indeed the improvement in housing conditions, the possession of country houses, private plots, automobiles, and consumer durables have led to the "privatization" of individual leisure time at the expense of time spent at public institutions and official functions. Since the 1960s, for example, the attendance of public functions has been declining; between 1970 and 1984, individual expenditure on public entertainment remained virtually the same, despite a 59 percent increase in real income (per capita) (*TsSU* 1985, p. 426). This process of the privatization of leisure time has been long recognized as a problem by Soviet officials (see Churbanov 1986, p. 57; Zinin and Diskin 1985, p. 186–87).

The Growing Role of the Family

With the decline in the use of overt coercion for social control in the three decades after Stalin's death, there emerged a greater emphasis on the family as the social unit with which individuals primarily identified. Hence the family has become the unit for which individuals seek to achieve benefits, even through illegal means, and now represents a refuge from state intervention and even the basis from which all sorts of activities directed "against" the state can be conducted. Indeed, as we shall argue later in this chapter, the family has become the major arena for legal (e.g. private plots) as well as semi-legal or illegal activity which makes up the "real" civil society in the USSR. Moreover, the family also performs important social functions, such as the principal source of information outside of official channels, a source of entertainment, and a forum for other activities that are impossible to perform under the aegis of the state.

Past sociological surveys on value orientations in the 60s, 70s, and 80s seem to bear this interpretation out. All these surveys demonstrated that the family as a value was ranked higher than any other values related to social activities (e.g. professional work, social prestige, active life, etc.) (Fainburg 1969, p. 93; ibid 1982, p. 73; Arutiunian 1972, p. 18; ibid 1980, p. 151; Iadov et al. 1970, p. 248; Iadov 1977, ibid p. 229, 1977, p. 56; Kharchev 1982, p. 17).

Friendship Networks as Major Private Institutions

Along with the family, the role of friendship networks in private life has increased dramatically in the post-Stalin era. During the Stalinist period, friendship bonds were weakened considerably, primarily because of the pressures of the totalitarian state. The destruction of strong personal bonds seems endemic to such societies, as demonstrated by several studies on Stalinist Russia, and Maoist China and Vietnam (see Orlov 1953; Grigorenko 1982; Terz 1984; Liang Heng and Shapiro 1983, 1986; Toai and Chanoff 1986).

However, friendship flourishes when there is a "softening" of such despotic regimes. During periods of "decompression" friendship networks complement the family as the principal shelter and basis for semi-legal and illegal activity directed against the state. For instance, friendship networks assist individuals in "beating the system" in a variety of ways—in the procurement of scarce goods; in the access to educational, medical, and recreational facilities; in locating employment; as well as in providing reliable information and company for social activities (see Shlapentokh 1984).

In Soviet society, like most other nondemocratic systems, friendship is highly valued as providing important social services. Indeed as indicated by survey research conducted in the USSR, friendship is consistently ranked higher in terms of values than other orientations. In Iadov's study of engineers, for example, friendship was ranked as sixth among eighteen values; by contrast, in a study of Americans with higher education respondents ranked friendship as twelfth in importance in a range of eighteen values (Iadov 1979, p. 90; Rokeach 1973, p. 64; see also Boiko 1980, p. 105; Titma 1981, p. 77; Babosov 1985, p. 145).

Moral Nihilism

Another negative trend, at least from the perspective of the Gorbachev regime, is the increasingly visible and militant individualism. This "moral nihilism"rejects the notion of moral obligations, and "sacred responsibilities."

So, the growing number of people attempt to avoid any work at all and become "social parasites." Journalists in *Literaturnaia Gazeta* supposed that these people made up a significant proportion of the Soviet population in the 70s, a fact that becomes even more significant if one takes into account the stiff penalties for those who have no permanent residence or permanent job.

THE "REAL" SOVIET CIVIL SOCIETY

The privatization of Soviet society would have remained at a rather modest level, and would not have radically altered the fabric of Soviet society, had it emerged only in such primary associational groups as family and friends. Moreover, this process has spilled over into other arenas of social interaction that are not bound by personal relations. Indeed having entered the wider arena of society, this "privatization" process has led to the creation of various institutions which together make up what can be referred to as Soviet "civil" society.

The Economy

The private plots of collective farmers have always represented the elements within Soviet civil society (although the official attitude toward them has oscillated enormously in Soviet history). Since the mid-1970s, the Soviet regime has moved toward the active support of peasant private plots. Moreover, the Gorbachev regime has sought to extend this right to urban dwellers as well, largely with the thought of increasing food production. By the early 1980s, private plots representing only 2–3 percent of the arable land, produced up to one-third of all agricultural products in the country (Levin and Petrovich 1984, p. 133; Rimashevskaia and Karapetian 1985, p. 84). According to Soviet economists, the total labor expenditure in the private plots is almost the same as for collective and state farms—about 20 million full-time workers (Dumnov et al. 1984, p. 107–08).

Another element is the activity of moonlighters, who include about 15 percent of the labor force. These private laborers of the second economy produce about half of the services rendered by the state sector (Shokhin 1986, p. 43). A third element of the second economy are the free-lance laborers, such as private construction teams, who sell their labor on a "market." Although concentrated primarily in the construction industry, they have been joined in recent years by free-lance agricultural workers, who are now utilized by collective and state farms as "shock" labor.

Finally, there are those private enterprises in the services, commerce, and industry that function as a "secret" branch of a state organization. These enterprises mushroomed during the Brezhnev era, especially at the republic level. Although briefly condemned after his death, there has been a growing resurgence in their use with the decentralization and privatization program espoused by the Gorbachev reformers in 1986–1987.

Culture

The scope of "private" (i.e. not directly controlled by the state) cultural activities is no less significant than that of the second economy. Civil society in this sphere emerged first in the 60s with *samizdat'* and the bard movement. In the 70s home theaters and concerts became important elements of private cultural activities (Litvinov 1976; Cohen 1982).

The most radical developments in private culture took place in the early 80s when so-called informal associations began to appear among young people throughout the country. Within a few years, these associations have embraced a considerable proportion of Soviet youth, and have offered a "private" alternative to the Komsomol and other officially sponsored clubs and associations.

Education and Health Services

The use of private tutors for children entering schools and higher educational institutions, as well as private instruction of foreign languages, music, the arts, and other "skills" has become an important element of Soviet civil society. Moreover, private health care, and private visits by physicians constitute an important feature of Soviet health care.

Political Activity

Until very recently "private" political activity has been the most dangerous element of civil society. Indeed, until the period of *glasnost* such activity was viciously persecuted and political life in the second culture remained rather limited. Nonetheless, although the number of active participants in illegal political activity (dissidents) has always been limited, their impact on future political development has always been great, leaving open the possibility of the expansion of "private" political activity in the future.

PRIVATE ACTIVITY WITHIN THE STATE

Although the time and energy an average citizen spends on activities in civil society outside of the state is considerable, the activities they spend on various semi-legal and illegal activities within their enterprises and offices is even more so. A major development in Soviet history after 1953 has been the transformation of official positions in the state and party into "commodities" for the benefit of self-interested individuals. In the last two decades the value of any job (at least from the perspective of the individual) was determined not by the size of the salary or legal privileges, but primarily by whether or not it provided opportunities for semi-legal or illegal benefits. In the post-war era, people have learned how to utilize their positions to extract additional income for themselves, to gain access to scarce goods and services, and to establish their own patronage networks.

At this point it is necessary to dwell briefly on the major forms in which people exploit their official positions in the state sector to expropriate private benefit. These range from relatively innocent activities to those that openly defy the Soviet state.

Self-Serving Sectors

In the 70s all enterprises began to tend to provide goods and services in the first place to their workers. Indeed it became "normal" for light industries and food services that had over 20 million employees to open their stores and supply of equipment in the first place to their employees (*Literaturnaia Gazeta*, July 16, 1986; *Sovietskaia Kul'tura*, October 14, 1986). This has established an important precedent for other spheres of society, especially in human services. Education institutions have offered preferential treatment in accepting the children of their professors and other employees. The same priority has been given to workers and their relatives and friends for hospitals, resorts, cultural facilities, etc. In fact the majority of Soviet families have the opportunity to exploit their position in the state sector to gain special access to such benefits.

The Exchange of Goods and Services

By having the opportunity to appropriate state resources for their own use, Soviet citizens use these resources to exchange for equivalent goods and services. The bulk of these resources are obtained through "under the counter" deals at speculative prices. Indeed the exchange of goods has become a thriving business, where desired goods, like blue jeans, scarce theater tickets, and caviar can be obtained by the average individual (Katzenellinboigen 1978; Simis 1982; Shokhin 1986).

Pilfering

The opportunity to pilfer goods from an enterprise in which one works is a major feature of any "job profile." Pilfering has become a society-wide problem involving things from food to writing paper. As one author notes, "we are moving to a nation of 'nesunov'" (those who carry something out of their factories or offices). Indeed Gorbachev himself has recognized this as a significant problem when, in his report to the Twenty-seventh Party Congress, he noted that individuals have a tendency to "grab everything they can" (Gorbachev 1986b).

Soviet media has discussed this problem at length, noting that petty theft was rampant throughout all sectors of the Soviet economy. In the housing industry for example, private homes are built that use up about 16 million square meters of utilizable space (about 20 percent of the total construction space built by the state each year). Most of these homes are built by private labor using stolen materials (see *Sotsiologicheskie issledovaniia* 3 (1987), pp. 26–27; Gudilina 1985, p. 34; *Strana i mir* 5 (1986), p. 37).

Black Market

The role of the black market is revealed in the fact that 83 percent of the Soviet population, being unable to get what they want in state stores, resort to paying much more than the official price for various goods and services (Belikova and Shokhin 1987, p. 7). The black market, especially important for young people, is where they buy 40 percent of all their goods (mostly of foreign material) (Shchekochikhin 1987, p. 13).

The black market has now become a fixture of Soviet everyday life and is closely intertwined with all spheres of Soviet society, having people from all walks of life among its main actors—from the daughter of a general secretary (it is well known that Galina Brezhneva was deeply involved in black market activity)—to people with the most humble of society's positions.

Corruption

The Soviet apparatchiks, or those members of the nomenclature, are in an especially advantageous position in exploiting their positions for personal benefit—ranging from clothes, to publication of worse than mediocre works, to sexual favors. As a result, corruption has permeated the country, encapsulating whole regions as well as entire branches of industry. The revelations in 1985–88 on the level of corruption in the country depicted a system where corruption had become a permanent fixture.

Indeed the corruption of the 70s led to the formation of what can only be referred to as corruption syndicates. This informal social structure controlled the cadres, the courts, and the police apparatus, and even made decisions concerning economic and social problems. Moreover, through these informal structures, bribes were used to influence apparatchiks, which in turn significantly improve the lives of officials at all levels—from the chairman of the collective farm to a member of the Politburo. Now, after the revelations of *glasnost*, it has become clear that even Brezhnev and his family was involved in mafia-like activity, in particular in connection with the Krasnodar "mafia" directed by Medunov, first party secretary (see Vaksberg 1987, p. 13, about the trial of Brezhnev's personal secretary involved in bribing. See also *Izvestiia*, January 16, 1988).

Of all of the forms of "privatization" in the state sector, corruption is the most dangerous, primarily because it has become the most entrenched within the system. Indeed, it is "standard operating procedure" in the eyes of many Soviet citizens, and to threaten that procedure may prove to be a hazardous venture.

Chapter 3
Soviet Society in the Early 1980s

The withdrawal of human energy, emotions, and time from service of the state and society, the loss of the authority of the state as employer, and the privatization of all spheres of Soviet life brought the USSR to a critical situation by the end of the 70s. The evaluation of the state of affairs as being dangerous and fraught with various threats to the status of the country was repeated many times by Gorbachev and other members of his team in the 1985–1987 period (see Gorbachev 1985, 1986, 1987a, 1987b, 1987c and Iakovlev 1987).

HARD DATA

There are a number of objective indicators of the decline of Soviet society in practically all its spheres, even if we do not have data about developments in military technology that could be, as will be shown later, of crucial importance for the political and ideological processes of the USSR in the 80s.

Since the beginning of the 70s the Soviet economy entered a period of steady decline and technological stagnation. Gorbachev even characterized the state of the Soviet economy as being "close to a crisis" (Gorbachev 1987b). The rate of economic growth (in terms of national income) strongly dropped—from 7.8 in 1966–1970 to 5.7 in 1971–1975 and to 3.6 in 1981–1985. The dynamic of the rate of labor productivity growth was the same—a decline from 6.8 in the first period to 3.1 in the last (*TsSU* 1986, p. 38).

The technological gap between Soviet and Western industries became much more pronounced by the middle of the 80s than in the 60s. The inability of the Soviet economy to produce personal computers, video recorders, and even reliable color TV sets—products that were on the assembly lines of Taiwan and South Korea—as well as the invitation of Yugoslavian or even Indian workers and engineers to build hotels in the country made the retardation of the USSR evident to the whole world.

In food production the USSR still could not adequately meet the dietary requirements of its population. Indeed, the Soviets have been compelled to import significant amounts of feed grain and animal husbandry products, an embarrassing situation from the perspective of the authorities. Agricultural productivity has continued to remain low despite the tremendous investments made during the Brezhnev era. Indeed private plots, whose production is based almost exclusively on manual labor, exceeded the productivity of mechanized state and collective farms by two to six times (*Moskovskiie Novosti* 35, September 20, 1987).

Coupled with the decline in economic productivity, there has been the increasing exhaustion of natural and "physical" resources of the country. By the early 80s it had become apparent that the Soviet economy could not sustain the reproduction and retooling of industrial capital. This has resulted in the increasing obsolescence of industrial capital and the decay in the Soviet ability to meet the demands of the population (see Val'tukh and Lavrovskii 1986, p. 19).

At the same time the Soviets have begun to face an increasing problem with the environment. The pollution of major lakes, bays, and rivers began in earnest in the 70s: Baikal, Ladoga, Balkhash, Aral, Issyk-Kul', Sevan, Azov, Kara Bugaz, Volga, Dniepr, and others. The air in virtually all of the major Soviet cities has become a major health problem. For example, the workers in the city of Bratsk, which had been glorified in the 60s as a "model communist city," complained that "their city was about to be turned into a crematorium" (*Pravda*, September 7, 1987). Soviet newspapers described the tragic ecological situation in many Soviet cities including Perm, Nizhnii Tagil and others, (*Komsomol'skaia Pravda*, September 23, 1987).

Soil, water, forest, oil and other natural resources have been exploited without any efforts at replenishment. The widespread use of chemical fertilizers and insecticides have contributed to the depletion of the soil. The health of many agricultural regions have been threatened as a result. In Moldavia, Central Asia, the Urals, and even in Ukraine, there were reports that the local populations were suffering shortages in "safe" water due to pollution (*Nash Sovremennik*, 1, 1987, *Novyi Mir*, 1, 1987, *Literaturnaia Gazeta,* July 29, 1987, *Pravda,* September 7 and December 9, 1987; see also the program "In the Light of *Perestroika*," Soviet television, December 17, 1987, about the tribulations of the people in the central Ukraine: The mining industry has destroyed subterranean water supplies and deprived hundreds of settlements of water).

There has also been a general deterioration in the health of the population over the last two decades. The mortality rate increased during this time from 8.2 in 1970 to 9.4 in 1983, with a significant decline in average life expectancy. Two trends during this period were especially alarming— the drastic increase in male and infant mortality.

Several factors contributed to these developments, but perhaps the most important was the general deterioration in the public health service. In the last two decades, the ratio of expenditures on medical services/ national income has steadily declined. Materials published in 1986-1987 revealed the decrepit state of the Soviet public health service, particularly in terms of services, dilapidated buildings, the lack of elementary equipment, the lack of training among paramedics, the low quality of physicians, and the demoralization of medical personnel (*Literaturnaia Gazeta*, February 5, 1988).

The 70s and 80s were also a period of increasing decline in the quality of intellectual activities in all spheres of the economy. Indeed Soviet scientists have been reduced (primarily because of a mass "inferiority" complex on the part of Soviet scientists) to merely imitating Western achievements. This sad state of Soviet science was recognized at the Twenty-seventh Party Congress in speeches made by Anatolii Alexandrov and other members of the scientific community (see *Materialy xxvii s"ezda* 1986).

The arts and literature also suffered during this period. "Hack" books have flooded the market, which are neither bought nor read. The prestige associated with writers and other intellectuals declined during this period, accelerating the process of artistic decline. Theater and Soviet movies have perhaps experienced their worst time since the end of the last war.

What has happened to the quality of life in the Soviet Union since the 70s? The answer to this question is exceedingly complex. In many respects the quality of Soviet life has declined in the period under consideration. In the first place it is true of services—public transportation, commerce, and others—not to mention medicine. The supply of food, of meat in the first place, was also deteriorating, despite imports. In any case, in this period rationing of many kinds of food was introduced or widened in many regions of the country. The deterioration of the quality of food was also an important tendency in this period.

The decline in quality was of even greater importance for nonfood consumer goods. This tendency was accompanied by the rising aspirations of the Soviet people—the result of the growth of education, access to the West, and the satisfaction of basic needs—which led to the growth of lines for any kind of decent consumer goods and the role of the black market and all other elements of the second economy.

At the same time, in some respects the standard of living of many Soviet people was improving, mostly because of an accumulation of durable goods—electronics, cars, furniture, and fashionable clothes. Housing conditions in this period also continued to improve as well as opportunities for tourism and vacationing outside the place of residence. The decline of economic activity and the corruption of managers also created an atmosphere of relaxation for millions who in this period did not fear their superiors and were sure that in case of conflict they could find a job at the next door.

In general, the decline of the material standard of living was impeded by the extraordinary efforts of the government, which by the export of oil, timber, and gold, and the waste of other natural resources, was able to prevent the quality of life from slipping too fast.

Along with negative tendencies in the "material sphere" of Soviet life, society underwent in this period a process of almost total demoralization. One heard tales of the deterioration of labor ethics, pilfering, and the participation of the majority of the population in various forms of corrupt activity. Moral nihilism (the rejection of all moral values), blatant consumerism, prestige mania—all these phenomena became typical for a growing number of young people entering adult life and preserving these traits as they grew older.

Of no less significance were other changes which, while typical for other countries, took especially harsh forms under actual Soviet conditions. The growth of crime, especially among the youth, is one of these changes, as is the significant deterioration of family relationships. The rate of divorce (per thousand people) increased from 1.3 in 1970 to 3.5 in 1983 (*TsSU* 1986, p. 30).

One of the most conspicuous forms of the Soviet demoralization is lying. The average Soviet individual in the 70s easily lied to his or her colleagues, subordinates, superiors, children, spouse, and neighbors. It was a period when a special type of mentality was shaped in the country. This mentality, with many levels and separated sectors, allowed the Soviet people to think, say, and do things that had nothing in common with each other.

But probably all these negative tendencies pale before alcoholism, which in this period, precisely, became a real national problem. According to the calculation of Igor Bestuzhev-Lada, the consumption of alcohol doubled in two decades, increasing the number of alcoholics and heavy drinkers among men aged sixteen to sixty by up to 20 percent (in some age groups even by 35–37 percent). Alcoholism was responsible for many extremely negative developments in Soviet society—from the rise of crime to the number of fires to absenteeism at work and industrial accidents (*Nedelia* 32 (1987): 12).

But of special significance is the influence of alcoholism on children. Alcoholism is regarded in the USSR as bearing the main responsibility not only for the rise in infant mortality but also for the increase in the number of children with inborn defects—physical and mental. According to a Soviet study, no less than one-half of the children born in a family of alcoholics are victimized in one or another way. Bestuzhev-Lada asserts that each year no less than 100,000 to 120,000 children who reach school age are sent to schools for abnormal children. Now these schools have as many children as the vocational schools (i.e., about 4 million students, roughly 10 percent of the number of children in "normal" schools) (*Nedelia* 32 (1987): 12; see also *TsSU* 1986, pp. 405, 496).

THE POLITICAL ATMOSPHERE IN THE COUNTRY

The process of decline in all spheres of Soviet life, which has characterized the last two decades, has had a significant impact on the mentality of the Soviet people and their attitudes toward the system and the state.

The majority of the population, due to a lack of objective information, was not aware of the state of affairs in their country. With their standard of living maintained and even rising in some areas, Soviet people, especially Russians and the other Slavs, combined in this period critical attitudes toward various concrete issues with a belief in the superiority of Russia and the Soviet system over the West. Moreover, the bulk of the Soviet people were sure, as Leonid Pochivalov a prominent Soviet journalist put it, that the Soviet Union had gained "the universal love of ordinary people in all countries of the world" who wanted "to imitate the Soviet order without reservations" (*Literaturnaia Gazeta*, August 26, 1987, p. 14).

Under the pressure of the official ideology with its pompous style, the Soviet people perceive the negative facts which they met in everyday life as rather unrepresentative of the society on the whole. Patriotic feelings inculcated over the decades have been deftly exploited by official propaganda, which seems so awkward to foreign observers.

The attitude of the average Soviet citizen to the public medical service illustrates how little "objective" developments have affected this particular mindset. The deterioration in the health of the Soviet people in the last two decades is perhaps the most tragic characteristic of Soviet life. However, as surveys of the population conducted during this time demonstrate, the majority of the population was satisfied with the amount and quality of health care they were receiving. A survey of residents of five major cities (Moscow, Leningrad, Kiev, Baku, and Alma-Ata) conducted in the early 80s revealed that only 9 percent responded that public medical service was "poor" (Bozhkov and Golofast 1985, p. 98). In another nationwide survey of 30,000 respondents, 78 percent evaluated the work of hospitals as "good" (Bednyi 1984, p. 217). Moreover, 43 percent of the respondents in the major city survey responded that they thought that medical service had actually improved by the early 80s.

Although the average Soviet citizen appears to identify with the tenets of the official line, his actual behavior contrasts sharply. Thus one can differentiate between a "mythological" level, which is what one wants to believe, and a "pragmatic" level of behavior, which is characterized by efforts to beat the system. The pragmatic level of the Soviet mindset, unlike the official line, is characterized by the common belief that everyone is naturally guided by private interest and that those who deceive or cheat the state are those who become the most prosperous.

A survey of Soviet youth in 1987, found, for example, that Soviet young people tend to believe that most rich people make their fortunes in the second economy. Asked who they thought earned the most in the country, the majority of respondents named speculators, service workers, taxi drivers, and so on, as those employed in the most profitable occupations 1.5 times more often than minister, diplomat, professor, and so on (*Literaturnaia Gazeta*, September 2, 1987, p. 13).

The combination of the belief in the "myth of superiority" with this sense of material inferiority vis-à-vis the West has manifested itself in a certain ambivalence among Soviet citizens. On the one hand there is an almost xenophobic attitude to the West in general and the United States in particular. On the other hand, there is a certain yearning, especially among the youth of the country, for Western life styles, Western dress, a trip abroad, and so on.

The results of a survey of youth (mentioned above) seems to confirm the existence of this ambivalence. An absolute majority of respondents seemed to be fascinated by Western life-styles. Asked what their peers value, 83 percent of Moscow students in high schools and vocational schools responded "fashion" (a Soviet synonym for Western goods). In addition 54 percent of them said that they dream about "firm goods" (or goods produced by foreign firms), and 25 percent responded that the imitation of everything Western was "good." Among Armenian respondents this figure rose to 35 percent (*Literaturnaia Gazeta*, September 2, 1987, p. 13; see also Alekseeva, 1983, p. 62; *Literaturnaia Gazeta*, August 26, 1987; *Komsomol'skaia Pravda*, July 20, 1984; ibid, September 5, 1987).

Though the intelligentsia in this period was strongly influenced by Russophile ideas, including the missionary role of Russia in the world, the disbelief in the ability of the country to solve its technological and scientific problems on its own became widespread in the country.

However, at the same time, Soviet people in their everyday contacts with the Soviet authorities display great dissatisfaction with how these authorities handle their problems. Each year in Moscow alone, 5 million complaints are received, which means that no less than 10 percent of all families ask for the help of central institutions (*Sovietskaia Kul'tura*, August 11, 1987).

As will be shown later, the main actors on the Soviet political scene, such as factions in the political establishment and the intellectual community, perceive the current state of affairs in the country very differently. As a result, by the beginning of the 80s, a variety of ideologies have emerged, each with different images and beliefs of the state of Soviet society, and each offering a different solution to the country's problems. The identification of these ideologies and the programs they offer will be the subject of the next section of the book.

WHAT THE SOVIET PEOPLE KNOW ABOUT THEIR SOCIETY

The critical situation in the country (Gorbachev labeled it an "impending crisis," Gorbachev 1987b) which had been taking shape by the beginning of the 80s was far from adequately perceived by various groups in the population. The existence of many systems of channeling information accounts for the fact that only the highest echelon of power, the ruling elite, got access to the real picture of the society.

However, not all members of the political elite, including Leonid Brezhnev, to begin with, wanted to have a full account of the developments in the country, and deliberately barred the flow of information that could reach them. The curtailment of objective sociological studies in the 70s is only one example demonstrating the unwillingness of the supreme leader to know some of the important elements about life in the country (regarding the attitudes of the political elite to sociology under Brezhnev see Shlapentokh 1985, 1988).[1] It was seemingly the KGB, headed by Iurii Andropov, which was in this period the depository of the most sensitive information about the real processes going on in the country, a supposition corroborated by the strong negative stance that Andropov took toward Brezhnev's heritage in the first days of his new position.

However limited the information that was available to the members of the ruling elite (and mostly because they eschewed it), in some cases the rest of the population—including intellectuals and the party and state apparatus—had to be satisfied with the official, very complacent image of life in the society. A considerable part of the population—including the mass intelligentsia and even intellectuals, (especially those who served the regime) and, certainly, most of the apparatchiks—even those who were critical about many aspects of Soviet society—all with reservations, as became clear later, after the revelations of 1985–1987—bought the major postulates of Brezhnev's propaganda.

Critical individuals, being largely well-informed only about the sector of society where they worked, had only sundry data about the situation in the country. In other words, those who worked in agriculture could have a relatively clear idea about the state of affairs in their sector, just as those who worked in science, culture, medicine, or some other sector, would be privy to their own group's dynamics, but not the larger picture.

However, personal experience, taken together with that of friends and relatives, was not enough for those who wanted to have a sober view of current developments. They could not claim that impressions and data they accumulated were fully representative even in their own area of activity. A biologist, for instance, could contend that his science was in very bad shape but he could not extend with certainty this judgment to physics, and those who found the situation terrible in metallurgy could not be sure that the same was true of the performance of the air industry. The control of the state over the evaluation of information, its monopoly with regard to proclaiming what is typical and what is an exception (a "deviation"), played an extremely important role in keeping the absolute majority of the population in darkness (on this control of data evaluation in the USSR see Shlapentokh 1986).

Communication between people with experience in different sectors of society only slightly helped to give a clear idea of the whole of society because there were people who did not want to have a gloomy view of life around them and who offered views more optimistic than were warranted by the situation in their area. Since only the state could determine the degree of validity of negative facts known to individuals, none outside the narrow circle of the Soviet rulers could pretend to have representative information about the situation in the country on the whole.

With political reaction well entrenched in the country since the late 60s, with the suppression of dissidents and repression of intellectuals who dared to express even the slightest criticism of life in the country, the possibilities for confronting the official propaganda with data objectively describing the state of affairs turned out to be very limited.[2] From the late 60s on, the authorities continually spread the veil of secrecy over all sorts of data. The cessation of the publication of many demographic indicators, such as infant mortality, life expectancy, mortality rates by age groups, and others is only one of many examples of the process that led to the publication of books and articles on economics, demography, health service, and sociology void of elementary data.

The leakage of information from those institutions possessing data, such as the Central Statistical Board or the Planning Committee (not to mention the KGB or the Ministry of Internal Affairs) was practically nil. Serious sociological studies that could provide the public with some insight into Soviet society were, in practical terms, either terminated or totally classified. In fact, the Brezhnev regime was very successful in blacking out all information that might gainsay the official picture of society.

The information situation in the country in the early 80s along with the repression of those who defied the monopoly of the state over information affected the ideological processes in the country very strongly.

RUSSIA AFTER NIKOLAS THE FIRST AND BREZHNEV: FIRST SOME SIMILARITIES

There are many features common to what happened in Russia in the 1860s and what took place in the early 1980s, because in both cases Russia, then clearly and now apparently, tried to liberalize itself, even if only in part.

Alexander and Gorbachev emerged as the leaders in these periods when nondemocratic societies tried to move towards liberalism. The similarities between the factions of the political establishment represented by Alexander and Mikhail Gorbachev begin with the condition of their country at the moment when each took command of it, the former from his father, Nikolas I, the latter effectively from Leonid Brezhnev. The historical backgrounds of both reformers were strikingly similar; each, for instance, followed a ruler who presided over a conservative stage of Russian history. Let us say a few words about their predecessors, which is very important for an understanding of the developments in their respective reigns.

It is only natural that in Moscow intellectuals as well as apparatchiks in 1985–1987 manifested a keen interest in the period preceding Alexander II's reforms in the middle of the nineteenth century, and indirectly (and even directly) compared these reforms with those of Gorbachev. The articles of Gavriil Popov are in this respect very characteristic (see Popov 1987b).

Nikolas I (ruled 1825–1855) and Leonid Brezhnev (ruled 1964–1982) created very similar historical contexts for Alexander II and Mikhail Gorbachev. Both came to power with a strong aversion for the liberalism of their predecessors, which they blamed for the troubles of society. Nikolas saw in the liberal policy of his brother, Alexander I, the cause of the Decembrist rebellion (1825) that shook the foundations of the monarchy during the interregnum following the latter's death. Seizing control of the Kremlin in 1964, Brezhnev's faction in the party apparatus laid the same accusation at the door of Nikita Khrushchev, whose anti-Stalinist campaign and flirtation with liberal intellectuals created a political atmosphere fraught with danger for the whole Soviet system. It is significant that the beginnings of both regimes were marked by political trials, of Decembrists (1826–1827) and of the writers Andrei Siniavskii and Yuli Daniel (1965). Both trials, the first in particular, conveyed a message about domestic policy to the population.

Each taking the reins of a society in turmoil, Nikolas and Brezhnev considered the dangers of anarchy and disintegration as their main nemesis, and proclaimed a renewal of conservative policy as the only way to save the state. However, despite their basically conservative orientation, both

Nikolas and Brezhnev were still partly under the spell of the previous regimes, thus feeling somewhat insecure and reluctant to appear too "reactionary," and therefore initially inclined to play with some ideas of reform. Nikolas tried to improve the judicial system, and even considered the idea of freeing the serfs. Brezhnev, in turn, dealt with the reform of economic management, claimed to have increased the autonomy of state enterprise, and even wooed the liberal intelligentsia for a few years.

With the regime increasingly solidifying after the period of uncertainty, both leaders moved toward overt reaction, persecuting everyone who demanded changes in any social domain. It is curious that both resorted to the psychiatric hospital as a repository for those very critical of their regime. Nikolas placed there Piotr Chadaiev, a brilliant Russian intellectual; Brezhnev used this institution much more generously, sending to it many scores of dissidents. What's more, the preservation of the status quo made both rulers the gendarmes of Europe. Nikolas quenched the Hungarian uprising of 1848, as did Brezhnev the Czech liberalization movement in 1968 (see Lincoln 1978, pp. 295–303).

Each of these actions became a critical event in the reign of these potentates, exerting tremendous influence on domestic life in Russia. The Soviet invasion of Czechoslovakia influenced Soviet life much more than the route of the Hungarian Revolution of 1848 by the Czar. The repressive actions against dissidents were drastically increased in both cases. The members of the revolutionary Petrashevskii circle, among them Fyodor Dostoevsky, were arrested in the aftermath of the Hungarian uprising, while in 1968 Brezhnev began a general campaign against intellectuals such as Alexander Solzhenitsyn, Andrei Sakharov, and many others, thus moving the country into a period of deep political reaction (see Lincoln 1978).

Both Nikolas and Brezhnev—especially the latter—to the bitter end did not wish to know the truth about life as experienced by the citizenry, and their staffs did their best to keep from them objective information about the processes going on in the country. Wrote Pogodin, a prominent historian of Nikolas' time: "The Emperor, fascinated by the brilliant reports, does not have the correct view on the actual condition of Russia. Being at an inaccessible height, he does not have any means with which to hear, and none with the truth dares, or is able, to reach him" (see Kornilov 1909, p. 9).

Using the most mild words, Gorbachev characterized Brezhnev's leadership as taken up "by the desire to ignore anything that did not fit into the traditional schemes," as unwilling to perceive "the dangerous growth of critical processes in society" (*Pravda*, January 28, 1987).

Knowing the reluctance of their bosses to learn the truth, the close associates of Nikolas advanced a special theory to substantiate the necessity of disinforming the tsar about life in the country: "His Majesty is getting old," contended Ivan Bibikov, the Vilna Governor-General, "and therefore we have to protect His Majesty and not utter the truth directly" (Zaionchkovskii 1978, p. 154). As is clear now, the old and ailing Brezhnev was also spared bitter information by his Politburo colleagues, including Yurii Andropov, who, while director of the KGB, had, as was revealed immediately after Brezhnev's death, a quite realistic picture of the country (Andropov 1983), much like Count Alexander Benkendorf, the chief of gendarmes, as well as some of his successors in Nikolas' secret police, like Buksgevden (Zaionchkovskii 1978, pp. 111, 123–24, 147).

It is remarkable that both potentates, at the end of their tenures, sponsored sumptuous campaigns glorifying the nonexistent achievements of their rule: Nikolas in connection with the twenty-fifth anniversary of his reign in 1850, and Brezhnev in connection with his seventy-fifth birthday in 1981. Nikolas apparently was much more honest, however, privately acknowledging before his death the decay of Russia, telling his heir, "I am handing you command of the country in a poor state" (Vernadskii 1966, p. 218) whereas Brezhnev, according to many unofficial Moscow sources, stuck to the same fanciful version even in communications with his closest aides.

It is remarkable how lying prospered in both regimes. The lie was considered by critics of Nikolas' and Brezhnev's times as a main cause for the stagnation of society. In 1855, the liberal landlord Alexander Koshelev insisted on the necessity of preparing special memos about "the lies of the government," "the lies of the Church," and "the lies of the landlords" (Kornilov 1909, p. 30). In 1986 two Soviet authors, Maia Ganina and Ol'ga Chaikovskaia, devoted their articles in *Literaturnaia Gazeta* to positing the lie as a leading Brezhnevian institution as well (*Literaturnaia Gazeta*, January 15 and April 16, 1986, January 13, 1988). The result of this policy was the emergence of the stagnant societies inherited by Tsar Alexander and Mikhail Gorbachev.

First of all, each inherited a country with a floundering and technologically backward economy, and a society paralyzed by egotistical bureaucrats, especially at the local level; in the first case by the nobility, in the second by Party apparatchiks. The technological gap between Russia and the West significantly increased during both regimes. Analyzing the developments in Brezhnev's period, Gorbachev pointed to 1970–1982 as a period of growing stagnation in the economy (Gorbachev 1987a, 1987b). The decay of society also accelerated in the last ten to fifteen years of Nikolas' reign—again the resemblance is amazing.

In both cases it was agriculture that was hit especially hard by the inertia and conservatism. The productivity in this branch of the economy, so vital for the country, did not grow in Nikolas' Russia, and the grain yield per hectare even had a tendency to decline (Liashchenko 1947, p. 522, Khromov 1950, p. 18). Literally the same thing happened in Brezhnev's

Russia: in 1982 the yield per hectare for nearly all crops was lower than in 1970, or at best equal (*TsSU* 1986, p. 33, ibid 1982, p. 228). Even more striking is that in both periods there were common complaints: the peasants produced much more in their private plots than on the landlords' estates. Both regimes proved incapable of promoting technological progress in Russia at the same pace as in the West, as in those countries which were Russia's potential adversaries.

The building of railroads, which were the prime symbols of the industrial revolution in Nikolas' time, was progressing extremely slowly in Russia, leaving the country far behind the West. By 1861 the extent of the Russian rail network was only one-tenth that of England and approximately one-seventh that of Germany. Technologically, Brezhnev's Russia was behind not only the United States, Western Europe, and Japan, but also such places as South Korea and Hong Kong.

However, the most spectacular similarity between the two Russias is in the rising level of mortality, a most accurate indicator of the quality of national life. In the last two decades of Nikolas' rule mortality rose from 27.5 to 39.4 per thousand. The same trend, extremely rare for a developing or developed country, took place in Brezhnev's period: mortality rose from 8.2 in 1970 to 10.4 in 1983 (Liashchenko 1947, p. 489, *TsSU* 1986, p. 31).

As well, Alexander and Gorbachev both received the legacy of a country worm-eaten by venality and nepotism. Descriptions of corruption in diverse parts of Nikolas' Russia, for instance Moscow, Penza, and East Siberia, mirror exactly the exploits of the Party's first secretaries in Rostov, Krasnodar, and Uzbekistan. In both Russias bribes opened the way to the highest positions outside the capital as well as to the solution of any problem. In both Russias the local administrator considered himself to be the absolute master of those living in his domain, and in no sense feared complaint to the tsar or to the general secretary (see Valuiev 1961, V. 1, p. 321–22). In both periods the interception of all suspect mail sent to the capital was a normal procedure for local officials. Local bureaucrats could afford to be petty tyrants because the judicial system also was completely manipulated by them. In the words of Alexander Khomiakov, a contemporary philosopher and poet, the court system in Nikolas' time was a symbol of "the black untruth, the yoke of slavery, godless flattery and all sorts of vile things" (Khomiakov 1969, p. 136).

In 1985–87 the Soviet press published a lot of material that, for the first time since the revolution, cast light on the state of the Soviet judiciary system. Accordingly, articles in the Soviet press, presenting Soviet courts as deprived by local authorities of any autonomy, strikingly resemble descriptions of mid-nineteenth century Russian courts in that they are completely under the control of local landlords and bureaucrats. Stories from Odessa, Baku, Tambov, Uzbekistan, Kazakhstan, and other locales recounted the imprisonment of individuals who dared to challenge the local bureaucrats by defending the interests of the state or their own dignity (see *Pravda*, March 14, 1988).

Of the greatest significance for both regimes was the defeatism and almost total immobility of the intellectual community. Liberal intellectuals were so terrorized or corrupted, then by reprisals against the Decembrists—revolutionary tsarist officers and the intellectual cream of Russian society—and today by the suppression of dissidents, that to the end of their reigns there was no visible resistance to the policies of Nikolas and Brezhnev in their respective capitals (regarding apathy and intellectual stagnation under Nikolas, see Lincoln 1978, pp. 320–24). Those few who did not recant their liberal views were exiled, or emigrated and could exert only a very modest influence on society from abroad.

The free-thinkers in Brezhnev's period were probably even weaker than under Nikolas. In any case, no legal Soviet writers could author and publish satires similar to Gogol's *The Government Inspector* (1836), a work portraying tsarist bureaucracy in a manner not possible even in the first years after Brezhnev's death. Some contemporary works criticizing Soviet bureaucracy, such as Alexander Gel'man's *The Prize* and *We, the Undersigned* are incomparably less aggressive than the Gogol play.

No less striking a parallel lies in the common harshness of censorship in both periods, and other covert policies deployed against contact with the West and the penetration of its liberal ideas. If under Brezhnev it was strictly forbidden to bring up the names of Andrei Sakharov and Boris Pasternak, so it was under Nikolas I the names of advocates of liberalization, such as Vissarion Belinskii, already dead, or Alexander Herzen, who had emigrated westward, and even eighteenth century story tellers such as Antiokh Kantemir and Ivan Khemnitser. Even the letters of Catherine the Great to Voltaire and other figures of the Enlightenment could not be printed in 1850 (Lincoln 1978, p. 321). There were also concepts that the press was forbidden to express as conceivably relevant to the Russian reality under Nikolas, such as "republic," "revolution," or "the abolition of serfdom"; likewise "pluralism," "democratization," "opposition," or even "reform" in the last phase of Brezhnev's rule.

Alexander Pushkin, the great Russian poet, conveys the atmosphere of his epoch in this way: "Our public life is a sad thing. This absence of public opinion, the indifference to justice and truth, the cynical contempt for human thought and decency." Today, Soviet intellectuals describe life under Brezhnev in exactly the same words. In both epochs, the single outlet for unofficial views was the *Samizdat*. Unlike Soviet underground literature, the *Samizdat* authors in the last years of Nikolas' reign were members of the tsarist establishment, like the aforementioned Koshelev and Pogodin, and the philosopher Yurii Samarin, who dared to circulate the memos they had sent, with devastating critiques of the national condition, to the Winter Palace. They all later became most active figures in the charting of Russia's new course (Kornilov 1909, pp. 8–12).

No Soviet dignitaries or intellectuals, with the sole exception of Sakharov, were brave enough to follow these examples from the previous century. Those who became champions of the criticism of Brezhnev after his death, such as Vitalii Korotich or Abel Aganbegian, were among those who had earlier sung hallelujah to the regime, if a bit less robustly than the others.

Both periods were astoundingly similar also in the role of the emigrant press, which informed an avid Russian reading public on national developments as seen from abroad. There is, however, a curious difference between these periods, again not favoring Brezhnev; if the number of emigrant Russian periodicals in the 1970s was much higher than in Nikolas' period, the influence of Herzen's *Kolokol* (*The Bell*) in Russia was significantly higher than such current magazines as *Kontinent*, not to mention other publications. Herzen's magazine, with its network of secret correspondents in Russia, among whom were some of Nikolas' courtiers (Eidelman 1973), could force Nikolas to remove bureaucrats, including despots like Panchulidzev, the governor of Penza, whose corruption had been exposed on its pages (Miliukov 1969, p. 15). Nothing like this was observed in Brezhnev's Russia; no articles in *Kontinent* or other magazines produced a comparable effect on Brezhnev's administration. Only radio somewhat breaks the almost perfect cultural symmetry of the two periods: there was no Voice of America or BBC for Nikolas' subjects to avidly use in obtaining information about the life of their own country.

NOTES

1. This tendency to avoid information that could be harmful to the vaunting image of Soviet society was revealed already in the late 60s. My own experience can be useful in shedding light on it. At this time, as the director of surveys conducted by the leading Soviet newspapers (*Pravda, Izvestiia, Trud, Literaturnaia Gazeta*), I possessed the most comprehensive information about the political attitudes of the Soviet population. However, I was never called to discuss them with anybody from the Central Committee or any other body. The greatest part of this information was never used, and when I was leaving the country in 1979, again, no one displayed any interest in obtaining my archive (for more about this case see Shlapentokh 1988).

2. In fact, the majority of the participants in the liberal and dissident movements in the 60s and 70s were involved mostly in the dissemination of information about the country, its present and past, in particular through legal and illegal (*Samizdat*) publications, seminars, conferences, and other means.

Chapter 4

The Political and Ideological Situation before 1985: The Search for a Solution

THE POLITICAL ELITE: THE ONLY ACTIVE PLAYER ON THE SOVIET POLITICAL SCENE

The fragmentation of the country and demoralization of the Soviet population, particularly the apparatchiks, was a heritage that Brezhnev's regime passed on to its heirs.

Those who came to power after Brezhnev had two options. They could continue prior policies while making small efforts to curb undesirable tendencies, or they could adopt a strategy of restoring centralized power and state discipline among apparatchiks and among ordinary people. Chernenko chose the first option; Andropov and Gorbachev, the second. In both cases the initiative came from inside the political elite.

Brezhnev's leadership had plunged the country into a period of stagnation that lasted about fifteen years. Yet there were no forces in the country capable of changing the leadership, nor even of countering, to some extent, these baleful tendencies. Neither the intellectuals (the element in the party apparatus worried about the fate of the country) nor the masses did anything to force Brezhnev's leadership to reconsider its policy. Even the KGB, a political force the importance of which was growing in the 70s, with all its information about the demoralization of the party apparatus, could not seriously influence Brezhnev's leadership. Only in 1982, when Brezhnev was almost completely incapacitated, and after Suslov's death, could Andropov and his people begin to move against the old leader.

The lack of any feedback mechanism in Soviet society was dramatically manifested after Andropov's death in February, 1984. Chernenko became general secretary and, after a short period of animation, the country was again immersed in a stupor which ended only with Chernenko's natural death. It was only the election of Gorbachev as leader after Chernenko that again activated the process of change in Soviet society.

The passivity of two political actors relatively active in the 60s—the working class and the intelligentsia—was conspicuous during the greater part of Brezhnev's regime. While the human rights movement reached its peak in the mid-70s, with the creation of a committee to oversee the observance of the Helsinki agreement, it was thereafter practically eliminated from the Soviet scene without arousing resistance from any part of the population (Alekseeva 1983).

The upsurge in intellectual activity that took place in the middle of 1985 was clearly promoted by the Soviet leader, who most likely sent personal signals to intellectuals with liberal reputations, such as Evtushenko, Efremov, and Zaslavskaia, encouraging them to write "brave" articles, plays, and movies. In this respect, the second "thaw" appears to have been much less spontaneous than the first one.

According to research conducted by Ludmila Alekseeva and Valerii Chalidze on mass rioting in the USSR, forty-eight strikes took place in the country in the period from 1975 to 1983. However, none of these strikes were even remotely similar to the Novocherkask city strike between June first and third, 1962. The majority of the strikes involved only separate enterprises and usually only portions of them. In most cases they were caused by dissatisfaction with piece rates and work norms. The duration of the strikes examined by the researchers was very short—from thirty minutes to a maximum of five days. More than half of all registered strikes were successful, and by all accounts were in most cases settled as "family affairs," remaining unknown even to local authorities (Alekseeva and Chalidze 1985, pp. 153–68).

The USSR in the 70s and early 80s not only failed to experience internal turmoil of the sort visited upon Poland, but also experienced no major defeats in its relations with the outside world. Whatever one's evaluation of Soviet foreign policy during this period, it clearly did not produce developments that were humiliating to Soviet prestige, to say nothing of the sort of military defeats that have triggered reforms throughout Russian history.

THE PREVENTIVE CHARACTER OF REFORMS

There is no doubt that in nondemocratic societies, especially those with political power as strong as in the Soviet case, the political elite is usually moved to serious reform only under pressure from actual threats, such as military defeats, antigovernmental demonstrations, riots, or mass strikes. At the same time, it is true that in some cases reforms may be instigated by the political leaders' perceptions of potential danger. The first type of reforms can be described as "reactive reforms," and the second as "preventive reforms." Of course, the difference between these two types of change depends on the political context. Some of Khrushchev's reforms, for example, his agricultural reforms in the mid-50s, were closer to being "reactive" (the country was on the verge of starvation) than were many of his other reforms.

Preventive reforms are also stimulated by hard facts, such as the stagnation of the economy, the retardation of technological progress, lagging progress in the military sphere, the grumbling heard in lines and reported by informers, a decline in international prestige, and other events and developments. Such facts make up the substance of numerous memos submitted to the leader (if he wants to know objective data), or may be collected by his rivals in the Politburo, the KGB, or the army.

However, as horrible as such facts may look in classified reports and memoranda, and however gloomy the predictions made (if the authors dare to include them in these reports), the leader can dismiss them (as did Brezhnev many times) as overly pessimistic, opposing such lugubrious predictions with much more optimistic estimates offered by another group of experts. In other words, as long as the position of the political elite is not physically endangered—by the masses, political rivals, or by foreign adversaries—all proposed reforms appear to be "facultative," debatable, and, what is especially important, vulnerable to the arguments of conservatives who contend that any significant change would jeopardize the whole system, which, whatever its flaws, continues to function.

There is no doubt that reactive reforms prompted by developments "on the streets" are as a rule much more radical than preventive reforms that are stimulated only by dismal predictions. For this reason, preventive reforms tend to be frail, inconsistent, and superficial. Moreover, they often fail, as was the case with Khrushchev's reforms in agriculture, the economic reform of 1965, and many other innovations of the post-Stalin period. Unlike reactive reforms, the fate of preventive reforms depends on an array of circumstances, including some factors that are very subjective.

Soviet history demonstrates a number of relatively successful reforms of both types. Lenin's New Economic Policy (NEP), adopted under the direct influence of the Kronstadt rebellion and peasant riots, was clearly a "reactive reform," as was Stalin's reform of the army during World War II, after initial defeats. However, Khrushchev's political reforms can be regarded as preventive because, in the aftermath of Stalin's death, there was no serious turmoil that jeopardized Soviet power even slightly, a circumstance which made the opposition to these reforms inside the Politburo so tenacious.

The reforms advanced by Andropov and Gorbachev definitely belong to the second type. In attempting to substantiate the necessity of radical changes in the Soviet economy and other spheres of life, reference is made to various potential threats, internal as well as external, to the Soviet state.

THE IMPETUS BEHIND THE PREVENTIVE REFORMS: POSSIBLE POLITICAL DESTABILIZATION

The threat related to political stability is clearly one of the most important. The peaceful Soviet political landscape does not delude the new Soviet leadership, who, unlike Brezhnev's team, are not inclined to take the political stability of the country for granted. Two speeches that drew the special attention of the delegates to the party congress—El'tsin's and Ligachev's—both directly suggested that they not overestimate this stability (*Pravda*, February 27 and 28, 1986).

What does the new Soviet leadership mean when it uses the term *political stability*? This is used in the Soviet lexicon (along with the adjective *political* in any other combination) only when it is assumed that political power is in danger. And by all accounts, the new leadership has in mind more than just the standard of living. Even the complacent Brezhnev, in one of his last speeches in December 1981, qualified "the food problem" as a "political" problem (see The New York *Times*, January 12, 1982).

There is substantial and fairly clear evidence that the new Soviet leaders are fully aware of the deep animosity of the Soviet people toward their superiors, the apparatchiks. They quite reasonably ascribe the origin of such feelings to the drastic increase in social inequality that occurred during the 70s, mostly as a result of the total corruption of the party apparatus.

Only in this way is it possible to explain why, after Brezhnev, the new Soviet leaders—first Andropov (1983) and then, with special emphasis, Gorbachev—advanced a new ideological concept, "social justice." This concept, regarded in the mid-80s to be almost the fulcrum of a new party ideology, was one of the most central in Gorbachev's report at the Twenty-Seventh Party Congress. It even becomes the title of one of the sections in this report (Gorbachev 1987).

There is no doubt that this concept is also directed against Soviet wheeler-dealers who exploit the countless sources of illegal income in the second economy. The swelling of corruption and of the second economy in the 70s accelerated the process of social differentiation which was completely beyond the control of the Kremlin.

What is more, this spontaneous development completely undermined the efforts of the Soviet leadership to mitigate differences in the standard of living among the Soviet population. Having exempted the party bureaucracy from this effort, the political elite tried to accomplish the task by increasing the income of lower-paid employees while leaving intact for decades the salaries of scholars, actors, journalists, and other members of the intelligentsia (on the egalitarian elements of Soviet social policy see Rogovin 1980).

The major factor in the uncontrolled differentiation of the Soviet population in the 70s was the movement of speculators, bribe takers, and operators, who had previously remained underground, onto the public scene, openly flaunting their wealth, connections, and bourgeois life-styles. A prominent Soviet journalist was prompted to write, at the beginning of 1986, that "present 'millionaires' are not embarrassed by their riches" (*Nedelia* 8 (1986): 13).

It was the real emergence of a new class in Soviet society that could only increase social tension in the country, not to mention its demoralizing effect on new generations. This very important social development was almost immediately registered by Soviet writers and especially dramatists who, like Arro in the play *Look Who Came*, described a new Soviet type: the self-confident wheeler-dealer who looks down on intellectuals and other people with legal income sources as being inept.

The rise of a new class of nouveau riches would have been impossible if the corruption in the party apparatus and the whole bureaucracy had not flourished so during the Brezhnev period. Therefore the concept of social justice, even if it is formally two-pronged, assumes (in line with public opinion) that behind the "deformation in the distribution of goods and services" lie corrupted apparatchiks, without whom the second economy could not have expanded so dramatically.

THE THREAT TO MILITARY PARITY: TECHNOLOGICAL RETARDATION

Along with the danger of political destabilization, another threat has stimulated (perhaps to a much greater degree) the preventive reforms of the new leadership: the danger of a return to U.S. military superiority.

This danger began to loom for the new generation of Soviet leaders immediately upon the installation of the new administration in the White House in 1981. Even earlier, in the late 70s, the increase in the technological gap between the USSR and the West had begun to scare Soviet military leaders such as Marshall Ogarkov.

However, with the proclamation of SDI by President Reagan, the danger of losing military parity became, by all accounts, an obsession of the leadership. Only this can explain the sudden shift in Soviet foreign policy from aggressive confrontation which reached its culmination in 1983 during the campaign against the locating of U.S. missiles in Western Europe, to a more conciliatory approach, which began with an unexpected visit by Gromyko to Reagan on the eve of the presidential election.

Brezhnev's leadership tried to conceal the growing Soviet retardation in science and technology in various ways. In the mid-70s, for instance,

Literaturnaia Gazeta organized a series of articles written by prominent Soviet scholars who were assigned the task of proving that Soviet science was not lagging, but rather was leading the world in many domains.

In 1955, the first central committee meeting since Stalin's death to discuss technological developments in the country, revealed to an amazed Soviet people (whose heads were still full of propaganda about the superiority of Russian and Soviet science) that "there is stagnation in science and technology in certain Ministries which impedes the development of industry and agriculture, condemns a number of branches of the national economy to backwardness, and seriously damages the interests of the state" (*KPSS v Rezoliutsiiakh* 1985, p. 506).

Practically the same thing happened in 1985 and 1986, when Gorbachev decided to evaluate the situation in the country more objectively than did Brezhnev, and expose what Abel Aganbegian graciously referred to as "the historically accumulated gap" between the USSR and the West, though avoiding specifying the period during which this gap increased (Aganbegian 1985, p. 6). But it was the Twenty-seventh Party Congress which disclosed the real state of affairs in science and technology. Complaint about the low level of Soviet technology and science was one of the leading themes at the congress. Delegates working in the manufacturing industries, extracting industries, building trades, agriculture, medicine, and service industries, all described the technological level as very low, and sometimes as desperate and unchanged for over fifty years.

The delegates who represented science at this congress could only assent to the harsh judgments of Soviet workers and engineers. A. Sozinov, director of an academic institute, who was singled out as a representative of science at the congress, described the situation in Soviet science in bleak terms. Using a typical Soviet euphemism, he said that he had heard at the congress "the bitter, but just words that Soviet science does not hold always and everywhere the most advanced positions, that there has been retardation in the solution to a number of scientific, and consequently technological, issues" (*Pravda*, March 6, 1986).

Anatolii Aleksandrov, president of the Academy of Sciences, was not only pessimistic about Soviet science, but also tried to shift responsibility to Soviet managers, who were accused of not trusting Soviet scholars, and of ordering everything new from abroad. Labeling this the "import plague," he argued that the emergence of the practice of buying production technology "leads in many cases to stagnation in certain branches of science and technology" (*Pravda*, February 27, 1986).

However seriously Gorbachev and those close to him view the threat to political stability, it is hardly disputable that they consider technological retardation an even more frustrating and alarming problem. In the end, the political order in the country can be preserved, although the price may be high. Military defeats, however, could be fatal to the regime.

TWO MAIN GOALS OF REFORMERS

It is now possible fairly accurately to reconstruct the major elements of the new party ideology that was gradually being forged among people close to Andropov, and that were expressed in more or less complete form for the first time publicly by Gorbachev in his published speech at the April meeting of the Central Committee in 1986, one month after his election.

In order to grasp the hierarchy of goals set by the Kremlin, it is extremely important to separate the issues that it regards as key problems from those it considers of less political significance.

Of various means that are available, if not to solve, at least to mitigate significantly the two main problems of the USSR described earlier—potential political destabilization and military retardation—the leadership has evidently chosen two as the most urgent and important: the cleansing of the party apparatus and the restoration of control over regional party committees, and the acceleration of technological progress. These means are, according to the Gorbachev leadership, fundamental to any resolution of these most important problems.

Certainly neither of these tasks can be isolated from a number of other objectives set by the new leaders. The cleansing of the party apparatus is closely intertwined with the decision to restore labor ethics—and morals in general—in all strata of the Soviet population, and with allowing ordinary citizens to express their accumulated grievances, thereby releasing political tensions. The anti-alcohol campaign is aimed not only at apparatchiks (even if they are the main target), but also at workers and peasants.

By all accounts, the new leadership sees in a rising standard of living, and in the radical improvement in the food supply and the quality of consumer goods, other ways of strengthening political stability.

At the same time, by accelerating technological progress and drastically improving the quality of Soviet industrial products, Gorbachev wishes not only to prevent military backwardness, but also to solve a number of other problems, including the food problems and the low quality of consumer goods and services.

Of the two main tasks—purification of the party cadres and accelerating technological progress—the first has preoccupied the new leaders most.

The emphasis on the cadre issue is quite understandable, because it is in this area that the leadership has faced its strongest and most dangerous resistance, and because, without a revamping of the party apparatus after the Brezhnev period, there would be no chance to accelerate technological and general economic progress.

While addressing the cadre issue in practically all of his speeches, Gorbachev has also pointed to the crucial importance of technological progress. The first big public meeting of the Central Committee that he convened in his new capacity (June 11, 1985) was devoted explicitly to "the acceleration of technological progress." Characteristically, his report at this meeting was titled "The Basic Question of the Party Economic Policy" (Gorbachev 1985). Continuing to expound his policy during the first months of his tenure, he repeated the same thesis two weeks later at a public meeting in Dnepropetrovsk: "It is necessary to accelerate the growth rate of our economy.... How to do it? We at the Central Committee and the government think the basic road is the acceleration of technological progress" (Gorbachev 1985). Gorbachev persisted in hammering away at the same idea in all subsequent speeches devoted to economic issues (see *Kommunist* 14 (1985): 13–40, and ibid. 15 (1985): 4–12).

THE IDEOLOGICAL RESPONSES TO CORRUPTION AND TECHNOLOGICAL RETARDATION

In its diagnosis of the situation in the country as it was shaped by the early 80s, the political elite was most unanimous. Perhaps even the dignitaries who had been supportive of Brezhnev's conservative ideology could not deny the analysis made by Andropov and then by Gorbachev.

However, the political elite and the nomenclature were far from united in the response to the major problems of Soviet society. The different factions offer differing ideologies as their vision of the future of Soviet society.

Soviet party ideologies differ from each other in various ways. First of all, some of them—Brezhnevian—are conservative, whereas others—Neo-Stalinist and liberal—are dynamic. Each has its own central value: for Brezhnevian and Neo-Stalinist ideologies it is the might of the state; for liberals, social progress. In the present Soviet context, liberal ideology, though not challenging the fundamentals of the Soviet system as it was shaped in 1917, nevertheless emphasizes humanistic values and the right of the individual to strive for happiness and to fight those who oppose its achievement.

Dynamic ideologies offer different explanations for the unsatisfactory state of society. Party liberals blame bureaucratization, and Neo-Stalinists point to the lack of discipline. The various ideologies also differ in their designation of the major culprit behind the problems of Soviet society: for Neo-Stalinists it is the masses, with their low labor ethics, for liberals the bureaucrats. Of course, each ideology also has its own vision of a better future. Neo-Stalinists seek a restoration of order, liberals favor the active participation of the masses in economic and political activity.

Analyzing various types of ideologies, the author is fully aware of their interaction and that they overlap with one another. However, at the same time he assumes that a leading factor in the ideological process is the conflict among party ideologies. As soon as a party ideology became dominant it would immediately change the dominant public ideology—affecting also the ideological mosaic among intellectuals as well as public opinion in the country. Simultaneously the dynamics of party ideology significantly depend on the ideological developments among intellectuals.

The analysis in this book is mostly concentrated on party ideologies as they function in the 80s. The objective is to discover how each of these ideologies responded to the critical state of affairs in the country and in particular what remedies they offered for rectifying the major problem of Soviet society— its incapacity to effectively evaluate the performance of individuals in all spheres of the society.

WHAT PROMPTED ALEXANDER: SOME SIMILARITIES WITH GORBACHEV

The motivation for radical change was practically the same for Alexander II as for Gorbachev. They both were inspired by liberal elements in their respective establishments. Aides to both bureaucrats—Alexander II and Mikhail Gorbachev—came early to the conclusion that the only way to save the country from stagnation and decay was to reduce the power of the bureaucracy, as well as landlords in one case, party officials in another, using for this purpose aspects of Western democracy. Here one sees clear evidence that both rulers, representing the liberal factions of the ruling class, personally exercised initiative in the radical change of domestic politics.

In underscoring the role of Alexander II and Mikhail Gorbachev in the initiation of liberal reforms in Russia, I do not in any way want to underestimate the ultimate importance of the economic, social and political factors that pushed these leaders toward the transformation of their country. However, I want at the same time to reject the views of those present historians who in their drive toward a more "objective analysis" of historical developments tend to underestimate the influence of the leader's personality, in particular that of Alexander II concerning the reforms of the 1860s (see, for instance, Lincoln 1982, p. XIII).

Of course, it would be more than trivial to point to economic and social factors that ultimately exerted the decisive influence on the historical process. However, Soviet intellectuals, including historians—who passed the Marxist test in shaping their views on "the historical process"—believe at the same time that each time society, with a given constellation of historical influences, faces various options and the personality of the leader, his mentality and character can exert tremendous impact on the choice among the options.

The role of the supreme leader is especially strong in such nondemocratic countries where the replacement of the potentate is an extremely difficult task for those factions of the establishment that are strongly dissatisfied with him, an element that helps those who already have access to the means for doing many things—even against the will of the ruling class.

It is remarkable that most of the intellectuals—activists of *perestroika*—strongly defend the idea of alternatives in historical developments, and the extremely great influence of the personality of the leader on the option chosen by society at this historical juncture (see Burlatskii 1988; L. Ovrutskii's article "History in conditional mood," and A. Butenko's article "Before the court of generations," *Sovietskaia Kul'tura* February 4, 1988; I. Bestuzhev-Lada's "Truth and only truth" in *Nedelia* 5, 1988).

Gavriil Popov, one of the leading intellectuals of *glasnost*, has analyzed in depth the origin of the reforms of the 80s in the light of *perestroika*, and came to the conclusion that the role of Alexander II, who was determined to implement his reforms, was of the greatest importance in overcoming the fiery resistance of the landlords. The charisma of the Tsar was a powerful force against the adversaries of the reforms.

Popov contends that "the personal properties of the Tsar, and his closest milieu, even the psychology of the emperor, were extremely important. The struggle for one or another approach to the reform, in many respects, turned into a struggle for the emperor's opinion, for his position. In some sense, it was the will of Alexander II, who wanted to preserve his dynasty, and the farsighted part of the bureaucracy devoted to it, which was one of the most important causes for the reform" (Popov 1987b, p. 78).

Popov also indicates that, along with the Tsar, it was his brother, the great Prince Konstantin (who also being supported by the great Princess Elen and the Tsar's aunt), actively defended the idea of reforms, and played an extremely positive role in the elaboration of the final draft of the peasant reform (pp. 79–80).

While avoiding these two sins—the Macaulean one of overrating the role of single individuals in history, and the vulgar Marxist sin of determinism—a researcher of Russia in periods of radical historical change should, of course, be aware that concrete historical circumstances determine the number of options as well as the distances between them. In every case, during the early 60s of the previous century and the early 80s of this century—as well as in some other periods (1917, the 1920s and 1960s) —the constraints have not been so strong as not to permit developments to evolve in very different ways.

It is more than remarkable that in both cases the idea of reform was not a direct response to internal developments. Under Nikolas I, as well as under Brezhnev, the country did not experience any significant strikes or rebellions, neither in the cities nor in the countryside. A few peasant riots did take place, but only in connection with army conscription, and these were never transformed into national events. In general, the peasants and workers did not dare to express dissatisfaction with their lives. The resistance of the intellectuals, as mentioned, was almost totally crushed; in both cases, however, the new rulers were not confident that the passivity of the population would last very long.

The determination of Alexander II and Mikhail Gorbachev to accomplish an overhaul ("*perestroika*") was dictated by the fear that political stability was only temporary. The tsar said, addressing his nobles, "it is preferable that such a move come from above rather than from below." However, the major impetus for reform in both cases was less a concern with internal affairs than a fear that Russia might develop into a state of secondary rank. Alexander and Gorbachev both saw as their historic mission the prevention of such a decline, and the preservation for Russia of her role as a great country in world affairs. They used the same concept to justify their reforms: "The interests of the state." Insisting on the necessity of the reforms, Alexander said, "further delay can be injurious to the state" (Miliukov 1969, p. 5). Gorbachev, in his turn, also substantiated the necessity of *perestroika* and even a "revolutionary transformation" for Soviet society with references to "the interests of the country" and "domestic as well as international developments." He has spoken of "the forces of inertia and deceleration, which are dangerous in their ability to draw us . . . into stagnation and the country's dormancy." He has also insisted that the defeat of the reforms "would be fatal for the country" (*Pravda*, January 30 and February 26, 1987 and January 13, 1988).

In one case it was Russia's defeat in the Crimean War (1853–1856) that revealed, as a recent Soviet history textbook admits, "the backwardness of Russia in technology and economics in comparison with two powerful states (France and Great Britain) that had highly developed industries. Historians attribute the Russian defeat, which culminated in the fall of Sevastopol, to the fact that the Russian soldiers were armed with smoothbore weapons, whereas their adversaries used a new weapon: guns with rifled barrels that assured a precise firing trajectory. Perhaps even more significant was that the Russian Navy, consisting of sailing vessels, had to confront steamships. The badly developed network of railroads also accounted for the inability to provide the army in time with ammunition and food" (Nosov 1978, p. 257).

It is curious that some American authors, in their recent tendency to focus more on economic and social factors than on political ones, tend to underestimate the role of the Crimean defeat as a major impetus (but, of course, not as the ultimate cause) in the reforms of the 1860s. Rejecting the explanation given by Russian historians, such as Alexander Kornilov—almost a contemporary of the events, they look for more "fundamental factors."

Arguing that the Crimean defeat was not an event which pushed the tsar and political establishment toward reform, Bruce Lincoln contends that "the Crimean defeat raised no unusual concern about national security in the mind of Russia's policymakers" (Lincoln 1982, p. XII; see also Field 1976).

To deny the crucial role of the Crimean defeat in the creation of conditions for reform is to ignore two other critical events in Russian history—the revolutions of 1905 and 1917—which were both directly connected with military defeats to the Russian empire. In all three cases the point was not so much the question of the territorial integrity of the country but its role as a power in the world's politics. This was especially true with respect to developments in the aftermath of the Crimean War. Lincoln himself quotes important documents that witness the willingness of Russia's adversaries to drive it back from Europe to Asia (Lincoln 1978, p. 353). It would be too narrow a view to consider the consequences of the Crimean War only in terms of territorial changes, ignoring Russia's pretensions to control significant parts of the world.

More recently we find the same fears, this time not because of military defeat, but due to the growing technological gap between the USSR and the United States. Reagan's SDI to some degree played the same role as the rifles of the Crimean War, because it is perceived by the Kremlin—as *Pravda* editor Viktor Afanasiev underscored after his trip to this country—as a way to gain complete and enduring military and technological superiority over the Soviet Union (*Pravda*, February 12, 1986; see also Mandelbaum and Talbot 1984).

The danger of the transformation of Russia into a member of the Third World club has been a leading Muscovite theme in the 80s up to this very moment, even spilling over into the press in 1986–1987, calling to mind a comparable mood in the St. Petersburg of Nikolas I. Discussing the tribulations of the Soviet economy and the vital necessity of developing private initiative in order to save the country from stagnation, a Soviet economist admonished his opponents to remember that "we are regarded as a great nation only so far" (*Literaturnaia Gazeta*, December 3, 1986).

The impetus toward reform was so strong for both figures that they could overcome the traumatizing influence of the insurrections that took place on Russia's periphery, and which were used by establishment conservatives as the strongest argument against any moderation of domestic policy. This episode came for Alexander in the form of the several European rebellions of 1848, beginning with France and Hungary; for Gorbachev it came as the Hungarian uprising of 1956, and even more so the Prague events of 1968.

Chapter 5
Conservative Ideology

As was true of practically all party ideologies, Brezhnev's ideology entered the Soviet political scene gradually, developing its content in the process of adjusting to the changing political and social context and making its substance known to the party apparatus (and all the more to the rest of the population) only bit by bit.

THE ORIGIN AND DEVELOPMENT OF BREZHNEV'S IDEOLOGY

The First Stage—The Cautious Attack on Khrushchev

Like many others, Brezhnev's ideology was born as an antithesis to the ideology of the previous regimes, which in the perceptions of many party officials shattered the fundamentals of Soviet political and social order and put the country in jeopardy.

In this case, as in practically all others, the new ideology almost could not reveal itself before the demise of the old regime. With Khrushchev in power, discontent could only be manifested in the closed circles of people who trusted each other. It is almost impossible to find any published piece before October, 1964, that could be interpreted as evidence of a new political philosophy. As is well established, the plot by the Politburo against Khrushchev was a total surprise for him, and his dismissal was prepared and carried out when the leader rested on the Black Sea (Crankshaw 1966; Tatu 1967).

However, it is obvious that the fundamentals of the new party ideology were elaborated before the coup because at the secret meeting of the Central Committee on October 26, 1964, the participants heard a rather detailed report on Khrushchev's blunders. This report has never been published, but all party members learned about it during closed meetings across the country—an eloquent illustration of the concept of internal, party ideology.

However, the new leadership started a campaign for the indirect discrediting of Khrushchev's ideology and also for the dissemination of the new vision of Soviet society and its future.

The term "voluntarism" was used as a code name for the party ideology under fire, and criticism of Khrushchev's policy without naming names became a part of all political and related publications after the second half of the 60s (see, for instance, Ponomarev 1982, pp. 617–19; Samsonov and Kovalenko 1978, pp. 530–31).

However, the adherents of Brezhnev's ideology (as was the case with Stalin's or Gorbachev's ideologies) did not dare to familiarize even party apparatchiks with all the ideas of their social and political program. In the first years of the new regime, the leadership felt quite insecure because of the coup that it had carried out. This coup revealed the weakest spot of the Soviet political system: the lack of legal, in Soviet terms, procedures for changing the leader. The plot once successful against Khrushchev could be repeated, and this time against those who plotted against him, and this idea hung over Brezhnev's team in the first years and forced it to conceal, even from the highest echelon of power, its attitudes toward many issues.

Brezhnev and his comrades came to power with clearly negative attitudes toward the liberal movement. They clearly wanted to restore the cult of Stalin, even if only partially, and in one of his first public speeches (on the occasion of Victory Day) Brezhnev gave a strong eulogy of the late dictator (*Pravda*, May 9, 1965). The course toward re-Stalinization aroused the anger and brave protests of the intelligentsia and compelled Brezhnev's leadership to retreat and abandon it.

What is more, Brezhnev's leadership started to flirt with the intelligentsia, making various concessions to it and winking at the activity of liberal intellectuals (including *Samizdat* and the publications of *Novyi Mir*, the magazine which became the mouthpiece of the liberal intelligentsia). In the person of Aleksei Rumiantsev, a party official, the former editor of *Pravda* and a vice president of the Academy of Sciences, the liberal party intellectuals even got their own official leader.

The leadership also supported some projects dear to the liberal intelligentsia, such as the building of Soviet sociology and mathematical economics (started under Khrushchev), trying to use scholars against Khrushchev's voluntarism (regarding the development in mathematical economics see Katsenelinboigen 1978; in sociology see Shlapentokh 1988).

However, with the consolidation of power and the dispelling of fears of the survival of the regime, Brezhnev's leadership gradually started to reveal in a more and more conspicuous way its nature, in particular its hostile attitude toward the intelligentsia. It is remarkable that Brezhnev's ideology, especially since 1968, was taking shape not so much in its critique of Khrushchev's policy and ideology but in the detraction of the intelligentsia. The evolution of this ideology over almost two decades was revealed mostly in the change of attitude toward the intelligentsia. For the party leadership this stratum arose as the major threat to the system and the Prague Spring could only strengthen this view. Only toward the end of the regime did the ideology soften its hostility toward the intelligentsia and start to use some "positive" (and not only negative) concepts in substantiation of its main postulates.

The Second Stage—the Campaign Against Intellectuals

The developments in Czechoslovakia in 1968 helped to develop the new ideology and make public those of its postulates which had been guarded as state secrets in the first years after the coup. The campaign for the glorification of the working class as the leading force in society—as the model for all others, combined with the denigration of the intelligentsia, allowed party officials to present Brezhnev's ideology in its true light (see Brezhnev 1971, pp. 89-90; ibid. 1972, pp. 483-84; see also the article of R. Kosolapov and P. Simush in *Pravda*, May 24, 1968).

This campaign, which lasted until 1974, was headed by Vladimir Iagodkin, the secretary of the Moscow Party Committee on Propaganda, and Sergei Trapeznikov, the head of the Department of Science and Higher Education of the Central Committee. Both of them published vitriolic and scurrilous articles and books against the intelligentsia and liberal ideas (see, for instance, *Novyi Mir* 1, 1976).

The political elite managed to involve in the development and popularization of the new party ideology hack authors (for instance, Ivan Shevtsov, who published strong anti-intellectual novels such as *In the Name of Father and Son* (1968) and *Plant Louse* (1969), and Stalinists (see, for instance, Vladimir Kochetov's novel *What Do You Want* 1969), and also even former liberal intellectuals who in their publications sustained the major elements of the new ideology, including its anti-intellectualism (see Bliakhman and Shkaratan 1973; Kolbanovskii 1978).

A special role in the denigration of the intelligentsia was assigned to the Russophile movement. In line with this tradition, intellectuals were not only opposed to the working class, but also to Russian culture and traditions (on Russian chauvinism see Yanov 1978).

The Third Stage—the Consolidation of the Ideology

During the next five to six years in Brezhnev's ideology conservatism and immobilism continued to evolve as its major values. The decision to introduce formal party control over science in 1971 was one of the hallmarks of this process as well as the new Constitution (1977) which openly proclaimed the dominance of the party in all spheres of social life and explicitly promulgated the limitation on the use of political freedom if it came into conflict with the interests of the state and society.

The Fourth Stage—the Concepts of "Mature Socialism" and "Soviet Style of Life"

Toward the end of the 70s Brezhnev's ideology became less aggressive toward the intelligentsia and was more involved in the elaboration of its image of Soviet society as prospering under the regime.

In this period the ideological center of the regime mobilized philosophers, sociologists and historians to develop concepts that proclaimed that Soviet society had entered the stage of "developed" and "mature" socialism and that the "Soviet style of life" manifested its superiority in all possible ways over the "Western style of life." Many hundreds of authors took part in the creation of this image of a society which had little in common with reality.

Using various data, sociologists described Soviet people as conscientious, hard workers for whom work mostly had become "the primary vital need" (see Changli 1978, Aitov 1981, Shkaratan 1978, and Osipov, et al. 1982). Other sociologists presented the majority of the Soviet people as highly involved in social work and ideological activity (Sbytov 1983, Plaksii 1982, Sokolov 1981). The Soviet people were also described as strong collectivists, active participants in the management of their enterprises, and as supporters of official policy in all spheres without any reservation (see Sbytov 1983, Smirnov 1979).

Now let me move to an analysis of the content of Brezhnev's ideology.

THE CULT OF POWER AND THE SYSTEM

Brezhnev's team came to power with an ideology that placed critical emphasis on power and the stability of the system as its central values. Watching Khrushchev's reforms this team saw in them a serious threat to the Soviet political system and deemed it vitally important to stop this process, which could undermine the fundamentals of Soviet society. The subsequent developments in Czechoslovakia four years after Khrushchev's dismissal could only confirm their apprehensions about the consequences of the liberal course.

With its glorification of power and order, Brezhnev's team seemingly returned to Stalin's ideology. As with Stalinist ideology, conservative ideology exalts power because it brings order and exterminates anarchy. Both ideologies were able to exploit the commendation of order in prerevolutionary tsarist Russia in their own interests, even creating the impression that yearning for order is an inborn quality of the Russian people (regarding foreign perceptions of the particularly Russian fear of anarchy see Smith 1976, and Shipler 1983). It is remarkable that Gorbachev's enemies in 1986–1987 attacked his course mostly by referring to the threat to order in the country (for more on this argument against *perestroika* see Drozd 1987, p. 13, and Ivanov 1987, pp. 6–7). There was a radical difference between Stalinist and Brezhnevian ideologies. The former personified power linked everything to the person of the leader, Joseph Stalin, whereas the latter emphasized the system as such.

Stalin (and to some extent also Khrushchev) tried to identify Soviet order with his personality and used the gigantic ideological apparatus in combination with political repressions to persuade the Soviet people that the survival of society was at stake. Many hundreds of thousands of people were sent to the *Gulag* accused of lese majesty, of insulting the top leader; in most cases these were people who had done nothing of the sort but were accused by careerists and vigilantes for words or gestures that could be interpreted as disrespectful of Stalin. Andrei Tarkovskii in his famous movie *The Mirror* (1975) showed the tribulations of a newspaper copy editor who did not notice some grammatical error which could be used as evidence of her hidden animosity to the leader. The *Gulag* was full of people who were sentenced for "crimes" like this.

However, whatever was the price, Stalin managed to inculcate in the minds of his subjects, even in those whom he kept in concentration camps (on such people see Solzhenitsyn's *The Gulag Archipelago* (1975) and Evgeniia Taratuta's article in *Ogoniok* 40 (1987): 23) idolatry of his personality and forced them to sob at the news of his death, mostly because they believed that without Stalin the whole society would crumble. As is well known, the tendency to identify a system with a charismatic leader is not at all a uniquely Soviet phenomenon and has been repeated many times in history and was even considered by Weber to be a normal stage in the development of authority in the history of many societies.

The divorce of the personality of the leader from the Soviet system started immediately after Stalin's death, but only under Brezhnev was it fully accomplished. The personal traits of Brezhnev—his evident mediocrity—accelerated this process and helped to develop the idea in the new party ideology of the strength of the system as such and its independence from the qualities of the leader.

Of course, in public ideology the cult of the leader persisted in Brezhnev's time as in the previous regimes. In view of the patent mediocrity of the leader, this cult took somewhat more ridiculous forms than under Stalin: Brezhnev was glorified as a great military commander, writer, theorist, and so on. However, in the 30s and 40s the cult of the leader was universal and a high party official no less energetically and sincerely than a bookkeeper praised the leader in private circles (regarding the attitudes of Soviet apparatchiks toward Stalin see Bek's *The Appointment* (1971) and Rybakov's *Children of the Arbat* (1987), as well as the memoirs of the Soviet dignitaries (see, for instance, Zhukov 1971).

In the 70s and the early 80s Brezhnev's cult was not accepted seriously by apparatchiks or by intellectuals along with many people from various other strata of the population. However, the large part of the nomenclature considered the cult of Brezhnev to be an important ritual that was necessary for the stability of the system. Brezhnev's public veneration was treated by Soviet officials in the same spirit with which nobles paid homage to their monarch, even if he was an insignificant personality.

Being deprived of any illusions about the personality of the supreme leader, Brezhnev's ideology at the same time suggested the high importance of the institution of the general secretary as the major guarantor of stability in the country and of coordination of efforts in the major political and economic actions. For this reason, this ideology demanded extreme caution in the process of replacing one leader with another, suggesting that any violence could undermine the system at its weakest point.

For this reason, it was in line with Brezhnev's ideology to continue the cult of the ailing Brezhnev and two of his successors—Andropov and Chernenko—who almost turned into mummies unable to influence the governing of the country. The prestige and the stability of the country demanded a demonstration of loyalty to those who personified them.

The highest respect for the position of the general secretary, and only derivatively, for those who held it, was combined in Brezhnev's ideology with a strong regard for the representatives of power at all levels of the hierarchy.

Unlike the party ideologies dominant in Stalin's and Khrushchev's times, Brezhnev's ideology wanted to recompense the lack of charisma of the supreme leader with the veneration of all institutions in the political and economic systems and of all the officials who directed them. In this worship of regional and even district leaders who comported as dictators in their areas, Brezhnev's ideology identifies one of the most important elements for the creation of the stability of the system.

Glorification of the party was a special feature of Brezhnev's ideology and regime. Of course, all ideologies praise the party as the leading force in Soviet society. However, with this common denominator there are serious differences between ideologies in their attitudes toward the party.

Administrative ideology in its Andropovian version, as well as liberal ideologies, want to curtail to some degree the role of the party and its local committees and allow other elements of the Soviet political system to play a more significant role. I will return to this issue later.

Contrary to both ideologies Brezhnev's ideology rejects any constraint on party activity, demanding the full submission of all other institutions—including the KGB, police, procurator's office, and courts, not to mention local governmental bodies—to the local party committee.

It is remarkable that in the early 80s, when the main procurator's office started its investigation of corruption in the Krasnodar region, party officials being interrogated by prosecutors slung accusations of an attack against the party in their faces: Corrupted party bosses such as Medunov, the First Krasnodar Party Secretary, were sure that taking them to task, whatever had been their deeds, was nothing but encroachment upon the leading role of the party in Soviet life (see the analysis of the Krasnodar affair in Arkadii Vaksberg's article "The Fate of the Procurator," *Literaturnaia Gazeta*, October 28, 1987).

In fact, in Brezhnev's times, as was mentioned in Chapter 2, local party secretaries were absolute dictators in their regions and could cover up any crime committed by their people as did, for instance, Rashidov, the first party secretary of Uzbekistan, or Bodul in Moldavia.

Along with allowing local officials—directors of enterprises and offices—complete discretion in directing people, and exempting them from the control not only of the masses but also from intervention by various controlling institutions such as the mass media, courts, procurator's office, and police, Brezhnev's ideology also assumed that the rotation of cadres should be minimal and that each member of the nomenclature should feel himself to be secure and free from any fear.

Brezhnev's ideology regarded privileges, legal and even semilegal, to be reasonable rewards for the managerial activity of the apparatchiks, for their readiness to work as many hours as necessary and especially for their political loyalty.

Therefore, this ideology substantiates and justifies the existence of a true dominant class that identifies itself with the system. In its millions of bosses, big and small (according to the data mentioned by Gorbachev they number 18 million, and with their families they make up no less than 15–20 percent of the population—*Pravda*, October 2, 1987), Soviet society gets its real strength, which surpassed in importance for the political order other alternatives—neo-Stalinist, neo-Leninist, or especially the liberal socialist one.

With its utmost veneration of the system in all its facets, Brezhnev's ideology extended its protection from the current holders of power to all those who ran the country in the past. Brezhnev's ideology supposed that any criticism of the rulers of the past was extremely harmful. Any denunciation of Stalin and his deeds is incompatible with this ideology, as it undermines the prestige of the system as such. With all its hatred of

Khrushchev and his iconoclastic ideology, Brezhnev's ideology did not indulge in berating this leader and his policies in public and demonstrated strong restraint even in the propaganda that was for internal party consumption.

THE EVALUATION OF HUMAN PERFORMANCE

With its preoccupation with keeping the existing political system intact, the Brezhnev ideology did not pay too much attention to the mobilization of human energy and talents for the achievement of the economic and social goals that it proclaimed. A real (and not verbal) focus on performance and efficiency requires the encouragement of individual achievements, individual initiative, and professionalism at the expense of those qualities which are compatible with political loyalty.

The ideology and the policies based on it clearly manifest their proclivity to rank, promote and reward people for their political loyalty to their bosses and the regime. Discipline with respect to superiors, the readiness to obey any orders, especially the most absurd (such as the praise of the literary values of Brezhnev's memoirs or his military feats during the war) were commended as major virtues by this ideology because they helped to consolidate the system and fight deviation.

For the same reason, Brezhnev's ideology was indifferent to professional performance in any sphere of society if good work was combined with independence in thought and deeds. It was only natural that the ideology look with suspicion at great talents, presupposing a high correlation between talent and potential for dissent. The ideology, with its praise of discipline and political fealty, almost directly supported mediocre people as the most reliable members of society. Therefore, despite all the necessary words about the respect for science and culture, Brezhnev's ideology was deeply inimical toward the intellectual community and could easily acquiesce to the flight of creative people from the country. The idea of the replaceability of any individual, whatever be his or her creative capacity, was incorporated in Brezhnev's ideology with contempt for intellectuals if they were unable to adjust to the corridors of power.

Having a strong distrust of the Soviet people (Brezhnev's ideology shared this with neo-Stalinist ideology), the ideology under discussion rejected any serious participation of people—including party members—in the management of society, totally relying on the bureaucracy. Not denying some abuse of power, this ideology however sought the solution to this problem in the expansion and perfection of the control apparatus which had to inspect systematically various institutions in the country, mostly on a secret basis, without making the results of their scrutiny public.

RUSSOPHILISM IN BREZHNEV'S IDEOLOGY

Brezhnev's ideology almost renounced the promises of Communism and other forms of the "radiant future." Khrushchev's declaration at the Twenty-second Party Congress citing 1980 as the year when the Soviet people would enter communist society was treated as another manifestation of his "voluntarism and adventurism." Brezhnev's own reports to the party congresses practically ignored communism as an issue relevant to the Soviet people—his contemporaries (Brezhnev 1971, 1976, 1981).

Filling public propaganda with empty and bombastic concepts such as "mature socialism," "developed socialism" or "the socialist style of life," this ideology could not claim that party apparatchiks would take this humdrum seriously. An ideology had to have spiritual values really appealing to the bureaucracy, especially the high echelons of power. In this respect Brezhnev's ideology followed Stalin's legacy, and from the end of the 60s, when the regime began to persecute the liberal movement, it strongly increased the role of Russophilism.

Devotion to Russia was blended with the commendation of the state and the system as being the highest values, which allowed the introduction of emotional feelings into the abstract idea of Soviet patriotism. The interests of Russia could be perceived by apparatchiks as something really tangible, in comparison with "internationalism," "internationalist duties," and other clichés that for some time had been treated by them with contempt or at best as code names that had nothing in common with the original concepts.

Russophilism combined with orthodoxy were important for Brezhnev's ideology as they were teachings hostile to individualism and aspiration for individual achievement, a high standard of living, and technological progress, and they emphasized the obligation of Russians to sacrifice everything including their lives for the sake of the motherland. The commendation of sacrifices, restraint in personal life, and the rejection of progress very much aided Brezhnev's ideology in vindicating the country's technological backwardness and low standard of living as being the price paid for the preservation of the existing political order.

With the refusal to regard individual performance as the major criterion for promotion and reward, Brezhnev's ideology highly appreciated Russophilism with its contempt for "businesslike people" who aspired to material success and believed in professionalism and science. Russophile ideology also coalesced very well with the idea of collectivism which is also strongly hostile to individual achievements and the differentiation of income.

In this respect an analysis of the movies which were made in Brezhnev's time and approved by the authorities (unlike a number of other movies shelved for many years) can help us to understand why Brezhnev's ideology incorporated exactly this element of Russophilism so willingly.

Ivan Il'ich Oblomov, the hero of Ivan Goncharov's novel *Oblomov* (1859/1986), which was extremely popular in Russia, became the epitome of the type of person who, being uninvolved in practical business, wastes his life on empty speculations and plans. Such an interpretation had been accepted by Lenin and Soviet official textbooks since the revolution. During industrialization in the 30s the image of Oblomov was widely exploited by Soviet officials (Stalin included) in the fight against passivity, inertia, and hare-brained schemes. But in 1980 Sergei Mikhalkov made the movie *A Few Days from the Life of I. I. Oblomov* and presented the hero as an extremely positive man who instead of fussing about trivial things is absorbed with reflections on sublime matters, in opposition to Andrei Stolz, his active friend, who in the movie became—contrary to the novel and the traditional Soviet interpretation—rather a negative person.

Other movies made and praised in Brezhnev's times can also be cited as conveying the same negative attitudes toward professional achievements. One of these movies is *Do Not Shoot the White Swans* (Kirill Rapoport and Rodion Nakhapetov 1982). The hero of the movie is a lad with very low professional training. He is not an achiever and not a particularly hard worker. He is not without creative skills, but exercises them only when he is in a good mood or if he likes his job. If both these conditions are not met, his professional performance is terrible. He does not read books and does not go to movies and, in general, does not display any interest in the outside world. Being incapable of performing any official job, he also cannot sustain his family, the poorest in the village. But, recalling Tolstoy's Karataiev from *War and Peace*, he is absolutely content with his life.

However, all the sympathies of the authors are on his side: He is absorbed with love, not only for human beings, but for all living creatures, and he is extremely generous and absolutely free of vanity and ambition. What is more, these qualities—despite his low professional level—allow him to be extremely efficacious when a noble purpose demands this from him. He is presented as a model for imitation.[1]

The main positive character of another Russophile movie, *Love and Pigeons* (Vladimir Menshov 1984) is almost a double of the forester from the other movie. He holds the same low professional skills and lack of desire to make a professional career, the same preoccupation with nature and the rejection of the modern style of life.

The idea of sacrifice, as opposed to the Western striving for material and egotistical success—to the evaluation of people according to their work—is even more strongly revealed in movies about the war.

The last war is strongly exploited by Brezhnev's ideology as an argument against individualism and egotistical preoccupation with one's own career, as well as for devotion to the common cause and discipline. The praise of sacrifices as the major theme in Russophile war movies could only serve the major tenets of Brezhnev's ideology.

Russophile movies about the war present soldiers and the civilian population mainly as suffering and making sacrifices for others, in a sense repeating the ordeal of Christ. In *The Shore*, a movie based on Iurii Bondarev's novel of the same name (Alexander Alov and Vladimir Naumov 1984), the main hero, Alexander Kniazhnin, sacrifices his life—and not even for friends, but for enemies—to save hoodwinked German youths from meaningless resistance to the Soviet army in the last days of the war. The same presentation of Russian soldiers as people inclined toward sacrifice and forgiveness is seen in the film *Back Home*, based on the story by Andrei Platonov (Gavriil Egiazarov 1983). As in the case of *The Shore*, the film's director ignores the hero's military valor but focuses on the circumstance that he forgave (for the sake of his children) his wife who betrayed him while he was at the front. The idea of sacrifice threads through many other, if not all, movies on the war made in the 70s and the first half of the 80s, including *Kindergarten* (Evgenii Evtushenko and Mosenko 1982), *I Will Never Forget You* (V. Sadovnikov 1983), *The Fall of Stars* (Viktor Astafiev and L. Menaker 1980), and others. Even the Russophile movies about present times manage to propagate the idea of sacrifice, making the conscription of a young man a turning point for all members of the family—ordinarily absorbed with fuss and vanity (see *Relatives*, Viktor Merezhko and Nikita Mikhalkov 1982).

THE IMAGE OF THE UNITED STATES IN BREZHNEVIAN IDEOLOGY

The refusal to consider efficiency and productivity as the major criteria for the evaluation of people's activity (even if these criteria continued to be hailed in public ideology) led the dominant party ideology in the 70s to change radically the image of the United States, a country that was admired even by officials as the model of human performance. The entire arsenal of Russophile arguments against efficiency which was described above was used in order to discredit the United States as a country that had been regarded by Soviet society in the past as the paragon of human performance, along with a strong belief that Russia would soon catch up with the United States at the economic and technological level.

The strong confidence that the USSR could catch up and even outrun the United States in this domain tempered to some degree the envy of U.S. well-being felt by officials and those who were under the influence of Soviet ideology. Khrushchev's party program (1961) was the last official document that expressed this optimism, as did his numerous speeches (Khrushchev 1957).

With the stagnation of all sectors of Soviet society in the Brezhnev period, both the Soviet bureaucracy and the intelligentsia lost all hopes of catching the United States. The new party program adopted in January, 1986, which reflected the spirit of the previous period although Gorbachev had already been in power for a half-year, avoided—in clear contrast to Khrushchev's program—all comparisons with the United States (see *Materialy XXVII S"ezda Kommunisticheskoi Partii Sovietskogo Soiuza* 1986).

Under such circumstances, American technological and economic superiority has gradually engendered an inferiority complex among Soviet leaders, intellectuals, and ordinary people. Stanislav Kondrashov, a prominent Soviet journalist who worked in New York for many years, revealed this strong "black" envy of America in his documentary novel about this country, *In an Alien Element* (*V Chuzhoi stikhii* 1985). He wrote, for example, that "since we are behind in the world of consumer goods and comfort, those who hate us—the bourgeoisie—feel justified in not treating us as equal to them in the world of interstate relations as well" (p. 26). Vera Tkachenko, a well-known *Pravda* journalist, recognized that "the plebian envy of other people born on more warm and abundant land" is a serious problem in Soviet society (*Pravda*, August 21, 1987).

It is remarkable that even the most committed haters of the West and especially of the United States among Russophiles are convinced of the absolute scientific and technological superiority of the United States and exhibit a clear tendency to overstate U.S. potential in various spheres. Thus, Vasilii Belov, one of the most aggressive representatives of this ideological trend, revealed in his vitriolic anti-Western novel his conviction that the CIA, with its sophisticated methods, knows much more about present and future Soviet life than does Gosplan, the State Planning Committee (Belov 1986).

The loss of optimism with regard to the technological and economic progress of the USSR pushed both officials and Russophiles to the psychologization and individualization of the American image in an attempt to take revenge in the spheres of culture and morals. As all other images of America, the image offered by this ideological alliance was also based on "hard facts" about American life, but again as with other images, its specificity lay in the weight attributed to them, that is, in the underscoring of data that fit and the disregard of data that did not match the desirable schema.

The dominance of the Russophile component in the American image which we discuss here manifests itself in the disregard for a major principle of the class approach to a foreign country, opposing the ordinary people as good to the capitalists as bad. As was the case during the war against Nazi Germany, the clear tendency of Soviet authors in the 70s and especially in the first half of the 80s was to express negative attitudes toward the American nation without making serious distinctions between the proletariat and the capitalists.

Grigorii Oganov, an active journalist who writes on foreign life, in defiance of the "class approach" contends that U.S. mass media are successful in controlling the minds of the American people and that the whole American population was "caught by chauvinistic euphoria under the impact of ABC's broadcast of the Olympic Games in Los Angeles" (Oganov 1985, p. 242).

Kondrashov, who did not spare many disparaging remarks about the U.S. people in general (Americans are, for instance, "boorish"), describes American workers with the same barely hidden disgust with which he treats the majority of other Americans—physically a miner's wife is "a pale and uncomely woman" and repulsive (Kondrashov 1985, p. 84). Only a few authors in the 80s, such as Iurii Iziumov (*An Unofficial Trip* 1983) dared to express some sympathy toward the American people or to treat U.S. issues in a mostly traditional Marxist way[2] (Zamoshkin and Batalov 1980, Evenko 1985, Sogrin 1983 and 1986).

The image bolstered by these two ideologies became dominant among intellectuals and the mass intelligentsia in the late 70s and early 80s. This image was transported to the Gorbachev era and only in 1987 could we witness a growing counteroffensive by democrats and Westernizers.

The image of American life held by Russophiles consists of three major clusters which describe the major goals of the average American, his cultural interests and his human relations.

Since the mid-70s the average American has been portrayed as a person absorbed with material interests, indifferent to others and far from real cultural values.

Money

Describing the Russian people as "the single carrier of the moral idea" and as the people ready to suffer for the sake of this idea (Davydov 1982), and contending that "the Russian national mentality was never bourgeois" (Seleznev 1986), Russophiles present Americans as a people completely absorbed with narrow mercantilistic interests and the accumulation of wealth and money. In this view, the "yellow devil" (money) which runs the country (a phrase coined by Maxim Gorky in 1906) resides at the core of U.S. life.

Genadii Gerasimov, a leading Soviet foreign journalist who, like Kondrashov, spent several year in this country, and who is the main mouthpiece of the Ministry of Foreign Affairs in Moscow, begins a chapter in his book on the United States with this sentence: "You can say that people in America speak only about money" (Gerasimov 1984). Another Soviet author, Vladimir Nikolaev, begins an article on American life in practically the same way: "The dollar is the first and most important symbol of the United States, the second is the automobile" (Nikolaev 1985).

Only a few of the Soviet authors who continue to adhere to orthodox Marxism are inclined to treat the "American dream" as more than the hunt for money and affluence, pointing also to a "democratic version" of this dream based on a yearning for social and national equality (Shestakov 1982).

Consumerism and Vanity

In the Soviet image of America, the passion for money is linked with blatant consumerism and vanity. The relentless desire to replace one model of car with another and the obsession with conspicuous consumption was presented by many authors as an essential part of U.S. life. The purposeful selection of American novels for translation, which included mainly those that cast a very critical eye on the life of the average American, helped to strongly buttress such perceptions of Americans among the intelligentsia.

Spiritual and Cultural Emptiness

In the Soviet view, Russian superiority over Americans is manifested most clearly in the different attitudes of both peoples toward culture. In the Soviet view, Americans—preoccupied with the accumulation of wealth, with consumerism, and the desire to "keep up with the Joneses"—are indifferent to high cultural values. As Gerasimov wrote, "they all embraced absorption with making money and achieving success. Thus, they have neither the time nor the interest for science, literature or the arts" (Gerasimov 1984, p. 66).

Iurii Bondarev, one of the most eloquent Russophile spokesmen of the 80s, put into the mouth of Viachislav Krymov, the hero of his novel *Play* (1985), the following words: "American ignorance and the madness of money became the invincible legislators of fashion in the world, leading to the degradation of taste in the world." His American friend, also a film director and a supporter of this view of America, came to Moscow in order to find salvation in Russian culture (Bondarev 1985, pp. 133 and 139). Vladimir Soloukhin, another representative of Russophilism, is sure that America lacks "clear national originality" (Soloukhin 1982, p. 84).

In general, Americans are portrayed as completely immersed in mass culture and deeply alienated from the high traditions of European culture and from high poetry and prose (see Kukarkin 1985, p. 86; Gerasimov 1984, pp. 74–97; and Zasurskii 1984, p. 478).

Human Relations and Morals

Human relations is another sphere where the Russians feel themselves superior to Americans. Those who built up the image of the United States in the 70s and 80s considered "jungle individualism" one of the most typical American traits.

According to Gerasimov, "in general everybody in the US is concerned only about himself, and only God is for everybody. . . . Such concepts as labor collectives or civic duties are alien to this country, and the concept of society is treated only as the arena for life's struggle" (Gerasimov 1984, p. 71).

With such egotism, Americans are deprived of altruism and compassion, and can easily tolerate the poverty and sufferings of their fellow citizens. Nikolai Popov, for instance, asserts that "the average American is educated to believe that the 'lower class' only consumes and does not work" (Popov 1986, p. 127). And certainly, Americans with their coldness, mercantilism and egotism have no real idea about genuine friendship or about romantic, self-sacrificing love.

American individualism, as asserted by the architects of this image, is directly accountable for the American love of guns which results in violent behavior and crimes (Nikolaev 1985, p. 187).

What is more, the same individualism combined with affluence makes Americans the most conceited people in the world and strongly self-centered. As Kondrashov writes, "America considers the whole world as its appendage, and this self-complacent imperial ethnocentrism cannot lead to good things" (Kondrashov 1985, p. 23).

It is remarkable that Soviet authors—including those who, being consistent Russophiles or Marxists, claim for Russia a missionary role in the moral rejuvenation of the world (the former) or in the creation of a new Communist society (the latter)—blame Americans for their pretensions to appropriate precisely this role, which makes the country "exceptional." Criticism of American "exceptionalism" is a leading theme in many publications on the United States (Zamoshkin and Batalov 1980, p. 386).

According to the authors of the late 70s and early 80s, American self-confidence and conceit is often combined with a hatred of other peoples, Russians most of all. This idea was a leading one in Gerasimov's book *Society of Consumption* (1984) and also in Vitalii Korotich's book *The Face of Hatred* (1985).

The Conspicuous Disregard of Two Phenomena

Presenting American life as deeply flawed and corrupt, those who managed this issue in the 70s and the first half of the 80s generally preferred to avoid addressing the role of religion in American society, which is many times greater than it is in the USSR. It is impossible to find diatribes against the pernicious influence of the Church on the minds of Americans, something which could be expected from intellectuals brought up on atheism and contempt for "the opium of the people," and especially from official propagandists who are eager to add to the list of flaws in U.S. society. However, such authors as Gerasimov, Kondrashov, and Korotich almost completely skirt this issue, making an exception only for Judaism.

The cause of this strange reticence of many Soviet authors to criticize the religiosity of Americans lies again in the fact that in the 70s it was Russophiles who held sway among intellectuals and who also very much influenced official ideology. Religion, even if mostly Russian Orthodox, is a very important element of Russophile ideology. To recognize the strong religiousness of Americans is to thus credit them with a very important virtue which Russophiles want to flourish in their own country.

In their inclination to avoid blaming America for its religiousness Russophiles could find support only among their major adversaries—liberals and Westernizers—who, even if not regarding religion as the salvation of Russia, nevertheless—in defiance of Marxist ideology—demonstrated their respect for religion and recognition of its positive role in society.

If intellectuals touched upon the religiousness of Americans they did so mostly to point out the secularization of the population, especially of the youth, the hypocritical character of American allegiance to religion, or the spread of nontraditional religions—Moonism, TM, various types of oriental religions, different sects, and so on (see, for instance, Ashin and Midler 1986; Furman et al. 1986; Gerasimov 1984, pp. 99–124; Balagushkin 1984; Mitrokhin 1985; and Ugrinovich 1985).

In addition to religion, Soviet intellectuals in the 70s and 80s also tried to ignore the political freedoms enjoyed by Americans in their presentation of American life.

Purely hack writers who flaunt their political cynicism, of course, simply denied the existence of real democracy in the United States. American mass media and pluralism are the most frequent objects of criticism in the derogation of democracy in the United States (see Smolianskii 1977).

It is typical for these authors to avoid crediting U.S. democracy and mass media with the discovery of the Watergate affair and the near-impeachment of President Nixon. Instead, they present this affair as having nothing to do with public opinion and as instigated by the monopolies that had come to view Nixon's foreign and domestic policies as being dangerous for the dominant class (see Vlasov 1985, pp. 191–209).

However, authors, usually with Russophile tendencies, who pretend to address the intelligentsia, but who are mainly concerned with their reputations and don't want to resort to straight lies, usually try to avoid this subject or at least to downgrade as much as possible the importance of democracy for the average American. It is thus not surprising that Russophiles, largely ignoring the role of political freedoms in U.S. life, are rarely successful in understanding the essence of American society, in particular American individualism and self-respect, and even the American yearning for wealth as a condition for independence.

THE ROLE OF PROPAGANDA IN BREZHNEV'S IDEOLOGY

Having rejected efficiency as the major criterion for the evaluation and rewarding of human performance and having acquiesced to intellectual and economic stagnation, Brezhnev's ideology tried to compensate for negative tendencies in "objective reality" with the creation of a mythological reality in which Soviet society flourishes and is moving ahead.

Those who espouse Brezhnev's ideology are sure that the imposition of the "mythological reality" on the masses is useful for them and for the country. According to this logic, the real picture of the world can only demobilize people and push them to reconcile with bad facts—instead of combatting them—and will encourage them to follow bad patterns of behavior.

Brezhnev's ideology assumed that with all the defects of propaganda it is possible to persuade the masses of the validity of many, if not of all, beliefs about Soviet society.

For this reason this ideology practically excludes any serious criticism of even minor negative phenomena in Soviet society. Drawing the attention of the masses and even of the party apparatus to some flaws in society brings, according to the logic of this ideology, more harm than benefit. In the end, many of these flaws, for instance the low labor ethics of workers (especially of the youth), or drunkenness, are organic features of the society and hardly could be removed even by some drastic measures. At the same time, publicizing these defects as well as others such as prostitution or drug abuse not only damages the prestige of the system and the leadership, in itself very bad, but in a way legalizes these phenomena in the public conscience and rather leads to their expansion: People who formerly believed in the dominance of good norms in public behavior will learn that this is not the case and will be in this way encouraged to follow bad examples.

For this reason, Brezhnev's ideology strongly favored the classification of all sources of information. Secrecy in this ideology played no less a role than in the pure Stalinist one. Secrecy is lauded not only because it deprives the people of data about the current state of affairs in the country but also because it contributes to the prestige of power which is hardly possible without the flavor of enigma.

In connection with secrecy as an attribute of power lies also the role of ritual in Brezhnev's ideology. It suggests the importance of all ceremonies (even if they might look amusing to sceptics) that aggrandize power and power holders. The ideology considers solemn meetings of various bodies organized according to studiously elaborated scenarios, which include the greetings and expressions of love and devotion of pioneers and the Komsomol to the leader and the awarding of the leader with numberless titles and medals, to be very useful.

NOTES

1. This "village fool" is shown to be the sole defender of nature against the offenses of civilization. Being appointed as a forester, he decides to repopulate a lake with swans which had left it many years ago. Using money given to him for buying various goods in the capital where he was sent to take part in an ecological conference, he buys swans for his lake and dies defending them from poachers. His death, full of religious allegories, was not in vain: Civilization retreated and the lake, as in the remote past, was once again filled with life.

2. With its strong focus on the life of the average American, Brezhnev's ideology does not abandon its critique of U.S. social problems, a list of which significantly lengthened in the 70s to include along with the "traditional" flaws of America, such as libertinism. American imperialism—economic, cultural and political—its aggressive foreign policy and subversive activity against socialist and other progressive countries, its desire to unleash nuclear war, its lying mass media, its intoxicating mass culture, and its persecution of "progressive people" were, of course, absolutely obligatory elements of any writings on America (see V. Agafonov 1985; G. Ashin and A. Midler 1986; S. Demkin 1985; L. Dolguchev 1986; Iu. Iziumov 1983; B. Marushkin 1986; and N. Zagladin 1984).

Primarily this type of critique rather than a description of the American style of life is presented to the Soviet mass audience—workers, peasants and clerks—who, as some surveys showed, almost completely accepted this vision of the United States. Grushin's study discovered that the average Soviet individual was sure that the standard of living in the United States was much less than in Czechoslovakia (55 percent of the respondents named the latter as the most prosperous against 15 percent who pointed to the United States) and that Americans enjoyed much less democratic freedom than Czechoslovakians (55 percent vs. 19 percent), whereas the United States ranked first in the extent to which political freedoms are suppressed (53 percent vs. 16 percent for China and 7 percent for South Africa) (Grushin and Onikov 1980), p. 312.

Chapter 6

Neo-Stalinist Ideology

STALIN AND STALINIST IDEOLOGY IN THE POST-STALIN ERA

Stalinism is certainly the most adequate ideology for the system shaped in the 20s and 30s. Perhaps, the Soviet system could have been much more effective in the subsequent periods of its history if it had been possible to preserve the political and ideological conditions when the system emerged.

Stalinist Ideology and Stalin's Deeds

Stalinist ideology should not necessarily be identified with all of Stalin's deeds. There were hardly people even in Stalin's entourage who approved of his terror against apparatchiks, since such a terror could at any moment be directed against them. Khrushchev wrote in his memoirs how practically all members of the Politburo trembled for their lives (Khrushchev 1970).

Iurii Andropov, who became, as will be shown later, the major sponsor of neo-Stalinist ideology, by all accounts rejected Stalin's methods of repression and remembered how he awaited his arrest in 1940 when he was the first secretary of the Komsomol in Kareliia.[1]

Even in 1987–1988, when the logic of an ideological struggle polarized the views of Stalin in Soviet society, and when many people came to his defense, only a few of them dared to justify all repressions (see, for instance, Andreeva 1988).

Stalinist Ideology in Khrushchev's Times

Rejecting Stalin's atrocities as "overkill" and not necessary for the Stalinist ideology and policies, many Soviet politicians since 1953 have defended them as the best for the existing society with its historical and cultural background lacking in democratic experience and traditions.

It is only natural that in the aftermath of Stalin's death Khrushchev's drive for a new party ideology and reforms was met with strong resistance from apparatchiks who were sure that a radical retreat from the principles of Stalin's ideology would be nefarious for Soviet society.

Molotov, Malenkov, Kaganovich, and other members of the Politburo who rebelled against Khrushchev in 1957, argued that his ideology and politics endangered the existence of Soviet power itself (regarding their views see Khrushchev 1970).

The defeat of the so-called "anti-party group" by Khrushchev in 1957 forced the Stalinists into hiding to await the time for the disclosure of their real views in the future. Only a few writers, such as Vsevolod Kochetov, could disseminate their Stalinist views (see Kochetov's novels *The Brothers Ershov* 1958, and *The Secretary of the Obkom* 1961).

Stalinist Ideology under Brezhnev

The ouster of Khrushchev in 1964 inspired Stalinists with the hope that their time had come. There were many signs to corroborate their expectations. As was said before, Brezhnev's regime from its very beginning announced its desire to rehabilitate Stalin.

However, this intention was misinterpreted in the country by Stalinists as well as by their fierce enemies. Brezhnev's team in no way wanted to go back to Stalin's ideology in substance, which of course does not imply that the new party ideology did not have many elements in common with the older one.

Brezhnev's ideology took the course of creating a stable dominant class with minimal interference in its activity and the minimal rotation of cadres, as well as tolerant attitudes toward work and the private lives of the ordinary people, which was strongly at odds with the spirit of Stalinist ideology.

As was indicated above, the rehabilitation of Stalin was necessary for Brezhnev's team mostly for the restoration of the authority of power as such but did not mean positive attitudes toward Stalin's ideology were firmly held.

By the middle of the 70s (after some oscillation), Brezhnev's ideology shaped finally a stable attitude toward Stalin and his ideology which persisted until the end of the regime.

This attitude manifested itself in the absence of any official material that revised the evaluation of Stalin given by the Twentieth Party Congress, in praise of all the major developments of the Stalin period—the struggle with opposition, industrialization, collectivization, the war against Germany, and the post-war period—and in downgrading Stalin's role as the organizer of all successes and the minimization (in comparison with Khrushchev's times) of his mistakes (see Samsonov and Kovalenko 1978; Ponomarev 1982).

Brezhnev's specific solution to the Stalin issue was manifested also in the official attitudes toward Stalin's victims. The small group of his major opponents in the 20s—Trotskii, Zinoviev, Kamenev, Bukharin and a few others—remained to be rehabilitated in the spirit of Khrushchev, but the circumstances of their deaths were dropped from all biographies (see, for instance, *Soviet Encyclopedic Reference Book* by Prokhorov 1979 and 1982).

Again, only some writers could go beyond the official line about Stalin and praise him out of proportion to the norms established by Brezhnev's ideology (Stadniuk 1970–74).

Stalinist Ideology in 1982–1985

In 1982, after Suslov's death, the ideological struggle in the country came to the surface. It was the Stalinist ideology that was the first to appear as a challenge to the conservative Brezhnevian vision of Soviet society.

The increase in Stalin's popularity was a natural reaction to the mounting disorder that was expanding in the country, embracing new and more areas. The demoralization of the population, the decline of labor ethics, alcoholism, mass corruption, and so on were highly visible to anybody who wanted to look at reality.

The liberal alternative, even in its neo-Leninist form, was practically obliterated from the political scene in 1982–1984. By this period the dissident (or human rights) movement had been almost completely exterminated. Liberal intellectuals were either corrupted or scared to such a degree that none of them, with isolated Sakharov as an exception in Gor'kii, offered any program through official or unofficial channels that could be even remotely considered "liberal."

In their legal activity Soviet intellectuals at best could include only hints in favor of milder attitudes toward ordinary people and some very light criticism of bureaucrats (see, for example, such movies as Mikhalkov's *Siberiade*, 1979, Il'ia Averbakh's *Declaration of Love*, 1977, and Popov's *Fall in Love at One's 'Own Desire,'* 1982).

At the peak of liberalism in this period were Aleksandr Gel'man's plays and movies with their critique of individual dishonest bureaucrats (see, for instance, the movies *We, the Undersigned*, 1979, *The Meeting of the Party Committee*, 1976), along with Fedor Burlatskii's article on Maoist

China, which evoked parallels with Brezhnev's Russia (Burlatskii 1982) and Evgenii Evtushenko's novel *On Berry Field* (1982), where the author attacks Russophilism and some corrupted bureaucrats. These works did not attract much attention in the country and in no way were able to challenge the official ideology or the mounting Stalinism.

The intellectual climate in this period was controlled by Russophile intellectuals, in particular, by the writers adhering to the so-called "rural prose" (Vasilii Shukshin, Fedor Abramov, Valentin Rasputin, and others), who objectively were in collusion with Brezhnev's ideology, supporting its anti-Western orientation, and avoided the necessity of any radical changes in the country in their publications.

At the same time, most authors who later became the activists of *perestroika*, in the late 70s and early 80s relinquished the ideas of the 60s and found refuge in Russophilism, usually in its mild form, in an ideology that was practically supported by the Brezhnev regime and that also could not arouse the ire of Stalinists (see, for instance, Daniil Granin's novel *The Picture* 1980).

The most important document of this period presented by the intellectuals—Zaslavskaia's Novosibiirsk memorandum (Zaslavskaia 1984)—became known in 1983 and attracted general attention because of its strong analysis of negative phenomena as well as its challenge of bureaucracy which was for the first time denoted as the major enemy of change. However, this memorandum fitted very well into the Stalinist vision of the state of affairs in the country.

Andropov's Ascension to Power

As he seized power, Andropov immediately challenged the Brezhnev regime and ideology, recognizing already in his first speech that the country was in bad shape and it was necessary to look for the way out (Andropov 1983).

Andropov's ideology, as did other new ideologies, evolved gradually mostly in 1983 but also in 1984 and even in 1985 after Gorbachev's ascension to power.

NEO-STALINIST (OR LIBERAL AUTHORITARIAN) IDEOLOGY IN THE 80S

In no way should neo-Stalinist ideology be equated with the pure Stalinism of the 30s and 40s. The historical experience of the past and the radical changes in the country and world deny to even the most staunch admirers of the past the possibility of demanding a duplication of the policy now fifty years old. To some degree, neo-Stalinist ideology, or liberal authoritarianism, even incorporates some elements of liberalism and a scientific approach to economics and other spheres of social life. Therefore, as a matter of fact, we saw in the late 70s and the 80s a new, liberal, version of Stalinism, which does not exclude the existence of a harsh one having repressions and fear at the center of its social and political program.

As a dynamic ideology demanding strong measures for the rejuvenation of society, neo-Stalinist ideology rejects Brezhnev's conservative authoritarian ideology which should guarantee the stability of the dominant class. The major distinction between neo-Stalinist ideology and other alternatives lies in a belief in the strength of central power and its capacity to radically improve the situation in the country.

THE DEEP ANTIDEMOCRATISM

Neo-Stalinist ideology inherited many aspects of Stalinism, in particular its strong antidemocratism and deep mistrust of human beings.

The Gloomy Image of Man

The profound antidemocratism of Stalinism, as of any other authoritarian ideology including neo-Stalinism, stems from (or is justified by) an extremely negative image of the ordinary man, in crass contrast to the public ideology in which he is endowed with all possible virtues (about this image in public ideology see Soviet textbooks on "scientific communism" or "historical materialism": Fedoseev 1985; Afanasiev 1987).

The authoritarian ideology, like Stalinism, assumes that Man is a greedy, lazy and treacherous being prone to violence, anarchy and all possible vices, and is deeply hostile toward order, culture, and the intelligentsia. For their own sake the masses have to be strongly controlled by the authorities, who have to have no illusions about the nature of Man. Therefore, the average Soviet individual can in no way be allowed to make a decision on behalf of an enterprise and all the more of society.[2]

Going in the direct polemics with Stalinists on this issue, Gorbachev accused them of an ideology which espouses "the lack of respect of the people, the disbelief in its wisdom, patriotism, its common sense, its creative capacities, in its responsibility and the devotion to socialism" (*Pravda*, April 10, 1988).

The contempt and disrespect of the ordinary people moved from old Stalinists to new ones. Past history could only reinforce these feelings because after 1953, becoming less and less frightened by the state and more and more cynical, the ordinary people manifested in the 70s and 80s those qualities that were rather rare in the harsh times of the 30s and 40s— consumerism, lying, vanity with prestige mania, and sloppiness in work. Even drunkenness did not reach such Homeric proportions. In evaluating the moral decay of the masses there have been no differences between neo-

Stalinists and their liberal opponents inside the political establishment since Brezhnev's death.

In this respect, both the old and the new Stalinist ideologies differ from Brezhnev's, which prefers to avoid a sober perception of the Soviet people, and rather shared with official public ideology an idealized image of the Soviet man. As was said before, the publications of Brezhnev's period, even addressed to professionals and apparatchiks, limned universal enthusiasm and high morals.

The low estimation of Soviet people, and their own low self-respect, was recognized by Andropov almost immediately when he became the general secretary and ordered the hordes of people who strolled the streets during working hours or were in public baths or theaters to get to work. People who could not come up with the documents that excused them from their professional duties at the given moment were dragged unceremoniously to police stations and their behavior was reported to their superiors.

At the same time, unlike Stalinist ideologues of the 30s and the 40s, their heirs do not have illusions about the possibility of radically changing human nature and creating a New Man. The colonel of police in Iulian Semenov's movie *The Confrontation*, (1985), an important source of neo-Stalinist features, viewed the ordinary people he met in his chase for a criminal with patent condescension, sure that they were all potential thieves, smugglers, and shirkers. He did not try to teach them how to live honestly, which his predecessor would have done in the movies of the 30s and 40s. He would not permit these people to infringe upon the law only in serious matters where the security of the state or the order was at stake.

The Cult of State

The real object of the cult for neo-Stalinists is not the party and the leader, but the state as such. The glorification of statehood provides a basis for the alliance with those Russophiles for whom the Russian state, and not Russian religion, represents the most valuable part of Russian history.

The author Alexander Prokhanov, who became known in the 1980s for his commendation of the state as holding the highest value for Russian people, expended a great deal of effort in creating a special philosophy of "statehood," and introduced as a special term "gosudarstvenniki," or "people of state" (Prokhanov 1988).

The Ideology of "High Cost"

With its deep contempt of the masses, Stalinist ideology assumed that any serious achievement justifies its high cost and human sacrifices. Without any scruples it accepted the numberless victims of industrialization and collectivization, not even to touch upon the mass terror in the 30s which was also justified with the concept of the sort that "you cannot make an omelette without breaking eggs."[3]

Soviet novels written in the 20s and 30s with the blessing of the authorities, such as Kataev's *Time Forward* (1956) or Ehrenburg's *The Second Day* (1934), suggested to the readers that the terrible conditions of life during the construction of new factories was "normal" in view of the great tasks set by the party. The authors even found some pleasure in detailing the squalor of life at the "great socialist constructions."

For this reason, the so-called "class approach" to any issue and the rejection of "all mankind values" were such an important part of this ideology. The extermination of any traces of the veneration of such values as kindness, altruism, tolerance, and all others which could suggest sympathy for human endurance was an extremely important part of the main ideological campaigns conducted in Stalin's times. At the same time, "hatred of class enemies" was a leading value in Stalinist ideology, and the lack of the ability to "hate the enemy," the manifestation of kindness, was considered to be incompatible with the position of the apparatchik.

Neo-Stalinists significantly tempered the mercilessness and callousness of their attitudes toward the masses and now they do not demand such mass sacrifices as their predecessors did in the 30s and 40s.

With far fewer means to scare people and with a relatively weak ideology, people like Andropov pay much more attention to material stimulation and to the standard of living of the masses, but with all this, the neo-Stalinists again focus on moral obligations, patriotic feelings, and ideological commitments (see Andropov 1983, p. 240).

Just for this reason, the attitudes toward the Stakhanov movement are a sensitive indicator which helps to separate neo-Stalinist ideology from others. Since this movement is strongly associated with Stalin and with his presentation of Stakhanovites as workers who were moved in their heroic labor activity in the first place by the desire to serve society, the accent on the Stakhanovites' traditions reveals the Stalinist ideal about the motives that should drive workers the best—ideological commitment based ultimately on fear.

It is not accidental that the celebration of the fiftieth anniversary of the Stakhanovite movement which started in 1984 was perceived by the Soviet people as an omen of the resurgence of Stalinism. As will be shown later, Gorbachev in his evolution from neo-Stalinism to a more liberal ideology also took part in the glorification of the Stakhanovites in order to forget it completely at the next stage.

The Contempt of the Masses

The implacability toward the masses and the readiness to accept millions of victims in collectivization as well as during the war against Germany precluded any interest in popular attitudes or public opinion without mentioning real participation of the people in management. It is impossible to find in Stalin's works, even if the Soviet dictator did not have an equal in hypocrisy, any speech or article that seriously suggested that the apparatchiks consult the masses and involve them in management.[4]

Unlike Hitler, preferring a democratic cover for his despotic regime (Stalin's Constitution of 1936 was formally extremely democratic), Stalin in no way mixed verbal allegiance to "socialist democracy" with the practical work of management.

Stalinist ideology always tended to consider the army to be the ideal organization for the whole society. In the post-war years Stalin's inclination to dress all employees in uniforms and to confer ranks on all of them was fully implemented as well as his yearning for other attributes of the old tsarist empire such as separate schools for boys and girls, and so on.

The direction of society in Stalinist ideology is carried out by the energetic, competent, incorruptible, and merciless manager who with an iron hand will implement the orders from above.

Speaking about his Constitution in 1936 and praising it as "the single consistently democratic constitution in the world," Stalin however said almost nothing about the participation of the citizens in government, focusing on the equality of people before the state (Stalin 1952, pp. 552–56).

Only with the utmost disrespect for ordinary people could Stalin insist in his report to the Eighteenth Party Congress (1939) that the party turn to the results of the first election after the adoption of the new constitution (99.8 percent of the citizens participated in the election) as evidence that there was support for the killing of leading party officials in 1937–1938 (Stalin 1952, p. 630).

It is only natural that Stalinist ideology considered sociology its fierce enemy, and considered it deeply hostile to the essence of the Soviet system because it defies the Stalinist taboo on interest in the opinion of the ordinary people. Sociology was treated by Stalinist ideology as superficial, volatile, and able only to bring confusion to the minds of the people.[5] Neo-Stalinists, by all accounts, are already not so hostile to sociological studies but they want them to be fully controlled by the party and the KGB, to be almost totally classified and available only to the political bosses.

If Stalin and his apparatchiks, following Lenin with his disdain for "bourgeois parliamentarism" and its "political games," probably really disparaged the democratic mechanism, their heirs in the 70s and 80s were much more sophisticated on this subject and realized much better the advantages and disadvantages of this mechanism. Some publications of Soviet experts on state and law as well as of Americanists reveal a rather earnest understanding of Western political systems (see, for instance, Zamoshkin and Batalor 1980).

Now quite often the ideologues of authoritarianism would argue that even if democracy is preferable to the present order, the Soviet masses are not prepared for it. This idea is clearly discernible in Andropov's article, written when he was general secretary and in the same Aesopian language as all other Soviet political texts, especially before *glasnost*. Writing about the importance of "the further deepening of socialist democratism" he continued, "We do not idealize what has been done and is being done in this area; there have been and, we assume, will be difficulties of growth determined by the material possibilities of society, *the level of consciousness of the people, their political culture* (stress mine—VS) and also by the fact that our society develops not in hothouse conditions but under the cold wings of the 'psychological war' unleashed by imperialism" (Andropov 1983, p. 242).

The Soviet leader who unanimously impressed everybody who met him as an educated and refined person with a sound comprehension of the world (see Andropov 1983) almost openly contends here that the Soviet people are not mature enough (especially being under the pressure of Western propaganda) to be trusted with full democracy which is left, rather, for the future.

Neo-Stalinist ideology inherited the deep antidemocratism of Stalinism. This ideology, assigning to propaganda the task of speaking about "socialist democratism," the importance of mass participation in the work of various official bodies, and appealing to make this participation "even more effective than in the past," keeps silence about these matters if outside the realm of pure propaganda. Andropov in his speeches and articles never raised seriously, at least as did later Gorbachev, the issues of the real, and not phoney, role of the masses in government (see Andropov 1983).

The article of I. Zal'tsman, the former director of a large tank construction complex during the war, and G. Edel'hous, his aide in this period, published in *Kommunist* in 1984, was very interesting because while referring to the successes of the military economy during the war it gave a rare, cohesive description of neo-Stalinist ideology.

Lauding the achievements of their enterprises, the authors attribute them mostly to good managers and their autonomy and initiatives, an effective system of stimulation, active cooperation with science, and many others. But presenting the experience of their complex as a model for the present economy (the title of the article directly points this up: "The Lessons of the Tank Complex"), they did not even mention the participation of the workers in management. Even the activity of the party organization of the complex was given no attention, as the authors were devoted to the advantages of the strong hierarchical structure of their enterprise (Zal'tsman and Edel'hous 1984).

Of no less importance in this respect is Semenov's movie *The Confrontation* as a very valuable source of information on Andropov's vision of

Soviet society. Full of various political hints (some in that time, in 1985, still looked politically titillating, including the good words for private business), the movie eschewed any issues that could suggest that the author favored people's participation in the decision-making process.

THE LIMITED RESPECT FOR INTELLECTUALS

In this sense neo-Stalinist ideology directly relies on Stalin's attitudes toward the intelligentsia. Stalin, by all accounts, respected this stratum much more than any other group of the population, without mentioning the peasants whom he apparently almost hated, or party officials whom he could send to their deaths without any hesitation.

Stalin's positive attitude toward the intelligentsia was closely combined with his deep-rooted antidemocratism and contempt for the masses and for any spontaneous movements. Later, this contempt for the masses— uneducated and stupid—was manifested in Stalin's attraction to dictators of all times as well as for imperial paraphernalia, which he introduced in his last years and which had to inspire awe in ordinary people.

There were two periods during which Stalin approved and by all accounts instigated campaigns directed against the intelligentsia: one in 1928–1931 and another in 1935–1936.

In both cases, however, Stalin used the campaign only to crush his political enemies and create an atmosphere of terror against apparatchiks, never taking a public stance against the intelligentsia.[6]

As soon as these goals were achieved, Stalin immediately demonstrated his high appreciation of the intelligentsia, mitigating or even stopping the attacks against it that were coming from revolutionary radicals (as was, for instance, the case with RAPP—the Russian Association of Proletarian Writers—in the early 30s) or from the masses (as was the case in 1931 when Stalin halted the assaults against the old intelligentsia) (see Fitzpatrick 1984).[7]

So, in his attempt to eliminate Bukharin's opposition Stalin endorsed in 1928 the campaign against "bourgeois specialists" but already in 1931 he demanded cooperation with them from the party (Stalin 1952).

In 1935–1936 Stalin also endorsed the mass media, which often detracted scholars and engineers as wreckers trying to impede the Stakhanovites in the revision of the obsolete technical norms and rules. However, already in November 1936 (Stalin 1952, p. 550) he commended the intelligentsia as an important stratum of the Soviet population, which generated elation among professionals (Chalidze 1981, pp. 20–21). He reiterated his support of the intelligentsia three years later in his report to the Eighteenth Party Congress, condemning "the views of party members hostile toward the intelligentsia" (Stalin 1952, pp. 646–48).

What is more, during the war, in 1943, Stalin made an unorthodox statement (and to such a degree that it was never again cited in Soviet literature, even when Stalin was alive—a rare case!) about "the intelligentsia which is lending assistance and support to the workers and peasants in their fight against Fascism" (Stalin 1945).[8]

With all his seizures of arbitrariness, whims and megalomania, Stalin liked to invite to the Kremlin the best brains, even if he could support such a swindler as Lysenko. There are many examples of Stalin's willingness to listen to the advice of prominent scholars such as the metallurgist Bardin and aircraft constructor Iakovlev.

One of the central episodes in Vasilii Grossman's novel *Life and Destiny* is Stalin's call to Shtrum at the end of the war, a physicist who was being persecuted by the authorities and on the verge of arrest. Stalin's attention immediately created fabulous conditions for Shtrum's work, which was connected with nuclear energy (Grossman 1980). This call from the potentate was rather typical since Stalin used to speak with prominent figures in science and literature.[9]

Sending many thousands of intellectuals to the *Gulag* (for instance, 500 writers perished in the 30s and 40s), in the middle of the 40s, in order to accelerate the creation of the new military technique, Stalin ordered the organization of special prisons for those inmates who were scientists and could be helpful for his purposes. In these prisons, so-called *sharazhki* (described by Solzhenitsyn in his *Second Circle*, see also Kopelev 1978, *Moskovskiie Novosti*, November 29, 1987), scholars were fed and housed much better than other victims of Stalin's terror.

What is more, Stalin released from the *Gulag* some prominent intellectuals, such as physicist Lev Landau, the future director of the first Soviet cosmic program Korolev, and leading plane designer Aleksei Tupolev. Such "happy endings" fell only to a few military people on the eve of the war but never to former party apparatchiks.

From the middle of the 30s Stalin increased the privileges for intellectuals. In the middle of the 30s (1936) Stalin introduced titles for actors and then for outstanding figures in other arts as well as degrees for scholars (1934). In 1946, again due to a desire to meet the military competition with America, in one stroke he raised the salary of scholars by several times, practically equating them in income with the nomenclature and substantially increasing the various benefits for intellectuals.

Such attitudes toward the intelligentsia reflected Stalin's interests in real performance, even if in most cases his inclination to appreciate successful performance yielded to his maniacal suspicion and malice, especially after the war when having won, Stalin practically lost contact with reality.[10]

Having respect for the intelligentsia, Stalinist ideology at the same time leaves no doubt that the Soviet system is ready to endow intellectuals with its blessing only on the condition that they be totally submissive to the political elite and abandon any idea about activity, even in private life, that is against the current policy of the government.

Just because of this, Stalinist ideology tended to make a strict distinction between natural and social science (the ironic communality with the neo-Kantians who strongly opposed one type of science to another), allowing some leeway to mathematicians and physicists and denying it completely to philosophers or historians. Yet, with respect to biology, this distinction did not work and it was about to stop working even for physicists in the last years of Stalin's life when a campaign against idealism in physics and against Einstein was almost inevitable and was presented only by the strong intervention of the military.

Neo-Stalinists followed Stalin in his elitist and positive attitudes toward intellectuals as people necessary for the accomplishment of state goals. It is Andropov who could say in one of his first speeches that he "does not know recipes for improving the situation in the country" and that it was necessary to search for them (Andropov 1983, p. 212).

Andropov wrote in his major article when he was the supreme leader of the country that "socialism guarantees an exceptional recognition of the creative activity of the intelligentsia" (Andropov 1983, p. 246). Moreover, he even said that "if to speak sincerely, we have not still studied really the society in which we live and work," a very dissident statement in comparison with the complacency of the previous period (Andropov 1983, p. 294).

Neo-Stalinists today do not want to follow all the old patterns of Stalinism in many respects, including the attitudes toward intellectuals. They want to be much more consistent in making a distinction between natural and social science, permitting the former complete freedom, which as a matter of fact is in no way at odds with the conservative Brezhnev ideology.

What is more, neo-Stalinists, being strongly hostile to the serious participation of the masses in management, are inclined to allow scholars, even social scientists, to discuss important issues in critical activity until the leadership makes the final decisions.

It was under Andropov when the Soviet media started in 1983 a very open (by the standards of the previous period) discussion on economic management (see, for instance, the articles which challenged the fundamentals of planning in *Pravda*, January 31, March 13 and 16, May 16, June 1, and August 23, 1987; see also Kontorovich and Shlapentokh 1986).[11] By all accounts, Andropov was in favor of businesslike discussions by professionals in various spheres of social life. The few issues of the magazine *Sotsiologicheskie issledovaniia* (*Sociological Research*) which came out under the auspices of the new leader (see, for instance, #3, 1983, especially Vladimir Iadov's article, and #2, 1984) contained much more interesting information then Brezhnevian issues. Some authors managed to publish relatively fresh books (see, for instance, Aitov's book *Workers*

Good and Bad 1983, which with its criticism could not have come out earlier).

The history of Tatiana Zaslavskaia's memorandum also was indicative in this respect. She presented in 1983 (seemingly, in the spring) a seminar paper (about the state of the Soviet economy) which surpassed in depth of analysis everything that had been done by official scholars in the previous fifteen years. The seminar only became possible in the atmosphere created by Andropov, who clearly encouraged intellectuals to conduct more objective analyses of Soviet reality than his predecessor.

The Stalinist position toward the intelligentsia and the intellectuals is different from the attitudes of Russophiles who are openly hostile toward them (see, for instance, Vasilii Belov's novel *All Ahead* 1986). It is possible to surmise that with the rapprochement of Stalinists with Russophiles, the former would move in the direction of more inimical attitudes toward the intelligentsia. The article in *Sovietskaia Rossia* (March 13, 1988), which in fact to the liberals was a declaration of the war by the enemies of *perestroika*, equated "neo-liberal socialism" with "socialism of the intelligentsia," and was conspicuous in its hatred toward the intellectuals; this was a step toward the capitulation of Stalinists before Russophiles on this very critical issue.

IDEOLOGY

All party ideologies recognize the important role of control over the human mind and of public ideological work. Ideology combined with the fear of sanctions for disloyal behavior make up the basis for legitimization of the system, the regime, and the supreme leader in the eyes of the population, and in view of the lack of free elections, there is no other means for the legitimization of the authorities.

Even when not conducted in the most efficient way, propaganda, as Soviet experience shows, can influence the minds of the largest part of the population. The propaganda in Brezhnev's period was carried out by very unsophisticated party apparatchiks who were afraid to enroll in their activity Soviet sociologists and psychologists who were willing to enhance the efficacy of propaganda. Those who directed ideological work in the 70s and 80s refused to measure the efficiency of their work as was done in the 60s, and were as complacent about their activities as Brezhnev's people in other spheres (see Iakovlev 1984; Uledov 1980; see also my book *Soviet Public Opinion and Ideology* 1986).

However, even this propaganda (as became clear in the middle of the 80s) was relatively successful. Gorbachev's *glasnost*, which shattered Soviet dogmas, stupefied many millions of the Soviet people, outraged the considerable part of them, and revealed that a significant part of the population was effectively influenced by Brezhnev's seemingly ineffective ideological apparatus.

Helping to enhance the legitimacy of the system and the authorities, efficient propaganda at the same time diminishes the efficacy of performance in all sectors of society. The mythological conscience that is nurtured by propaganda hinders a sober evaluation of reality and correct appreciation of human efforts and talents. With great ideological activity the regime tends to use criteria for rewarding and promoting people that have little in common with real success in performance.

The central issue in ideological policy is the attitude toward negative phenomena in society, and how propaganda is to treat them; ignore them completely as was done before *glasnost* toward drug abuse, prostitution, or ethnic conflicts, to present negative facts as not typical or accidental (as was done concerning the low quality of goods or the corruption of officials), to recognize the existence of some negative phenomena such as alcoholism or crime but to ascribe them to the past or to Western influence, or to acknowledge their existence as well as their "structural origin" but profess a strong belief in their elimination in the near future, as is the ideological policy of Gorbachev's team.

Each party ideology and each regime considers for itself in cost-benefit terms what ideological strategy will be the most profitable for it. Conservative ideology definitely prefers a strategy that presupposes a strong emphasis on propaganda and that is ready to black out almost all societal problems in order to maintain the positive second reality in the human mind. The important thing is that at its height Brezhnev's regime almost did not make a distinction between various channels of information and often fed the party apparatus with the same fake data as the population at large.

It seems that even Andropov, the former chairman of the KGB, with all his sources of information, did not have a full picture of the state of affairs in the country. What else could prompt him to say, as was already cited, that the leadership did not know "the country in which we live and work"? Vaksberg's article in *Literaturnaia Gazeta* (Vaksberg 1987) about the corruption of the party leadership in Krasnodar only confirms this supposition and betrays that in 1983 Andropov did not have a clear idea of the situation in one of the most important parts of the country. Gorbachev also in his speeches avowed indirectly that his regime only gradually was taking stock of the state of affairs in various sectors of the country. At the same time it seems that Stalin's heirs, Khrushchev, for instance, were better informed about life in the country.

The attitudes of dynamic ideologies toward negative phenomena are different. Stalinist ideology, like the conservative authoritarian one, paid very important attention to public ideology and distorted the picture of the present and the past. With all this, the multiple channels of information were developed fully in Stalin's times, and the high echelons of power were getting relatively reliable data.

Stalin did not tolerate deceptive data if he himself did not suggest them, like the data about Soviet agricultural production which was estimated in a way which significantly increased the reported output of grain. At the same time, Stalin harshly punished those who distorted data about the real state of affairs. In the early 1950s he, for instance, punished Goremykin, a minister, who did not report the actual amount of equipment in the stores of his ministry.

With their determination to introduce many changes in a society demoralized under Brezhnev, and with their high appreciation of the role of propaganda, neo-Stalinists could only be ardent advocates of the multichannel system of information. In strong contrast to party liberals they oppose the redefinition of Soviet reality as it has traditionally been presented to the Soviet masses. They agree with the adherents of conservative ideology that the redressing of Soviet history and presentation of it as "a chain of errors and disappointments" (Ligachev's words) is a great error which can significantly weaken the legitimacy of the Soviet system.

Neo-Stalinists are in favor of a businesslike approach to various negative developments in Soviet society like low efficiency, low labor ethics, mass stealing, alcoholism, drugs, prostitution, and corruption, but they argue against publicizing these societal flaws for a number of reasons.

First, such divulging in the mass media hurts Soviet patriotism and weakens the feelings of pride in socialist society and in Russia, feelings that are the basis for the loyalty of Soviet citizens to their state, their motherland. The destruction of the self-respect of the Soviet people in conditions when the defects cannot be removed quickly would have many negative consequences—from lowering morale in the army to an increase in the influence of Western propaganda, and ultimately to dangerous dissident political activity, especially on the part of young people.

Second, the ideological striptease will significantly undermine the prestige of the USSR in the world, providing the arch enemies of socialism and Russia with data that they were formerly only able to dream of, and will render Soviet foreign propaganda almost meaningless. Such disregard for the interest in public ideology will seriously damage the position of Soviet allies abroad, in particular, Communist parties and Western liberals.

Third, the publicizing of negative phenomena as being endemic to Soviet society and therefore "normal," "typical," and "widespread" could only legitimate the violators of Soviet laws and morals and push many people, especially the young, to imitate them. Articles on prostitutes in the Soviet press, with their description of the secrets of the trade, could only serve to increase the ranks of the army of representatives of the most ancient profession.

Glasnost was openly attacked by neo-Stalinists for its damaging patriotism, and the feeling of Soviet and Russian superiority over the West. A leading theme in their manifesto was "I can not retreat from the principles," published in *Sovietskaia Rossia* (March 13, 1988). The same accusations against liberal ideologies were leveled by numerous other authors in 1987–1988 (see Leonid Ivanov's article in *Ogoniok* 46 [1987]).

BUREAUCRACY

Both main dynamic party ideologies—neo-Stalinist and liberal—are strongly at odds with conservative, Brezhnevian ideology in terms of their attitudes toward bureaucracy. If the latter ideology represents the position of the political elite that identifies itself completely with the party apparatus and regards the stability and the loyalty of the bureaucracy to be the major basis of the system and the regime, the former look at apparatchiks as servants of the political leadership who should be under strict control and who should be demoted and punished mercilessly if they do not implement diligently the orders of the Kremlin.

It is difficult to imagine a crueler master of the party apparatus than Stalin who sent many hundreds of thousands of them to death during his tenure. There was not a single period (the war was a relative exception) when the rotation of the cadres ceased for a moment. Even the last years of Stalin's life were marked with the mass purge of the Leningrad party apparatus and with the elimination of the bureaucracy in Mingrelia (a Georgian region), without mentioning the killing of Nikolai Voznesenskii, a member of the Politburo, and the imminent arrest of some other people from his circle (see Khrushchev 1970). The implacable treatment of bureaucrats ran from the peak of power to the lowest rung of the hierarchical ladder.

As was mentioned before, the permanent fear that apparatchiks felt in Stalin's times was a very important element of the system, and is accountable to a very great extent for the relative efficiency of the state machine.

Along with harsh control over bureaucrats, Stalinist ideology also supposed many privileges for apparatchiks. Along with the additional pecuniary allowance (it was handed to apparatchiks in special envelopes along with their formal salary which was not greater than that of professionals—a trick that was supposed to conceal the growing social inequality in the country), already in the 30s apparatchiks enjoyed special stores, hospitals, and rest homes (see the description of the life of apparatchiks in the 30s in Ginzburg 1985). The combination of fear (real, and not imaginary) and privileges could not but make the loyalty of apparatchiks to the leader, the regime, and the system, extremely strong.[12]

Heaping up apparatchiks with various benefits, Stalin's ideology is, however, hostile to any semilegal or illegal favors and Stalin severely punished those who violated the rules. Thus, at the end of the war Stalin fired a number of officials who were too greedy in grabbing wealth in occupied Germany.

Keeping apparatchiks in fear for their lives and privileges, Stalin was concerned with maintaining the high prestige of the party in the country. Even at the height of the wild hunt for apparatchiks in the 30s, at times when he replaced one layer of officials after another, Stalin never publicly inveighed against the apparatchiks as a species, as Gorbachev did in 1986–1987. In 1939 Stalin said in his report to the Eighteenth Party Congress, "As soon as the correct, tested-in-practice political line is established, the cadres of the party will become the decisive force in party and state management." Stalin urged the delegates of the congress and the country to "appreciate the cadres as the golden stock of the party, take care of them, hold them in respect." Stalin also required that the young as well as old cadres be valued, even if the latter sometimes "have the habit of looking obstinately to the past" (Stalin 1952, pp. 634–36).

It would be very superficial to consider these words simply another manifestation of Stalin's hypocrisy that really did not know a limit. However, the declaration of homage to the party apparatus was an important element of the ideology that regarded bureaucracy as the pillar of the command society. Stalin was really concerned about the authority of his people, catering at the same time to the masses who, leading a terribly harsh life, watched with delight—at least in the beginning of the purges—as their superiors were arrested and exterminated (for more on the popular attitudes of the masses toward the purges in the Smolensk archive, see Fainsod 1959).[13]

NOTES

1. The movie *The Confrontation*, made in 1983–1984 by Iulian Semenov, is very interesting in this respect. The author, well known in the USSR for his connection to the KGB (he wrote many novels and movies with KGB officers as the main heroes—see Semenov 1983-1984), openly bragged during his trip to the United States in the fall of 1987 about his friendship with Andropov. *The Confrontation*, which clearly reflects Andropov's ideology, unmistakably distances itself from Stalin and his admirers. The main hero, a police colonel, speaks with contempt about those who desired a return to the times when all problems were solved by fear and violence.

2. In a conversation with a Moscow intellectual in the late 70s the secretary of a Moscow district party committee was persuading his interlocutor of the necessity for the intelligentsia to support the regime, whatever its dissatisfaction with official policy. "You have to understand that without us the masses which hate you will destroy you in a moment" (a personal communication).

3. The Russian equivalent of this proverb—"you cannot hew wood without making chips"—became a symbol of Stalinism for decades. In Chingiz Akbuladze's movie *Repentence* (1984)—the strongest attack on Stalin in the So-

viet film industry to the end of 1987—one of the central scenes (and emotionally probably the most loaded) is an episode in which the wife of an artist who perished in a concentration camp desperately seeks, among logs felled by prisoners, one chopped by her husband who (as other inmates did) could make an incision of his name. The scene directly appealed to the associations of the "hewn wood" with Stalin's terror.

In the period of *glasnost* this proverb definitely migrated from Stalinists to their opponents, who often willingly use it on any occasion if someone tries to vindicate some sacrifices, for instance, in the struggle against private activity, or demands the elimination of all big savings as being of suspicious origin (see, for instance, Lisychkin 1987).

4. It is remarkable that in his speech at the first congress of the activists of the collective farms (1933), which supposedly should have been run by farmers themselves, Stalin did not even mention their so-called democratic character, the right of farmers to elect their superiors and so on (Stalin 1952, pp. 445-58). One year later, in his report to the Seventeenth Party Congress, dwelling rather at length on the theoretical differences between commune and kolkhoz, Stalin again said nil about self-management (Stalin 1952, pp. 505-11).

In the same report he also named fourteen requirements necessary for the improvement of "the organizational work" and the struggle against bureaucratism, but again nothing about the participation of the masses in management except demands for "the mobilization of the workers and peasants for the implementation of the slogans and decisions of the party and the government," "the purges of the party and Soviet apparatuses" and "the development of self-criticism and the discovery of the flaws in our work" (ibid., pp. 515-16).

5. I remember the reaction of the old party journalists in *Izvestiia* when my colleagues and I were preparing the first survey of the newspaper's readers. They regarded our work a sacrilege, a time bomb which sooner or later would damage the fundamentals of the system based as it was on the assumption that only the party leadership could know what people thought and felt (for more on this see Shlapentokh 1988).

6. In his speech in 1931, three years after the Khakhty trial and one year after the "trial of the Industrial Party," Stalin not only exonerated the majority of the old technical intelligentsia, which continued in his words to be more or less loyal to Soviet power, but demanded that Soviets "change their attitudes toward the engineers of the old schools, demonstrate to them more attention and concern, and bravely involve them in work" (Stalin 1952, pp. 377-78).

7. Even at the height of the Stakhanovite venture in November, 1935 Stalin, while holding up vanguard workers as models for scholars, nevertheless also praised science and in no way manifested anti-intellectualism (Stalin 1952, p. 540).

8. All of the defendants at the trial of the Industrial Party (1930) were professionals including some scholars and engineers well-known in the country, like Evgenii Tarle and Leonid Ramzin. However, unlike that which took place during the Cultural Revolution, these people were accused not for their knowledge but for being "bourgeois" specialists faithful to old capitalists and harboring the idea of overthrowing the new regime. The trial was exploited by Stalin as an impetus for

the creation of a new Soviet intelligentsia as an extremely important group of the population.

Stalin then soon pardoned many of the defendants who later became leading figures in the country. Ramzin received the Stalin Prize for his boiler, and even Tarle won three prizes: in 1942, 1943, and 1946.

9. Stalin clearly made a strong distinction between intellectuals who were party members and nonparty intellectuals, directing his suspicion and wrath mostly against the former. Writers who were close to party activity had a much higher probability of disappearing into the *Gulag* than those who conspicuously remained outside the political establishment, even if the latter also had a decent chance, like Kharms, of ending their lives in concentration camps.

Consider the fate of Isaak Babel, Aleksandr Voronskii, L. Averbakh, S. Rodov, or Vladimir Kirshon, all very politically active (many of whom belonged to the radical organization of "proletarian writers") who perished in the 30s and the lives of Mikhail Bulgakov, Boris Pasternak, or Anna Akhmatova—not at all easy, even tragic, but that they could physically survive (using Nadezhda Mandel'shtam's bitter words) to "die in their own beds."

It is also typical that all presidents of the Academy of Sciences under Stalin—Aleksandr Karpinskii, Vladimir Komarov and Sergei Vavilov—were not party members. Even Trofim Lysenko, Stalin's favorite, was never a formal party member.

It is possible to conjecture that in Stalin's paranoid mind too great an involvement by an intellectual in political activity could cast doubt on his devotion to professional duties.

10. One episode in Rybakov's *Children of the Arbat* (1987) conveys such a perception of Stalin's personality. He was served by a dentist whom he highly appreciated for his professionalism and especially for his readiness to insist on a procedure which Stalin wanted to avoid and which however turned out to be successful. Stalin even held up the doctor as an example of one devoted to duty and his colleagues. However, as soon as he found out about the doctor's positive attitude toward Sergei Kirov, his imagined enemy, Stalin immediately dismissed the dentist from the Kremlin hospital even if he did order "not to touch him," that is, not to arrest him.

11. It is notable that Andropov in the 60s, working at the Central Committee, created the institution of consultants, which was a recognition of expertise as important for the party leadership.

12. It is known that people from the NKVD (political police) in the 30s and probably later had special priority rights to take the apartments and belongings of the people they arrested (see Ulanovskii 1982).

13. Before 1937 Stalin even allowed cults of local party leaders. The portraits of such regional secretaries as Mendel Khataevich or Robert Eiche hung on the walls of all the offices of their regions along with those of Stalin and the members of the Politburo.

Chapter 7
The History of Liberal Ideology

Having seized power in a big country, the bolsheviks could not avoid differences in views on how to keep it and how to promote their cause. Seemingly, Lenin himself was not certain about the ways that the country should be governed, and the speeches and writings of his last years are full of contradictions—from the virulent rejection of self-management advanced by "labor opposition" (A. Shlapnikov, A. Kollontai, S. Medvedev, and others) and the prohibition of free interparty discussions (the famous clause of the Tenth Party Congress about "the unity of the party" which forbade party members to organize, so that groups defending their own views could not arise), to the introduction of NEP with the restoration of private activity, to virulent attacks against Soviet bureaucracy (Lenin 1965; *KPSS v rezoliutsiakh* 1953, pp. 527–33).

With all his contradictory commands and suggestions, Lenin's political will was unequivocal with respect to political order, which he considered foremost with respect to all other spheres of society, including the economy: Under the guise of a dictatorship of the proletariat the party apparatus had to preserve its monopoly of political power at any price, however allowing some controlled debates inside as well as outside the party on important social and political issues—with the exception of those which related to the existing political system.

With such a view of Lenin's political philosophy it would be a delusion, it seems to me, to treat Gorbachev's ideology as being neo-Leninist as the heralds of *perestroika* tried to suggest in 1986–88, presenting Gorbachev as the Soviet leader who was the first to decide to follow Lenin's ideas. Indeed, this ideology shares many common elements with Lenin's ideology as it was manifested in the words and deeds of the Lenin leadership in the early 20s (the positive attitudes toward internal party democracy and to private activity in agriculture and industry) and is much closer to it than to the Brezhnevian conservative or repressive neo-Stalinist ideologies. But with all this Gorbachev's ideology with its internal, if hidden, inferiority complex toward the Western political system (this feeling was completely alien to Lenin) gears toward the vision of a socialist society that is much more democratic (in the Western sense of this word) than Lenin's.[1]

The post-Lenin ideological and political struggle for control over the party apparatus practically did not touch the fundamentals of the new political order (no one of Stalin's opponents advanced any liberal political ideas directed against the monopoly of the party and its apparatus), but were concentrated mostly on the role of the world revolutionary movement, on the attitudes toward individual farming, on the rate of industrial growth, and—of special significance—on internal party discussions, on the possibility of using coercion against political opponents inside the party.[2]

With all this, it is impossible to find a program (if we are ready to apply this term to the aggregate of ideas advanced by the major figures in the debates of the 20s) that was similar to that of Khrushchev and all the more to that of Gorbachev.

This is not to deny that there are some common elements in the concepts advanced by Trotsky and Bukharin on the one hand and Khrushchev and Gorbachev on the other. For both Trotsky and Gorbachev the bureaucratization of the party was a major threat to the fate of the country, while Bukharin and Gorbachev shared many similar opinions on the role of private initiative in the economy (especially in agriculture), the necessity to use "economic methods"—the market, in particular—running the economy, as well as the inevitability of social differentiation in the countryside as a result of agricultural progress, and the necessity to pay serious attention to the well-being of the population (see Medvedev 1974, pp. 75–162).

However, none of Stalin's adversaries, nor Bukharin, and even less so Trotsky, advanced against Stalin a program that was liberal in its essence and that demanded decentralization in economic management (along with support of private initiative in agriculture and other sectors of the economy), or that suggested the election of managers, elements of democracy in the election of local governmental bodies, encouragement of intellectuals to discuss major flaws in social life, and so on. Of course, if one looks for the predecessors of the liberal party ideology of the 80s, Bukharin is closer to it with his economic ideas than any other, though he and his group were not concerned, as was Trotsky, with bureaucratization and the lack of inner party democracy.

Whatever the differences between Stalin, Trotsky, and Bukharin, they all support the major tenet of Bolshevism: the monopoly of the single political party and the total rejection of civil society with its independent associations ready to protect citizens against the arbitrariness of the state.[3]

The real precursor to Gorbachev's liberal ideology in the party was Nikita Khrushchev, who advanced an ideology that challenged, if extremely timidly, the political order of the system as it was shaped in the 20s. However, the real roots of Gorbachev's liberal party ideology (like the ideology of liberal bureaucrats headed by Alexander II) lie not inside the country, in its traditions, but in the West.

It was the successes of the West in economics and technological progress that forced dynamic party apparatchiks to look for serious liberal modifications for Soviet society. Soviet liberal intellectuals performed the role of information channels about the West, even though Soviet high officials themselves possessed access to the West and relevant data about Western achievements.

What is more, it is possible to contend that this direct acquaintance with the West was the major factor that pushed a part of the Soviet political elite toward the liberal model, whereas liberal intellectuals could only strengthen the tendencies for liberalism at the top of the power structure.

THE FORMATION OF LIBERAL PARTY IDEOLOGY UNDER GORBACHEV

The liberal party ideology did not emerge immediately with the appointment of Gorbachev as the general secretary. Having set its major goals—rejuvenation of the economy and the fight against the corrupt bureaucracy—Gorbachev's regime oscillated in the choice of the means for achieving these goals, means that really differentiate liberal ideology from a repressive one.

From the very beginning a number of controversial issues forced the hand of the Gorbachev regime. One goal of the new regime was the reduction of political tension in the country that had been engendered by the gap between the rulers and the ruled. But this goal demands not so much changes in personnel as it does the curtailment of various privileges enjoyed by the party apparatus. One category of privilege, illegal and semilegal benefits, could at least theoretically be eliminated through the expulsion of corrupt apparatchiks. But what about legal privileges? On this point, as we shall see, the political elite could not come to agreement, and it was exactly this issue which became the most controversial at the next party congress.

The new regime was even less specific about its policies concerning economic and technological progress. Of the various issues related to this, two were of special importance: economic reform, and attitudes toward intellectuals.

Gorbachev's regime faced two options with respect to technological progress and increasing the quality of manufactured goods. It could give emphasis to various administrative measures, ideological fervor, and new cadres—a sort of neo-Stalinist model—or it could take the path of radical economic reforms, using Hungary or even China as models. As will be seen below, the new leadership was evidently not immediately able to take a clear stand on this subject.

The issue of the status of the intellectuals was no less complicated. Again, Gorbachev's leadership, in the beginning, was seemingly determined not to allow the process of liberalization to go so far as to permit the creation of a dissident movement. However, even in the first months of his rule, the new leader made it clear that he did not imagine that economic problems could be solved, and technological progress accelerated, without an upsurge in the activity of intellectuals and public criticism of various flaws in the society. But in this he had been faced with the problem of how to prevent legal criticism from evolving into illegal opposition activity, as happened in the 60s. Again, as was the case with economic reform, the political elite came to the Twenty-seventh Party Congress apparently without a clear program.

Now let us move to the major political developments prior to the congress.

DEVELOPMENTS IN 1985

The first speech in which Andropov addressed his program showed clearly that this leader saw in the change in management of the country the key condition for improvement in the economy. Even more noticeable was Zaslavskaia's famous Novosibirsk memorandum (1984) which bluntly stated that the success of economic reform depended upon coping with the resistance of the bureaucracy. The circumstances of the appearance of this memorandum suggest that it reflected views supported in the Kremlin.

Gorbachev's April, 1985 speech, which raised dozens of problems plaguing Soviet society, clearly stated that the leadership envisioned the radical restructuring of the party apparatus (Gorbachev 1986). The subsequent actions of Gorbachev's leadership could only confirm the seriousness of its determination to carry out a purge of cadre on a scale unknown probably even in Stalin's time.

Gorbachev's campaign against alcohol, in May of 1985, which was perceived by most Western students of Soviet society as directed against the Soviet worker, was in fact aimed at party officials. In the end, it has not been the ordinary worker who has suffered most from this campaign, but his superior.

Pravda directly assailed the sexual libertinism in Soviet offices, with special emphasis on illegal sex among apparatchiks and superiors (*Pravda*, March 17, 1985).

The role of so-called "hunting lodges" is only one item of evidence of the role of revels in the lives of Soviet apparatchiks. Beginning generally at the district (*raion*) level, each first secretary of a party committee has had a special house which was used for fun by party apparatchiks—from relatively decent receptions to real orgies. The Soviet mass media have perhaps twice mentioned the existence of this institution (of course, with opprobrium, especially under Gorbachev). Once in connection with debaucheries in the Tatar republic in the mid-70s, and once again in 1985, during the Gorbachev anticorruption campaign (*Pravda*, September 4, 1985).

The anti-alcohol, and especially the anticorruption campaign (the May 1986 decree against illegal incomes targeted apparatchik bribe takers) each significantly impaired the quality of life of the dominant class in the Soviet Union, a fact of the greatest political consequence.

However, the intentions of the new Soviet leader and those who are his close supporters in the Politburo went further than the elimination of corruption among party apparatchiks and the boosting of their morals. The leadership raised its hand not only against illegal, but also against legal privileges of the party bureaucracy.

In this, the new Soviet leader took the same direction as did Khrushchev when the latter abolished the notorious packets containing secret income supplements for party officials which had been handed out each month together with other privileges.

As was noted, "social justice," along with "the acceleration of economic growth" was proclaimed by the new leadership as one of its major concepts. This concept has been used not only against corruption, but also against excessive legal inequality not justified by the contribution of the individual to the common wealth.

PRAVDA, FEBRUARY 13, 1986

If the campaign against corruption had been going on openly and at full speed long before the congress took place, the offensive against the legal privileges of party apparatchiks began only on its eve, and culminated in the now famous survey of readers' letters in the February 13, 1986 issue of *Pravda*, two weeks before the beginning of this gathering. With the characteristic title "The Cleansing: Candid Talk," this article, published by the number one Soviet newspaper, was an attack against the party bureaucracy which would have been unbelievable not only in Brezhnev's period, but even in the 20s, when *Pravda* published serious critical materials. Even then, such an article would have been assessed as a Trotskyist attack against the party.

This article, which only a few days later would become one of the major issues at the party congress, contained a number of statements, any of which, repeated in public, would have earned the author the keen interest of the KGB only a few months earlier.

To begin with, the author reported that the article was based on a reading of letters from "thousands of readers," suggesting in this way that it reflected the opinion of the Soviet masses. For the same reason, the article referred to letters coming from eighteen different regions of the country.

The main target of the article was the party bureaucracy. It was accused of many cardinal sins, including: (1) corruption, (2) the protection of its members from prosecution in those rare cases in which they were caught (the citation of Lenin's words, "This is the highest shame and outrage: a party, which is in power, defends its 'own' scoundrels" was by itself an extraordinary event in the given historical context), and (3) numerous social privileges.

The climax of the article was, of course, a sentence ascribed to a worker with the typical Russian last name Ivanov, from the famous chemical plant in Shchekino (Tula region): "The idea has been shaped in my mind that it is the immobile, inertial, and tenacious 'party-administrative stratum' which does not want radical changes and in fact stands between the Central Committee and the working class."

ECONOMIC REFORM: THE EVOLUTION OF VIEWS FROM APRIL 1985 TO JANUARY 1986

Gorbachev began his tenure as general secretary as an ardent advocate of the revamping of the national economy as the primary condition for the acceleration of technological progress. He at first avoided, as had his two predecessors, the term *reform*, which emerged for practically the first time in his report to the Twenty-seventh Party Congress (the heritage of Brezhnev's ideology).

If Gorbachev's position with respect to his two main goals—the cleansing of the party cadre and the acceleration of technological progress—did not change in the period between March, 1985 and February, 1986, his public attitude toward economic transformation underwent significant oscillation during the first year of his regime.

In his first big speech (April, 1985), Gorbachev was unequivocal in his vision of the radical modification of the Soviet economic structure in the direction of decentralization. However, by the following month, this theme had already almost completely disappeared from his economic speeches. Rather, all or most of these speeches focused purely on technological and investment policy, and on the necessity of improving the current management of the economy.

However, the apparent retreat of the general secretary from the road of economic reform became truly convincing when he joined the propagandistic campaign glorifying the Stakhanov movement on the occasion of its fiftieth anniversary, a campaign which had begun under Chernenko late in 1984, and continued to rage during the next regime. What is more, he himself convened the meeting with the veterans of this movement in September, 1985, and made long introductory and concluding speeches in which he praised socialist emulation and moral stimuli (*Pravda*, September 21, 22, 1985).

THE POLITICAL ATMOSPHERE ON THE EVE OF THE CONGRESS

The excitement in the few months preceding the opening of the Twenty-seventh Party Congress embraced not only the intellectuals and the mass intelligentsia, but also the rest of the population. One indicator of this was the drastic increase in the number of letters sent to newspapers and television and radio stations, mostly demanding radical measures against the bureaucracy and guarantees against persecution for criticism of the apparatchiks.

Against the backdrop of all the somewhat contradictory developments described above, the Soviet intelligentsia and bureaucracy, as well as active people from other strata of the population, awaited the beginning of the party congress in an atmosphere of some tension and amid sundry speculations.

Those who were skeptical about the serious changes that the new leadership and the party congress would bring about referred primarily to the drafts of the new party program and the new party statute published in November, 1985 (*Kommunist* 16 (1985): 3–73).

Indeed, both documents, which presumably contained the party's new ideology, could only disappoint those who yearned for structural changes. In many respects, the relative proportions of pragmatism and mythology (i.e., statements which refer to social reality but have nothing in common with it) are the most sensitive indicator of the real orientation of the leadership toward reforms.

The new program, as well as the statute, made it unequivocally clear that the leadership would run public ideology, literature, and the arts according to the same patterns as the previous regimes. The program proclaimed again that "the art of socialist realism is based on the principles of faithfulness to the people and the party" (*Kommunist* 16 (1985): 33–42). The new statute contained no hints that internal democracy would be installed even modestly within the party.

What is more, even the most realistic part of the program—the portion dealing with economics—failed to reveal any promise of radical economic reforms. Being in concordance with Gorbachev's speeches in the last months preceding the publication of the draft, the new program was no more than lukewarm about economic reforms and did not say a word about the role of the market in a socialist economy.

Of no less importance in the view of the pessimists was the harsh stance taken by Gorbachev's administration toward dissidents, particularly Sakharov, and his refusal to allow the resumption of Jewish emigration.

Optimists among intellectuals who continued to believe in a new era could point to the outburst of criticism in the press, to the bold plays in the theaters, and to the publication of incredibly challenging novels. They also pointed to the mass purge of apparatchiks, to the atmosphere of criticism in the country, and to a number of other positive developments.

GORBACHEV'S REPORT TO THE CONGRESS: A COMPARISON WITH THE PARTY PROGRAM

Generally, the differences between the draft of a party program and the content of the general secretary's report to the congress are minimal with respect to the spirit of the documents. This was true of the Twenty-second Party Congress, but was not completely the case at the Twenty-seventh.

Of course, the strategy adopted by Gorbachev, which was discussed above, was reiterated in his report. Both documents confirmed that the improvement of cadres and technological progress were considered the main goals of the new party ideology. The most significant differences were revealed in the economic domain.

Gorbachev presented himself, almost suddenly (in view of the developments of the preceding months), as an ardent advocate of structural economic changes. For the first time he declared the necessity of "a radical reform" and came out against mending the existing system (Gorbachev 1987a, p. 212).

Contrary to the program, in the analogous section of Gorbachev's report centralized planning was mentioned only once. This is even more significant when we consider that this section in his report was almost twice as long as that in the draft programs (Gorbachev 1987a, pp. 199–223). Unlike the neutral approach taken by the program's authors toward both types of economic regulation, Gorbachev blatantly chose an anti-centralist stand. Practically the whole section on management was written in an anti-bureaucratic spirit reminiscent of the Novosibirsk memorandum of 1983 (Zaslavskaia 1984, pp. 27–42). If the party program treated the organ of centralized management with full respect, those who prepared Gorbachev's text did their best to lambast the Central Planning Committee (Gosplan) along with the Committee of Supply and Ministries (Gorbachev 1987a, p. 213).

But the differences between the program and the report were far more extreme in another respect. The program practically kept silent about any changes that might touch upon property relations, the most sensitive question concerning economic reforms in socialist society. Unlike the program, Gorbachev was innovative on this crucial issue also.

Gorbachev supported in particular the idea of the family farm, a concept that is a radical one for Soviet ideology, and that theoretically opens the way for private businesses in service and other spheres (Gorbachev 1987a, p. 20). What is more, Gorbachev attacked conservatives who portray any new economic idea as a "deviation from the principles of socialism," and proclaimed, as *Le Monde* aptly noted in February, 1986, a Deng Xia-Ping criterion for a socialist economy: "The acceleration of social-economic growth" (Gorbachev 1987a, p. 218).

Returning again to the purely pragmatic approach which he demonstrated in April, 1985, and as if rescinding his involvement in the Stakhanov movement campaign in August and September, 1985, Gorbachev (again in contrast to the program—see *Programma KPSS*, 1986, p. 122) almost completely ignored socialist emulation. The absolute absence of even a word on socialist emulation was especially striking in his first speech following the end of the congress, which he delivered in Tolliati, presumably before an audience of workers (*Pravda*, April 9, 1986).

Aside from the part dealing with economics, Gorbachev's report did not contain any real novelties in comparison with the draft of the program or his speeches prior to the congress. However, this does not imply that the general secretary did not want to amaze the world with other ideas. For this purpose he, by all appearances, decided to use Boris El'tsin, a new man on the Politburo. El'tsin had just been appointed first secretary of the Moscow party committee, an excellent position for any party career.

EL'TSIN'S SPEECH: FEBRUARY 26, 1986

All who try to discover changes in Soviet policy through the reading of the Soviet mass media and official documents—from sophisticated Western sociologists to rural Soviet citizens with incomplete secondary educations—actually use the same method: measurement of the deviation of a current statement from the traditional cliché.

If we employ this method to El'tsin's speech (El'tsin was the third speaker after Gorbachev's report—*Pravda*, February 27, 1986), we must come to the conclusion that it was an extraordinary event. The difference between this speech and all other materials from the congress was enormous; probably only Mikoain's speech at the Twentieth Party Congress in 1956 could be regarded as something of a precedent. In fact, El'tsin's speech was much more unorthodox, and can only be linked to the February twelfth article in *Pravda*, which was cited earlier.

El'tsin's speech was the fiercest attack against Brezhnev's leadership, much sharper than Gorbachev could seemingly afford to deliver himself.

He declared outright that stagnation had become a "normal term" in the party lexicon. What is more, he noted that "the same problems" continue from one congress to another thus undermining the legitimacy of the party. The way in which he assaulted the apparatus of the Central Committee, directly accusing it in connection with the corruption of party cadres, was unprecedented.

But El'tsin did not stop there. He raised the question of the cult of the leader, and described it as a recurrent disease that regularly strikes Soviet leaders. Moreover, repeating almost literally the famous sentence from the February twelfth issue of *Pravda*, he referred to "the inert stratum of careerists with the party card," who resist radical change in Soviet society.

With all this, El'tsin saved his major blow for the end of his speech, when he attacked the social inequality generated by the privileges of apparatchiks. He demanded "the abolition of the privileges of superiors at all levels, if they are not justified," thus unequivocally endorsing the *Pravda* article cited above.

APPARENT CONSENSUS ON THE MAIN GOALS

As far as it is possible to judge on the basis of available information, the new leadership is almost unanimous concerning the two main goals originally set by Andropov and accepted by Gorbachev. In this respect, analyses of speeches made by regional party secretaries at the Twenty-seventh Party Congress are quite remarkable. As was mentioned before, in view of the relative freedom that speakers enjoyed, analysis of the content of the materials from the congress is not as futile as it would be with the materials of many previous congresses. Of course, the influence of the general secretary's report should not be underestimated in this analysis.

Cadre issues and technological problems predominated over all other topics in the speeches of regional party secretaries, a group who, unlike those speakers responsible for specific branches of activity (ministers, national secretaries, scholars, writers, and so on), are direct local homologues of the general secretary. Forty-one party secretaries devoted (if we take the space given to ideology as one unit) twenty units to cadres and thirteen to technological problems. The standard of living was the subject of two, and the discipline of workers and the anti-alcohol campaign, of one.[4]

DISSENT ON THE MEANS

Something different, however, happened with respect to the means necessary to reach the two proclaimed goals. Dissent in this sphere turned out to be, as could be expected, especially strong concerning policies toward party cadres, and more specifically on the issue of their privileges.

In fact, El'tsin's speech, along with the *Pravda* article of February thirteenth, was at the center of the congress. The most significant speeches were those which one way or another mentioned the speech or the article. While his speech was the sharpest and most significant, only two speakers—the regional party secretaries Vedernikov (*Pravda*, February 28, 1986) and Polozkov (*Pravda*, March 1, 1986)—declared their support for some of the more uncontroversial ideas that El'tsin advanced, and none expressed support for his attack on privileges.

While no one criticized the Moscow secretary directly, he came under indirect fire each time the *Pravda* article was attacked.

The attack against *Pravda* and El'tsin was begun almost immediately by Andrei Gromyko, who spoke on the same day, soon after the first secretary of the Moscow committee. Gromyko was quoted as saying that "nobody should be allowed, under the pretext of the encouragement of healthy and useful criticism and self-criticism . . . to resort to the fabrication of cleavages in our party and Soviet society" (*Pravda*, February 27, 1986). The next day, Egor Ligachev, the second-in-command in the Kremlin, followed Gromyko in this role, stating that even "*Pravda* did not escape blunders" in the campaign of criticism before the congress (*Pravda*, February 28, 1986).

The two Politburo members were supported in the following days by two regional party secretaries: V. Kalashnikov of Volgograd ("One cannot, in the chase for sensation, under the pretext of a 'candid conversation,' denigrate the cadre as a certain immobile, inert, and tenacious party-administrative stratum"—*Pravda*, March 2, 1986); and N. Ermakov from Kemerovo ("We highly support the critical comments addressed to the press by Egor Kuz'mich Ligachev. It is forbidden to lose a sense of proportion! It is intolerable that single journalists without experience, or professional knowledge of party work, give their subjective estimates of great party undertakings"— *Pravda*, March 5, 1986).[5]

REACTION TO GORBACHEV'S ECONOMIC IDEAS

The party cadre issue was not the only stumbling block for Gorbachev and those very close to him. His program of economic reform was accepted by the majority of speakers only in a very reserved way. None of them (except for Nikolai Ryzhkov, chairman of the government, who presented the second report to the congress), for instance, used terms such as "radical reform," which, according to the old rules, all the speakers would have had to repeat after the report of the general secretary (such was always the case in previous congresses). In general, the party secretaries and ministers avoided discussing structural changes in the economy. Many party secretaries, including those who were members of the Politburo, practically ignored the issue of economic reform. Among this group were Kunaiev from

Kazakhstan (*Pravda*, February 28, 1986), Grossu from Moldavia (*Pravda*, March 2, 1986), Fedirko from Krasnoyarsk (*Pravda*, March 5, 1986), Usmankhodzhaev from Uzbekistan (*Pravda*, February 28, 1986), and many others. It was also true that some ministers failed to say practically anything about managerial problems, for example, Maioretz of Energy and Electrification (*Pravda*, March 5, 1986), Dinkov of Oil (*Pravda*, March 3, 1986), and Nazarbaiev, the chairman of the Khazakhstan government (*Pravda*, March 5, 1986).

Those who raised the question of structural change did so in a very technocratic way, emphasizing improvements in the system of material stimuli and the cost-benefit approach in enterprises and ministries. In most cases, speakers developed various administrative ideas for the improvement of economic efficiency which related to the coordination of branch and territorial planning.[6]

But the most striking fact is that none of the speakers, including Ryzhkov, supported the ideas of family farms and the development of private initiative in the economy, or even mentioned an idea as innovative as the family farm. The speakers turned out to be much more conservative than the general secretary. In no other party congress in Soviet history have speakers distanced themselves to such a degree on economic issues.

SOVIET INTELLECTUALS AND THE CONGRESS

As mentioned before, the Twenty-seventh Party Congress began work in an atmosphere of intense intellectual agitation called forth by strongly critical articles in the mass media, ideologically very aggressive plays, and the involvement of many people in almost open discussions of many Soviet internal issues. Unlike any other congresses in Soviet history, this congress practically ignored the new intellectual atmosphere in the country, which had been, it was underscored, triggered by the Kremlin.

Almost all speakers on ideological issues—Demichev, Minister of Culture (*Pravda*, March 2, 1986), Markov, secretary of the Writers' Union (*Pravda*, March 1, 1986), Igor Gorbachev, theater director (*Pravda*, March 2, 1986)—defended very conservative views and in no way reflected the mood of their colleagues. Only Kulidzhanov, the leader of the filmmakers, stood out with his pledge to soften control over scriptwriting (*Pravda*, March 1, 1986).

But of course it was Viktor Chebrikov's speech which was in clashing contrast to the intellectual atmosphere planted by Gorbachev in Moscow. In many cases, Chebrikov used almost Stalinist language; for instance, when he demanded "irreconcilable attitudes toward any harmful ideological manifestations, toward any hesitations and vacillations which could help the class enemy in his attempts to weaken the stability of Soviet society."

He warned the delegates against the danger stemming from video cassette recorders (VCRs). What is more, in the spirit of the 30s, he told the congress about the discovery of a network of spies in the Soviet ministries. At the same time, he found no words to support Gorbachev's thesis on the development of criticism and publicity in Soviet life (*Pravda*, March 1, 1986).

In addition, not a single speech was given that was really consonant with the public atmosphere on the eve of the congress. A press conference devoted solely to cultural issues, which was convened after the congress, also set a very aggressive tone, giving vent to such ideological troglodytes as Markov and Chakovskii (*Sovietskaia kul'tura*, March 7, 1986).

In this respect, a comparison with the Twenty-second Party Congress is again appropriate. Whereas all speakers fervently supported Khrushchev's scathing attacks on Stalin, Moscow intellectuals were also involved in the new phase of the anti-Stalin campaign. There was considerable unity between the atmosphere of the congress and the public mood. This was not the case in 1986. Having strongly influenced intellectuals, Gorbachev failed to do the same with the apparatchiks.

THE SHAPING OF THE NEW IDEOLOGY AFTER THE CONGRESS

Like earlier Soviet leaders attending their first party congress, Gorbachev could be fairly confident that he had the support of a majority of the Politburo and would be able to win formal endorsement of his new program. However, with his direct challenge to the party bureaucracy (Khrushchev did not dare this at the Twentieth Party Congress), Gorbachev was perhaps overconfident about the congress's support of his new party ideology. Apparently realizing this, he decided to publish the draft of the party program and the statutes, which were much more conservative than the ideas he was promoting. In his report at the congress, as well as in an article in *Pravda* on February thirteenth, he made some significant steps forward, but has gone considerably farther since.

As we have seen, having revealed only parts of his program, Gorbachev met significant (by Soviet standards) resistance at the congress. However, in general, he had achieved his goals and legitimized, through the congress, the essence of his new vision of Soviet society.

DEVELOPMENTS IN 1986 AFTER THE CONGRESS

Encouraged by this success, Gorbachev sweepingly accelerated the process of public formulation of the new party ideology, introducing new accents and developing new ideas that were only vaguely present in his speech at the congress. It was in the aftermath of the congress that the term *perestroika* (restructuring) became the key word of the new ideology. Soon going further, he upgraded the dynamism of his program and himself declared that he "would equate *perestroika* to revolution . . . because the innovations and reforms designed at the April meeting of the Central Committee and at the Twenty-seventh Party Congress require a genuine revolution in the whole system of social relations, in the mind and heart of the people, in the psychology and understanding of the contemporary period, and, primarily, of the tasks generated by stormy scientific and technological progress" (*Pravda*, August 2, 1986). Following their leader, the Soviet mass media also began to apply the term *revolution* to the process triggered in April, 1985 (Sovietskaia Kul'tura, September 23, 1986).

During the year following the congress, Gorbachev made two moves: one in September, 1986 and the other in January, 1987. His speech in Krasnodar (*Pravda*, September 20, 1986) was a significant milestone in the unfolding of the new ideology. In his speech Gorbachev radically intensified his attacks on the corrupted bureaucracy as a major obstacle to "restructuring," advancing for the first time the idea of pluralistic democratization of Soviet society as an antidote to bureaucratic resistance.

THE JANUARY AND JUNE 1987 MEETINGS OF THE CENTRAL COMMITTEE

In the next six months Gorbachev did little to develop the "democratic part" of his program, instigating the mass media only casually to raise this issue. Again, as with the party congress, he saved disclosure of new portions of the emerging party ideology for the meeting of the Central Committee in January, 1987 (Gorbachev 1987b, pp. 5–47). Almost unexpectedly, he turned the question of democratization into the central issue of *perestroika*, demanding significant changes in the electoral process inside the party as well as outside it.

During the January meeting, Gorbachev and his supporters at the highest echelons of power took the considerable risk of almost completely revealing the new ideology, one that is in sharp contrast with its predecessor under Brezhnev. As of the spring of 1987, it appeared to be very dynamic, with an orientation toward strong modernization of all parts of Soviet life. It clearly supports decentralization in the economy and a serious expansion of private initiative. This ideology also calls for the active participation of ordinary people in the political process, and supposes close collaboration with the intellectuals. At the same time, this party ideology, like all previous ones, leaves intact the fundamentals of the Soviet system, such as the political monopoly of the party and the ultimate control over the economy and other sectors by the state.

Gorbachev's speech at the January meeting was a new spurt in the elaboration of liberal ideology and, in the first place, in the drastic increase of the role of democratization as a leading element of *perestroika*. The speech gave birth to avalanches of articles in newspapers and magazines as well as a string of new TV programs that highlighted ideas deeply hostile to Stalinism and conservatism.

In this period the revision of the official history of the Soviet period became a leading theme in the mass media. The publications of strongly anti-Stalinist novels, such as Rybakov's *Children of the Arbat*, Dudintsev's *People in White Robes*, Bek's *The Appointment*, Mozhaev's *Peasant Women and Men*, and Platonov's *Pit* came in this half-year as well as the opportunities for millions of people to see Akbuladze's *Repentence*, a film denouncing Stalinism.

Nikolai Shmelev's article in *Novyi Mir* (Shmelev 1987), Iurii Koriakin in *Znamia* (Koriakin 1987), Gavriil Popov in *Nauka i zhizn'* and *Znaniie* (Popov 1987a, 1987b), and Seliunin and Khanin in *Novyi Mir* (Seliunin and Khanin 1987) made significant contributions to the development of the major issues of the liberal ideology. Along with them came the publications of such journalists as Streliannyi (1987a, 1987b), Ivan Vasiliev (1987a, 1987b), and Iurii Cherednichenko (1987).

The popularity of *Ogoniok* and *Moskovskiie Novosti* reached its peak in these six months. Each issue of these periodicals became scarce immediately with their price on the black market attaining an unbelievable level (up to one hundred rubles for an issue).

It was also a period when the Soviet mass media started to change their attitudes toward the West, publishing more and more articles which depict the United States and other countries in a more restrained way. The space bridges between Soviet and U.S. citizens were also big political events which pushed the limits of *glasnost* further and further.

The June meeting of the Central Committee, when Gorbachev made a new strong push for the development of liberalism, marked the further deepening of liberal ideology (Gorbachev 1987c). The speech stood out with its new attacks against apparatchiks as the main enemies of *perestroika* and again underscored that democratization was at the core of *perestroika*. The elevation of Alexander Iakovlev, who had just published an article in *Kommunist* with the most consistent advocacy of democracy ever written by a Soviet high official (Iakovlev 1987) to the rank of full member of the Politburo, was also a sign of the continuing offensive of the shapers of liberal ideology.

However, even more important were the steps in decentralization and privatization of the economy declared by the Soviet leader, who started to speak about the "radical reform" of management in the country (Gorbachev 1987c).

The first months after the June meeting of the Central Committee did not differ very much from the first half of 1987, and the heralds of *glasnost* and *perestroika* felt as confident as they had in the earlier period. Some important publications that could be regarded as geared to the further development of the liberal ideology came out in the summer of 1987.

The ousting of El'tsin after his speech at the October meeting of the Central Committee (1987), in which he accused the leadership for the slow rate of *perestroika* as well as the pressure being applied by Gorbachev's political opponents, clearly slackened the growth of the liberal ideology and its expansion into new spheres and solidification. Gorbachev's speech on the occasion of the seventieth anniversary of the revolution (Gorbachev 1987f) was rather a retreat from the peak of June, 1987.[7]

In the half year after El'tsin's affair, the harsh struggle between liberals and Stalinists (supported by Russophiles) resulted in only temporary successes for one or the other side. Despite having retreated somewhat after the October meeting of the Central Committee, the liberals soon went into an offensive, mostly concentrating on Stalin, his myrmidons, and his victims.

A number of important publications came between November of 1987 and March 1, 1988, including the articles on Stalin and Stalin's times (see Bestuzhev-Lada's articles in *Nedelia* 5 [1988]; the discussions in *Ogoniok* 12 [1988]; Mikhail Shatrov's play "Further, Further, Further," *Znamia* 1 [1988]; the publication of Nikolai Bukharin's speech on Lenin (1929) in *Kommunist* 5 [1988]; the articles on Bukharin—*Moskovskiie novosti*, February 21, 1988—and *Nedelia* 51 [1988]; as well as the articles on Aleksei Rykov, chairman of the Soviet government (*Izvestiia*, March 5, 1988), on Nikita Khrushchev (Fedor Burlatskii's article in *Literaturnaia Gazeta*, February 24, 1988), on Lavrentii Beria (*Nedelia* 8 [1988]; *Komsomol'skaia pravda*, February 21, 1988), on Alexander Chaianov, a famous economist perished in the Gulag—*Komsmol'skaia pravda*, January 29, 1988, *Ogoniok* 10 [1988], on the "doctors' plot" (*Moskovskiie novosti*, February 7, 1988), on Aleksei Kuznetsov, secretary of the Leningrad party committee, killed by Stalin in 1948 (*Komsomol'skaia pravda*, January 15, 1988).

As a result of the offensive on the part of the liberals on the historical front, they managed to discredit the whole of Soviet history after Lenin, and presented Gorbachev's program as an attempt to save Lenin's heritage and to build up a real socialism, a socialism with a human face.

On March 13, with the article of Nina Andreeva's entitled "I can not retreat from principles" in *Sovietskaia Rossia*, Stalinists made an impressive blow to liberals. The article, clearly inspired by Ligachev, was reprinted in many local newspapers, as well as disseminated in the form of Xerox copies across the country. What is more, many local party committees ordered its use as a directive material for political education. Everything smells of a real state coup (see the analysis of developments between March 13 and April 5, 1988, in *Moskovskiie Novosti*, April 24, 1988).

However, after three weeks of uncertainty that spread chills among *perestroika* activists, Gorbachev struck back, forcing *Pravda* to publish a strong rebuttal against *Sovietskaia Rossia*, which restored, to some degree, belief in his strength (*Pravda*, April 5, 1988).

However, whatever might be developments in the future, including strong counter-reforms and political reaction, party liberal ideology as it was shaped in 1986–1987 is already the property of History, and like Dubchek's ideology of 1968, even the adverse course of political developments, even the betrayal of its founders cannot deprive it of the role of an important factor in world history.

NOTES

1. It is interesting that on the eve of and during his visit to the United States (December, 1987), Gorbachev used every available occasion to not oppose the Soviet political order to the Western one as its superior, an unusual practice for Soviet leaders under similar circumstances (see, for instance, the materials about Khrushchev's visit to the United States in 1961 in Adzhubei 1962); rather Gorbachev suggested that Soviet society is as democratic as America's, in procedures for the election of the government or the treatment of officials as well as in the realm of human rights (see Gorbachev's interview with NBC on December 1st, also see the report on his press conference of December tenth in *Pravda*, December 11, 1987).

The willingness to prove that the Soviet political system is not worse than the Western one was manifested in 1986–1987 in various innovations in Soviet political life—from the introduction of briefings for foreign journalists to the experiment with elections having several candidates on the ballot.

2. Trying to persuade us that Bolshevism and Stalinism are phenomena of two different natures, and seeing in Bukharin's ideology an alternative to Stalinism, Stephen Cohen, however, could not demonstrate that Bukharin's program presupposed even a modicum of political pluralism or liberalism in society (see Cohen 1973 and 1977; also see Levin 1974; and Tucker 1973). It is well-known that although Bukharin was far from Stalin's cruelty, he advocated capital punishment for the defendants of the phoney trials of the early 30s).

3. Stephen Cohen (1981) and Moshe Levin (1968a and 1968b) argue that Stalinism was not at all an inevitable product of the October Revolution and Bolshevism. Of course, Stalin's personality affected very much the developments in Soviet history and a victory of Bukharin in the political struggle of the 20s could have shaped Soviet history very differently. But to what degree? An analysis of the history of other socialist countries—China, Vietnam, Cambodia, Cuba, as well as the Eastern European countries (Albania and even Yugoslavia are of special interest because of their autonomy with respect to the USSR) shows that the Stalinist model, with various variations, became the dominant one in the aftermath of the seizure of political power by communists.

With their reluctance to place emphasis on the political order in socialist countries, both authors (using a very sophisticated argument against those who consider Stalinism to be an unavoidable path in Soviet history) ignore the comparative approach, which could enable them to look at the personality of Stalin in an appropriate perspective.

4. *Pravda*, February 27 through March 5, 1986. The indifference of the party secretaries to the well-being of the Soviet people contrasts sharply with the high profile of this issue in Gorbachev's report. Workers and peasants speaking as representatives of the masses dwelled on the quality of life much more, sometimes making this issue a main subject (see, for instance, the speech by Koroleva, a milkmaid, in *Pravda*, March 5, 1986; or Kostenko, a builder, also in *Pravda*, March 5). To some degree this was also true with respect to another group of speakers: directors of plants and chairmen of collective farms (see, for instance, the speech of Gorin in *Pravda*, March 5, 1986, or of Isakov in *Pravda*, March 1, 1986).

5. As is well-known, comments in a Soviet newspaper referring to a speech being accompanied by applause (or even a storm of applause) is an important political indicator of the mood of both the audience and those who control the mass media. This indicator acquires special importance for a gathering such as the Twenty-seventh Congress, whose participants could, as was mentioned before, express their attitudes much more freely than during analogous meetings in the past. Analysis of this indicator confirms that the congress was rather split on the issue of party cadres, especially on their privileges. On the one hand, El'tsin's speech was interrupted eleven times (including once with "long applause"), and was ended with "long applause." None of the other speakers, including all members of the Politburo, except for those who made reports (Gorbachev and Ryzhkov) and Gromyko, who spoke mostly on international issues, were honored with such a reaction. (Ligachev received the same number of applauses; however, he received no "long applause," even at the end of his speech.) However, each time an orator delivered barbs against *Pravda* for its famous article, or indirectly criticized El'tsin, he also was rewarded with applause.

6. The majority of party secretaries demanded an increase in the role of regional planning; see the speeches of Maniakin of Omsk in *Pravda*, March 1, 1986, and Volodin of Rostov in *Pravda*, March 3, 1986.

7. El'tsin's case was a sensitive blow to the spirit of *glasnost* and cast doubt on the vitality of Gorbachev's political course. From the very beginning the case was handled in the style not of Brezhnev's but rather Stalin's times. El'tsin's speech was not published and was declared a party secret, a direct challenge to the essence of *glasnost* which spurns all the old excuses—state secrecy, the prestige of the country, the exploitation of information by foreign propaganda and so on—and demands openness in everything but data of direct military relevance.

What is more, El'tsin was exposed to a show party trial where he, as had the defendants at the show trials of the 30s, had to recant and profess his loyalty to the supreme boss—who presided over the meeting where former El'tsin subordinates suddenly discovered thousands of flaws in their former master (see *Pravda*, November 13, 1987). Gorbachev's explanation of the El'tsin case in his interview with NBC (*Pravda*, December 11, 1987) was hypocritical and demagogical and did not differ from old Soviet clichés used on such occasions.

One can only speculate what happened behind the Kremlin walls and what prompted Gorbachev to reverse his policy so drastically in this case. However, the lack of this information (at least, at the time when this book is being completed during April 1988) is not a great impediment to this text, which is devoted not to the real politics of Gorbachev's regime but to its ideology, whatever the gap between them.

Chapter 8
Gorbachev's Ideology: A Version of Liberal Authoritative Ideology

As was mentioned in the previous chapter, Gorbachev's ideology went through a number of stages and by the middle of 1987 it completed its development as a liberal program for the rejuvenation of society. If conservative ideology puts its major focus on support of the bureaucracy, and the repressive authoritative or Neo-Stalinist ideology on the restoration of discipline and order, the liberal ideology has its major accent on the control over the bureaucracy from below. The first ideology completely ignores the defects in the evaluation and reward of performance in Soviet society, the second wants to solve the problem through the radical improvement of administrative control, and the third through an increase in the role of the people in management and in the control of the bureaucracy. It is, of course, liberal ideology which is the most concerned with the efficiency of human performance and which is ready to make the greatest changes in the Soviet system for its enhancement.

IDEOLOGY AND POLITICAL RISK

The three party ideologies among other things differ strongly in their attitudes toward political risk. Conservative ideology, by definition, is afraid of any action that, even if it promises success in the future, can put in jeopardy the existing political order. This ideology fears the difficulties of a transitional period and supposes that the dangers of this period are so great as not to vindicate the future benefit of reforms. It is only natural that to the end of Brezhnev's period the word "reform" was expunged from the Soviet political lexicon.

The Stalinist ideology supports the idea of changes but, as was emphasized above, this ideology encourages only those modifications which do not touch the political system and public ideology. This ideology is ready to expose to risk only the economy and some other spheres of society.

The liberal ideology is the bravest, and is not frightened of undertaking serious changes even in the political spheres and propaganda. This ideology assumes that the Soviet state machine is strong enough not to be afraid of spontaneous developments which could be engendered by reforms in any area of Soviet life. Being more confident (in some sense) in the strength of their system, the advocates of liberal ideology are ready to expect that there would be some mistakes and even some dramatic events that could be exploited by domestic and foreign enemies, including their political rivals. These people believe that they could weather such calamities, which are unavoidable in the restructuring of society, and that ultimately they would be rewarded by the significant strengthening of the state.

Gorbachev and his people many times in 1986–1987 inveigh against dogmatics who present all the ideas of the liberal ideology as deviations from socialism and as concepts that frighten the party and the people with visions of anarchy, the resurrection of capitalism, and total collapse.

Gorbachev defended his program against conservatives in almost all his major speeches. He did this in his report to the Twenty-seventh Party Congress, mentioning those "who see in each change of the economic mechanism almost a retreat from the principles of socialism" (Gorbachev 1987a, p. 218). He rejected the ideological arguments of his opponents in his speech at the June, 1987 meeting of the Central Committee as well (Gorbachev 1987c, pp. 29–30).

Alexander Iakovlev, the main official ideologue of Gorbachev's regime, was more rabidly incensed by orthodox ideology than his chief. He called for disregard of the ideology of "universal admiration" (a hint at Brezhnev's complacency) and accused dogmatism (in particular, its praise of centralism and its negative attitude toward the market mechanism) of being responsible for many flaws in Soviet society (Iakovlev 1987, pp. 6–7).

BUREAUCRACY: THE MAIN ISSUE OF LIBERAL IDEOLOGY

As was said before, the major thrust of the conservative (Brezhnevian) ideology is the pampering of the nomenclature, providing it with life tenure, various legal and illegal privileges, and immunity from the judicial institutions in case of blatant violations of the laws. Both dynamic authoritative ideologies—repressive (neo-Stalinist) and liberal (Gorbachev's)—took a different position toward the bureaucracy, denying it the almost feudal autonomy that apparatchiks enjoyed in Brezhnev's period. Both these ideologies assume that without strong control over apparatchiks the state could not escape the degeneration that was manifested so clearly in the 70s and the first half of the 80s.

Bureaucracy as the Major Culprit

However, there are radical differences between the two dynamic ideologies in their attitude toward the bureaucracy. If for neo-Stalinists bureaucrats share the responsibility for the stagnation of the country with the masses, for liberals the blame for it should be laid only at the door of the nomenclature. For them the workers, the peasants, and the intelligentsia were disenfranchised by the social climate created in the country by the apparatchiks. Some liberals treat Gorbachev's political course as "an antibureaucratic revolution" (Karpinskii 1987b) or even suggest that "capitalism and socialism have the same fierce enemy: bureaucratism" (Arab-Ogly 1987, p. 7).

Gorbachev in his speeches in 1986–1987 was very cautious in reprimanding ordinary people, but did not mince words when he talked about officials of various ranks. For him all the negative developments in labor ethics and morals in general were a direct result of improper party policy, of bureaucratic conservatism, and corruption (see, for instance, his sparkling and sharp denunciation of apparatchiks in his speech in Krasnodar (*Pravda*, September 20, 1986). Pointing, of course, only at bureaucrats, Gorbachev said in his speech at the January, 1987 meeting of the Central Committee—when he made his decisive jump to liberal ideology—that "the contemptuous attitude toward the law, the faking of reports, bribery, the encouragement of obsequiousness and glorification exerted a deleterious impact on the moral climate in society" (Gorbachev 1987b).

In his denunciation of the bureaucracy Gorbachev cast in doubt the usefulness of each apparatchik, pointing in his speech in Murmansk in October, 1987 to the size of the bureaucracy—18 million people, including 2.5 million in the party and state apparatus—which makes, as Gorbachev underscored, 15 percent of the Soviet labor force, or again—in his own words—every sixth to seventh person is a manager. Citing these figures as well as the amount of money spent each year on the sustenance of the bureaucracy (40 billion rubles, which, as again Gorbachev himself said, makes two times more than the increment of national income per year), the general secretary patently pitted the masses against their superiors again (Gorbachev 1987e).[1]

He spoke in another speech about "the legitimate ire of the laborers toward leading officials who, being called to guard the interests of the state and its citizens, abused power, hushed criticism, and enriched themselves while some of them became the participants in and sometimes even the organizers of criminal activity" (Gorbachev 1987b, pp. 10–11).

Gorbachev counterposed the masses, presenting them as being rather good, to apparatchiks, who are often bad, even more plainly at his next big speech at the June meeting of the Central Committee, which was again a milestone in the evolution of the liberal ideology. Praising the working class for its vanguard role in *perestroika* (restructuring), Gorbachev put to shame those "who for selfish interests impede social transformation and arise as the snag on the path of *perestroika*" (Gorbachev 1987c). It is obvious that the general secretary was aiming at apparatchiks.

In the speeches Gorbachev was beside himself while commending the masses for their activism and taking their side against "party, state and economic cadres . . . who are not imbued with a comprehension of the new tasks, who continue to stick to the old order and who with their immobility in fact sabotage *perestroika*" (Gorbachev 1987c, pp. 8, 10, 11).

It is remarkable that in his first speech as the general secretary in April, 1985, when he was still under the spell of Andropov's ideology, Gorbachev meted out responsibility for the retardation of the Soviet economy among both apparatchiks and the masses, even slightly in the direction of the ordinary people (Gorbachev 1985, p. 18). It is only natural that the authority of the party apparatus, especially at a local level, has sharply declined in the period of *glasnost*, as confessed by Piotr Dorofeev, the first secretary of the Kemerovo regional committee (*Ogoniok* 24 (June, 1987): 5).

Two Major Sins of the Bureaucracy

Liberal ideology blames the bureaucracy for two major wrong developments in Soviet society: the catastrophic decline in the efficiency of human performance and the great gap that separates superiors, the nomenclature, from the rest of the population.

First, Soviet apparatchiks turned out to be bad managers unable to organize the activity of the masses for the accomplishment of the tasks set by the leadership. They could not even guarantee that goods and services of a moderate quality would be produced under their direction in all spheres of society—from the economy, to health service, to culture.

Second, they lost contact with the masses, having transformed themselves into a special caste separated from the ordinary people not only by their privileges but also by a rarity of communication between them. Liberal ideologues openly spoke about the class antagonism in Soviet society, about the growing animosity between people, about "we" and "they" (see the articles of Anatolii Butenko 1982, 1984, 1987).

The enmity between the nomenclature and the masses, in the opinion of liberal ideologues, forcasts serious political troubles, and Polish events in the 70s and 80s as well as developments in Czechoslovakia in the 60s and even the riots in Russia before the introduction of NEP were directly or indirectly evoked by them in order to convince their audience that it is necessary to be aware of all inferences inherent in the social tension in the country.

The Degeneration of the Bureaucracy

Not only neo-Stalinists but even the advocates of conservative, Brezhnevian, ideology do not deny that party cadres can deviate from the main line and even commit crimes. However, both these ideologies are united in considering the party and state bureaucracy to be a healthy organism, differing only in the methods of supervising it.

Liberal ideology radically broke with this tradition, and has advanced the theory of the inevitable degeneration of the bureaucracy in a command society. They name bureaucrats after Lenin as "the worst internal enemy" (*Pravda*, October 12, 1987). Liberals compete with each other in making charges against apparatchiks, attribution to them as a species hostility to any progress, disregard of human interests, persecution of their critics, inimically to *glasnost* and the mass media, a propensity to exploit their positions for personal gain, permanent lying, the creation of a mythology which distorts reality, and many other sins (see, for instance, Shmelev 1987b, p. 11).[2] In fact, belief in this theory is the most important specific feature of liberal party ideology. In its attitude toward the Soviet bureaucracy liberal ideology likes to cite Lenin profusely, who really in his last years was confounded by the fast growth of bureaucratism in the new society (see, for instance, *Pravda*, October 12, 1987), but say no word about Trotsky who was the first to raise the question of the degeneration of the party apparatus—already in the early 20s.

Liberal ideologues recognize that after the short postrevolutionary period Soviet party cadres gradually stated to sacrifice the interests of the state to their private goals, in the beginning related to career, later related to illegal privileges and enrichment (see Butenko 1987, p. 8; Karpinskii 1987a, pp. 36–43). The privatization of the bureaucracy became, in the eyes of Gorbachev and his people, especially rampant in Brezhnev's times. For them, corruption embraced practically the whole party and state apparatus in this period, having penetrated even to the highest echelons of power, including the Politburo.

The Collapse of Administrative Control

Those who share the liberal ideology hold in high contempt the whole system of control which is supposed to check and rein in the bureaucracy by administrative measures. As was mentioned, the Soviet system of control engages in auditing activity a tremendous apparatus of full-time workers and no less than 10 million so-called volunteers. However, this gigantic system could not even slightly impede the spread of corruption in the country and what is more became itself a part of the mafia-like group at the regional and Moscow levels.

Gorbachev underscored many times that this system completely failed to prevent corruption and deter the violation of laws by apparatchiks, that "a focus on administrative control demands a permanent expansion of the apparatus of control." He did this in his speeches at the January as well as the June meetings of the Central Committee (Gorbachev 1987b, pp. 23–24, 1987c, p. 23; *Pravda*, July 30, 1987).

The introduction of the State Inspection of Quality (*Gospriemka*) in 1986 was in fact also recognition that the whole system of control over the quality of goods, which engaged many hundreds of thousands of people working in the departments of technical control in enterprises and in Ministries, had utterly failed (see Gorbachev's speech at the meeting of the Central Committee devoted to *Gospriemka* in *Pravda*, November 16, 1986).

THE PARTICIPATION OF THE MASSES IN MANAGEMENT AND CONTROL

"Democratization" in Liberal Ideology

Liberal ideology, in sheer contrast to both other party ideologies, proclaimed itself to be the advocate of democratization, of active mass participation in management and control. Demanding radical changes in the attitudes toward the role of ordinary people in the government, liberal ideologists present themselves as genuine supporters of democracy.

As was mentioned, in his speech at the June, 1987, meeting of the Central Committee Gorbachev proclaimed "democratization as the decisive condition of *perestroika*," as the core of the processes of change initiated by the party (Gorbachev 1987b, p. 22). He repeats this again in the aftermath of the El'tsin affair in November, 1987 (*Pravda*, November 21, 1987).

In its demand for the democratization of Soviet society, liberal ideology encountered a number of almost insurmountable theoretical difficulties which all practically converged on the question of the attitudes of Gorbachev's people to the previous regimes, and especially to Stalin's model of society and ultimately to the ideological cost which liberal ideology is ready to pay for the sake of real changes in the Soviet political order.

Indeed, since the middle of the 30s public ideology has contended that the Soviet people enjoy the most democratic system in the world. As a matter of fact, the conservative Brezhnevian ideology (not to mention the Stalinist ideology) accepted to some degree this thesis even for its internal consumption, and seemingly even in communication with each other the members of the political elite pretended that they were ruling a democratic country (see how Arkadii Shevchenko describes his conversation with Andrei Gromyko, Shevchenko, 1985).

However, unlike the Stalinist ideology with its total refusal to acknowledge some facts of reality, Brezhnev's ideology tried to be more realistic, at least at its beginning, and for this reason it introduces the concepts of "the expansion of democracy in the country" and of "the gradual widening of the participation of the workers in management of the country," pointing out that this is a main task of the party. These concepts were included in the Brezhnev Constitution (1977) and in his reports to party congresses (see Brezhnev, 1976, 1981).

With its radical rejection of Brezhnev's regime and its ideology, the liberal ideology tended to present the whole period under Brezhnev as a negative, in this respect as well, as deprived of any real participation of the masses in government. Even stronger is the tendency to describe Stalin's times as a period of total fear and repressions when words about democracy were only a mockery of common sense. Advancing democratization as the major task of the country, Gorbachev and his ideologues spoke about it as a process (democratization!), which itself supposes that democracy has not yet been achieved.

However, at the same time, to reject completely any claim on democracy in the Soviet past is to incur the serious risk of the delegitimization of the Soviet system as such. Just for this reason Gorbachev himself and his people vacillate in the definition of the political order which they want to change—as totally undemocratic (at least, as it was under Brezhnev or Stalin) or as already possessing well developed democracy (at least in comparison with inconsistent and curtailed Western democracy).

So if Gorbachev in his speeches in 1987 persistently suggested that the Soviet people "learn how to work and live according to democratic principles" (see Gorbachev 1987b, 1987c, 1987d), he at the same time in his interview with NBC (December 1, 1987) could claim that Soviet society is already democratic and pretend that the USSR belongs to "the world's democracies."

However, whatever are the ideological problems for liberal ideologues, they are the advocates of the real, and not fictitious, involvement of the masses in the social life of the country and see in them the first ally of the central power for control of the bureaucracy. They are also sure that the attitudes of the ordinary people to the existing economic and political order influence seriously the performance of the Soviet people. They are sure that "the failures" of economic reforms in the past should be ascribed to the passivity of the masses (see Gorbachev's speech at the meeting of the Central Committee in November, 1987 in *Pravda*, November 21, 1987).

The Party in Liberal Ideology

Those who advance the liberal ideology in no way can be defined as advocates of democracy in Western terms. They are far from offering the masses the right to choose their government or to take a real part in the decision-making process at any level of management, even if they do want to curtail the everyday intervention of the party in the activity of various institutions. They are unflinching supporters of the monopoly of the Communist party and do not envisage any change in this crucial issue even if they understand, contrary to the adherents of other ideologies, the role of political pluralism and civil society (see below).

As their opponents inside the political establishment, Gorbachev and his lieutenants continue to ascribe to the party all the positive developments in society, in particular, the course toward liberalization and the critique of the past. The party was credited by Gorbachev with "courage" for the critique of the cult of Stalin (of course, after Stalin's death). The party was also praised by him for "the candid analysis of the causes of the situation" and "exposure of the mechanism of braking and evaluation of it on a principled basis" (again, only after the death of Brezhnev who is blamed for all this) (Gorbachev 1987c, p. 3). At the same time, the bravest liberal ideologues do not dare to rebuke the party for all the troubles with which it has to cope so valiantly after the party itself created them. Only Alexander Gelman was so brave as to contend that the Party owes democracy to the Soviet people (Gelman 1988).

Liberal party ideologists, with all their criticism of the party apparatus, insist that the party in Soviet society continue to be the main coordinator of all social activities in the country, especially at the level of the Central Committee and the Politburo and the institution of the General Secretary. For them a change of the leading position of the party in Soviet society at least under actual conditions could only bring the country to chaos and catastrophe.

Certainly, liberal ideology supposes that the party should be less involved in routine economic business and should allow more freedom to managers as well as to the state organization, but in no way can the party and its apparatus be relieved even for a moment from its duty as the main guardian and leader of the system. As in the past, Gorbachev and his people in all their speeches devoted to real issues appeal to the party committees, laying on them the responsibility for everything in their regions, including the development of private business.

What Liberal Ideology Expects from the Masses

With all these reservations Gorbachev and other advocates of the liberal ideology desire a radical activization of the masses in the social and political life of Soviet society. They want it because they recognized that administrative control over bureaucrats failed, and they hope that the participation of the people in the control of managers from "below" will significantly raise the efficiency of management. As Gorbachev said, "with all the importance of control from 'above,' an increase in the role and efficiency of the control from 'below' has a special importance" (Gorbachev 1987b, p. 24; Iakovlev 1987, p. 7).

Liberal ideologues are almost candid in their substantiation of their ideas about "democratization." They do not refer usually to inalienable human rights to be free and to participate in the governing of society in which one lives. They mostly refer to "democratization" as a necessary condition for economic and technological progress, and for nurturing the might of the state in general.

Speaking about the failures of economic reforms in the past, Gorbachev said directly: "Historical analysis helped us to see more clearly also the roots of those phenomena which are covered with the name 'the mechanism of hampering'. . . . We came to the extremely important conclusion that we suffered many losses because our reforms were not backed by wide political changes such as the democratization of Soviet society" (*Pravda*, November 21, 1987).

Liberal ideology presupposes the creation of conditions for real (and not phony) mass critique in factories, offices, and institutions. This ideology especially wants to promote criticism inside primary party organizations as well as at party meetings, conferences, and so on.

With the broad participation of the masses in the control over managers, liberal ideology also pursues another goal—to make as many people as possible involved in the functioning of the state machine, a policy which was forged at the very beginning of Soviet society and which is supposed to turn millions of people into small (heads of small shops, a party secretary in an office) or partial (for instance, an activist who directs propagandistic work in a factory) decision makers. The involvement of millions of people in the process of *perestroika* by itself, whatever will be the results of the process, will make them more supportive of official policy and will give safe vent to their grumblings about their lives.

The Election of Managers

As a part of the involvement of the masses in the control over managers, liberal ideology proposes to put into practice the election of managers. Gorbachev's leadership launched in 1987 a great campaign for the election of directors of enterprises, the heads of departments and shops, presidents of colleges, and so on. The election of the director of a Riga factory in 1987 became a big national event which was televised and debated in all the central newspapers.

Gorbachev and his supporters in the Central Committee in no way wanted to introduce a really free election of managers. Ultimately, the nomination of candidates and the outcome of the election is supposed to be under strict control of the party committee. The crux of this policy is however to shift the control over the cadres from one level of the hierarchy to a higher one, diminish the danger of corruption, make out workers to be participants in the supervision of managers and in this way to strengthen the control over managers.

Thus, if in the past the appointment of the director of an enterprise was completely in the hands of the first secretary of a district party committee, now it is supposed that workers have the possibility of choosing between a few candidates (some of them even from other districts) who are not necessarily recommended by this committee. People would be able even to reject the candidate of the committee (and also of the Ministry, if it is a big enterprise). The competition between candidates would also help to unearth the hidden flaws in the activity of an enterprise or office.

However, it is the regional party committee which would watch the developments and would interfere at any moment if a candidate is undesirable for the authorities. Such procedures have to slacken the collusion between managers and local party committees, and make managers responsible, even if only partly, to their workers—who know much better than any outsiders what is going on in an enterprise. As in other cases, here liberal ideology proposes to make the control over managers more sophisticated and more effective, at the price of some inconveniences which could pop up for local party committees.

The Election of Government

With their willingness to modernize Soviet society and remove the stigma of an authoritarian state, liberal ideologues also want to get rid of elections with only one candidate on the slate, the butt of jokes inside as well as outside the country (Gorbachev 1987b, p. 22; on elections with several candidates see the discussions in *Literaturnaia Gazeta*, October 28, 1987).

However, not only a desire to update the ideology is behind the intentions to modify Soviet elections. Liberal ideologues see in elections with a real choice among several candidates (as well as in the case with managers) another way to introduce real control (even if of modest efficacy) over Soviet officials from below.

Again, against the fears of conservatives or neo-Stalinists, liberals do not see in these innovations a serious threat to the monopoly of the party. They simply want to transfer the final decisions on cadres to a higher level of the hierarchy, forcing local party committees to reckon also with the mood of the masses. Without ignoring the price which the party apparatus has to pay for the activization of ordinary people in the election process, liberals are sure that the benefit would outweigh it by a wide margin.

Party Internal Democracy

Liberals are determined to build up internal party democracy. In no way do they propose the installation of a genuine democratic order that would make the election of party leaders a free process in actuality.

Being concerned primarily only with the continuity and authority of power at the top of the Soviet hierarchy, liberal ideologues suggest that the introduction of real debates and elections in local party organizations can very seriously enhance control over the party bureaucracy (see Gorbachev's speech at the meeting of the Central Committee in November, 1987 in *Pravda*, November 21, 1987). Certainly, of all the other elements of the liberal program, this one is the most hostile to apparatchiks, putting in jeopardy not only low-rank officers of the party corps but even party generals such as first secretaries of regional and republic committees.

GLASNOST AND THE ROLE OF THE MASS MEDIA

Liberal ideologues are inclined to recognize that the lie became an organic feature of Soviet society, and that deception of each other, from the bottom to the top of the hierarchy is regarded as a normal phenomenon. These ideologues are sure that without combatting the faking of reports, the concealment of negative facts and the ignoring of unpleasant developments, there is scant chance for the leadership to rescue Soviet society from stagnation.

Enumerating the major lessons from the Brezhnevian past, Gorbachev in his report to the Twenty-seventh Party Congress named as the first "lesson of truth" (Gorbachev 1987a, pp. 201–02). He repeated this thesis at the January, 1987 meeting of the Central Committee, saying that the Communist party firmly holds the opinion that "the people know everything. . . . The people need the whole truth" (Gorbachev 1987b, p. 50).

It is remarkable that such words as "honesty" and "lie" were almost prohibited from usage in the mass media and propaganda in Brezhnev's period. The authors of a textbook on ethics for teenagers failed to mention honesty among seventy moral virtues included in their text (see Kon 1983, p. 433).

The fight or rather the reduction of lies and coverups of the misdeeds of bureaucrats was regarded by liberal ideologues to be the major task in the reorganization of Soviet society. With Gorbachev's regime both terms become the most frequently used in the articles and speeches of Gorbachev's people (Iakovlov 1987, p. 5; Iavorivskii 1986, p. 3; Shatrov 1986, p. 88; Chaikovskaia 1986, p. 13).

Having declared at the Twenty-seventh Party Congress that "there should not be any zone in the country closed to criticism" Gorbachev invited an extension of criticism to all spheres of society and to any official (beyond himself and his allies in the Politburo) for wrongdoing (Gorbachev 1987a).

Considering bureaucracy and its permanent tendency to corruption and deception as the major impediment to the transformation of the USSR into a state with an efficient economy and fast technological progress, liberal ideologues see in the mass media an extremely powerful means for keeping apparatchiks in tight rein. With the failure of the administrative control mechanism to check the degradation of Soviet society, the intensive critical activity of the press, TV, and radio becomes an extremely important element for the prospering of Soviet society in the eyes of liberals.

The *glasnost* concept as a policy that supposes open discussion and critique of any issue as well as the access of the people to information about all developments in society has to be implemented, according to liberal ideology, in the first place through the mass media, which has to be free to scrutinize all serious Soviet problems, and to investigate the state of affairs in any sector or region of the USSR. In its efforts to create real objective control over the bureaucracy, liberal ideology lends the mass media much more importance than any other Soviet institutions that could theoretically also perform the same role—the Soviet parliament (*Verkhovnyi Sovet*) and local soviets, party organizations, and others (on the role of the mass media in *glasnost* see Ul'ianov 1987, p. 3).

Probably, in assigning the Soviet mass media the role of the main public supervisor of the nomenclature, liberal ideology approaches the Western political system most closely. Indeed, by the middle of 1987 Soviet journalism, with its divulging the corruption and criminal activity in the Soviet police and courts, psychiatric hospitals and in the army, achieved the level of Western "investigative journalism." According to a high official in the Ministry of Justice, who was complaining about the Soviet press to *Pravda*, in 1986 and the first half of 1987 the central newspapers alone published two hundred negative articles about the procurator's office, and eighty about the courts (*Pravda*, August 7, 1987).

INTELLECTUALS AND LIBERAL IDEOLOGY

Even if liberal ideology tries to preserve its allegiance to the basic dogma of Marxism on the leading role of the working class (references to this can be found in all major documents prepared by liberals, see for instance Gorbachev 1985, 1986, 1987a, 1987b, 1987c), the real heroes for this ideology are the intellectuals.

There are very serious reasons for party liberals to regard intellectuals, the creative part of the intelligentsia (scholars, writers, artists, actors, film and theater directors, journalists), to be their most faithful allies. First of all, the whole idea of *perestroika*, as based on the liberalization of society, is by itself enough cause to look at intellectuals with sympathy. Indeed, what other groups in society could appreciate *glasnost*, the new, critical, role of the mass media, the drastic breakthrough in the publication of works prohibited in the past, the expansion of cultural contact with the West, the cessation of the persecution of the people for their political views, but intellectuals and the mass intelligentsia? All these values matter to people with higher education significantly more than to others.

But liberal reforms are especially dear to intellectuals because they promise to create favorable conditions for creative activity, and not only for journalists, social scientists, and figures in the arts and literature, but also for natural scientists, engineers, doctors—for all those who are devoted to their vocation and for whom professional achievements are very important.

The intelligentsia is also important for the liberal ideology because the liberal regime can improve its life with the introduction of *glasnost* much more easily than other groups of the population that need radical progress in the standard of living, which the regime cannot even hope to achieve in its first years.

But this is only a part of the explanation of the intelligentsia's important role in liberal ideology. This stratum, and of course, liberal intellectuals in the first place, in fact, gave birth to the liberal party ideology itself. Almost all the main elements of Gorbachev's ideology were advanced in the 60s and early 70s by members of the so-called "democratic (or human rights) movement" which in the persons of Andrei Sakharov, Iurii Orlov, Valerii Chalidze, Valentin Turchin, Ludmila Alekseeva, Roy Medvedev, and many others demanded openness, the strict observation of laws, respect for the individual, liberal reforms in the economy, the removal of old myths from the official ideology and many other things that emerged in the liberal party ideology (see Sakharov 1967, Turchin 1977; Chalidze 1981 and 1982; and Medvedev 1971 and 1975).

Of course, the immediate links between the democratic movement of Soviet intellectuals and liberal party ideology were party intellectuals such as Fedor Burlatskii, Alexander Bovin, Vadim Zagladin, Aleksei Rumiantsev—the so-called generation of the Twentieth Party Congress, who even if having strongly betrayed their convictions in their publications and activities in the 70s were however faithful to the liberal ideas of the 60s and managed to take an active part in the shaping of a new party ideology in 1985–1987.

Gorbachev has in various ways demonstrated his appreciation of intellectuals. He has met with them in the two years of his tenure much more often than Khrushchev and even more than Brezhnev. He not only did not heap reproach on them, as Khrushchev did in almost all his meetings with intellectuals, but even pushed them to be more critical of social life.

In his first years Gorbachev met with writers, filmmakers, theater directors, regularly visited theaters and with his presence backed unorthodox plays (such as Misharin's *Silver Wedding* and Shatrov's *The Brest Treaty*).

In all his public speeches he displayed respect for intellectuals, referring regularly to concrete intellectuals as authorities and was usually beside himself in praising the role of the intelligentsia in *perestroika* (see, for instance, Gorbachev's statements about the intelligentsia during his meetings with the participants of the Issyk-Kul' Forum in *Literaturnaia Gazeta*, November 5, 1986).

What is more, Gorbachev in an unusual turn during his press conference in Washington on December 9, 1987, when the question was raised about the origin of *perestroika*, spurned the traditional cliché about the decisive role of the party and pointed to Soviet scholars and other intellectuals who with their analysis of the developments in the 70s paved the way for the changes in the USSR (*Pravda*, December 10, 1987; see also Gorbachev 1987d and 1987f).

It is remarkable that Alexander Iakovlev cited in his article in *Kommunist* the famous novel of Alexander Iashin, *Leverage*, on the double-thinking of Soviet people, the novel which was one of the leading symbols of the democratic movement at that time (Iakovlev 1987, p. 10).

Intellectuals are prominent figures in the liberal ideology also because they are the moving force of *glasnost* as well as debunkers of adversary political ideologies. Journalists in the first place, then theater and film directors, as well as writers and social scientists (and not workers or peasants even if simply because of their inability to deal with written words) were in the forefront of *glasnost* in 1986–1987.

SOVIET HISTORY AS PORTRAYED BY LIBERAL IDEOLOGY

Both ideologies, conservative and repressive, are united in their unwillingness to revise the portrayal of Soviet history as it was shaped in the 70s and early 80s. The reason for such attitudes is obvious—both ideologies too highly evaluate the importance of the "second reality," that is, of the images of the world imposed by the elite on the population. History is one of the most significant parts of this reality, and with their cynical ideas about truth the representatives of these two ideologies do not see any ground for shattering the deeply rooted beliefs in the Soviet mind.

Liberal ideology takes a radically different stance. Undertaking a very risky social and political experiment, liberal ideologues have to substantiate themselves in the eyes of the Soviet people, especially apparatchiks and the intelligentsia.

The revolutionary changes in Soviet society can be justified only if propaganda can demonstrate the great scale of mistakes and deformations made in the past. It is notable that the radicalization of the approach to Soviet history followed with a small lag each new development in the major section of liberal ideology.

In the beginning, liberal ideology cautiously tried to change the official views on the immediate past, declaring that the last years of Brezhnev's regime were a period of stagnation. Then, already by the end of 1985 the negative evaluation of Brezhnev's period was extended to the whole decade of the 70s. A few months later, the same negative characteristic was applied even to the first years of Brezhnev's rule.

However, in Gorbachev's first year, Soviet history before Brezhnev's period was not touched. In 1985, for instance, history before 1964 as an issue was practically skirted by Gorbachev and his people. As was mentioned above, Gorbachev even took part in the celebration of the fiftieth anniversary of the Stakhanov movement, which was presented in the most orthodox Stalinistic way, in blatant conflict with actual historical facts.

However, already in the spring of 1986, after the Twenty-seventh Party Congress, where liberal ideology made significant steps forward, party liberals began their offensive against the old dogmas concerning Soviet history.

This campaign moved in the beginning along the line of the Twentieth Party Congress and was concentrated mostly on the victims of Stalin's terror such as Raskol'nikov, as well as on the authors who could not publish their works when they were written, such as Platonov's *Pit* or Akhmatova's *Requiem*.

In Khrushchev's time, after the Twentieth Party Congress, many of Stalin's victims were officially rehabilitated. Gorbachev's liberals not only took the initiative of the first thaw but made more of the rehabilitation process, turning much more attention to the terror of Stalin's times.

Thus, for instance, at their suggestion the hundredth anniversary of the birth of Nikolai Vavilov, a famous botanist who died from hunger in a Saratov prison, became an international event with numerous publications in the Soviet press demonstrating what Stalin's terror did to science and outstanding people (see *Pravda*, November 25, 1987; *Nedelia* 46, pp. 1, 6, 7; and *Literaturnaia Gazeta*, November 15, 1987).

Liberals were not satisfied, as Khrushchev had been, with the reenthronement of party officials and intellectuals who perished in 1935–1940. They also went back to the late 20s and early 30s and restituted the good names of Nikolai Kondratiev, A. Chaianov, A. Chelintsev and other agrarian economists killed by Stalin (see *Literaturnaia Gazeta*, August 5, 1987, p. 10, *Moskovskiie Novosti*, August 16, 1987, p. 12).

What is more, liberals gradually returned from nonexistence Stalin's political rivals, such as Nikolai Bukharin, Grigorii Zinoviev, Lev Kamenev, and even Leon Trotsky (see Egorov and Loginov 1987; Afanasiev and Shatrov 1987). If the Soviet encyclopedic reference book still in 1987 (it was edited in 1985–1986) did not yet contain any articles about these figures (Prokhorov 1987), the third edition of the reference book *The Great October Revolution*, or the second edition of the reference book, *The Civil War and the Military Intervention in the USSR* (Golub, Korablev et al., 1987; Khromov 1987) which came out in the middle of 1987, already contained articles on all Stalin's foes.

Gorbachev himself in his report devoted to the seventieth anniversary of the revolution did not politically rehabilitate any of these politicians as had been expected, however at least with respect to Bukharin he nevertheless mentioned that the struggle at the top of the party was seriously colored by personal motives and in this way did not close the opportunity for party liberals to continue the gradual revision of Soviet history (*Pravda*, November 3, 1987).

Then Gorbachev's intellectuals moved to the next stage, delving more and more into the major developments of Stalin's period. The two targets of their attacks soon became evident—collectivization and the struggle between Stalin and his foes in the aftermath of Lenin's death. Stalin's personality became as never before the center of many works, from newspaper articles to novels.

A great number of intellectuals, Westernizers as well as Russophiles, united in the scathing assault on collectivization, finding no grounds for the justification of this of Stalin's deeds (see Mozhaev 1987; Vershinin 1987; Burlatskii 1987c; Afanasiev 1987c; Ananiev 1987; and Voskresenskii 1987).

A few historians, led by Iurii Afanasiev, volunteered to revise also the most dramatic episode of Soviet history, 1923–1928 (and even earlier), suggesting that the real character of the conflicts in the party leadership about various "models" for the building of socialism had not so far been studied and that it was vitally necessary to look with a new perspective at all the major party figures active in this period.

Soviet writers took a very active, in some cases the leading, role in the revision of official Soviet history. Mikhail Shatrov, a playwright, ever since the 60s has been a very prominent figure in this process, in particular with his plays *We Will Win in This Way*, *Dictatorship of Conscience*, *The Brest Treaty* and *Further, Further, Further*, which presented such figures as Bukharin, Trotsky, and Stalin in a new way (see the dialogue between Mikhail Shatrov and the American political scientist Steven Cohen in *Moskovskiie Novosti* 24 (June, 1987): 9; see also regarding Shatrov's plays, *Sovietskaia Kul'tura*, March 15, 1986, *Moskovskiie Novosti*, October 4, 1987, p. 8, and *Literaturnaia Gazeta*, November 4, 1987).

Rybakov's *Children of the Arbat* forced millions of Soviet people to reconsider their views on the thirties and on Stalin's personality (Rybakov 1987a, 1987b), whereas Pristavkin's novel did the same for views on the removal of many people (in this case Checheno-Ingushes) after the war for their supposed collaboration with Nazi Germany (Pristavkin 1987). The novels of Daniil Granin (*Aurochs*, 1987) and Vladimir Dudintsev (*People in White Robes*, 1987) disclosed many facts about the last decade of Stalin's regime, mostly related to the famous Lysenko case (regarding these novels see *Literaturnaia Gazeta*, May 27, 1987; *Sovietskaia Kul'tura*, February 17, 1987), while Viacheslav Kondratiev concentrated his attention, in his novel *The Red Gates*, on the difficult fate of Soviet soldiers who were prisoners of war and were cruelly treated by Stalin after returning home (*Moskovskiie Novosti* 35 (August 30, 1987); see also Viacheslav Kondratiev's story in *Iunost'* 3 [1987]). A number of other writers also took part in the revision of official Soviet history, especially in the restoration of the place of writers who perished or were persecuted in Stalin's times, such as Oles Adamovich (1987), Evgenii Vinokurov (*Literaturnaia Gazeta*, October 21, 1987), and others.

THE LIBERAL IDEOLOGY AND CIVIL SOCIETY

The interest of party officials in *glasnost* and the activity of the mass media are linked also directly with their attitudes toward political and economic *pluralism*. For their opponents in the party this term was anathema, a bad word used in Soviet publications addressed even to a narrow audience in a pejorative sense (see, for instance, the article "Pluralism" in the Soviet *Philosophical Encyclopedic Reference Book* (Il'ichev 1983, p. 503; see also Momdzhian's *Pluralism*, 1983).

Party liberals took another stance toward this phenomenon. Analyzing the causes of the degradation of Soviet society, they pointed to the intellectual uniformity and the lack of real debates that were typical for the Brezhnev era.

Thus, then by all accounts began to understand that the existence of parallel and independent institutions is a very important guarantor against the monopoly and ensuing degradation of political power.

Even more important for them was the theoretical substantiation of the radical changes toward private initiative and the surrogates of private property in the economy, and the idea directed against the monopoly of social (or state) property in Soviet society. Since liberal ideology recognizes many flaws in the Soviet economic system (I will discuss this issue later), its advocates must also find a theoretical ground for radical change in economic policy.

Since pluralism has had a very bad reputation in Soviet ideology, the mouthpieces of *perestroika* had to move cautiously and they started with the praise of diversity as an important virtue in social life, a term which also sounded eery to Soviet ears when applied to politics and related topics. Commending diversity as a new positive value, Iakovlev condemns the previous period when "the concept of homogeneity was hammered at with enviable persistence in practice and theory" (Iakovlev 1987, p. 7).

However, gradually party liberals rehabilitated the term pluralism itself, and in August, 1987, Gorbachev already could speak about "socialist pluralism" in a positive sense (*Pravda*, July 16, 1987). Along with pluralism another prohibited term was rehabilitated: *tolerance*, especially "tolerance of the opinions of others." This term was hailed by Albert Beliaiev, the editor-in-chief of *Sovietskaia Kul'tura*, an organ of the Central Committee (and an interview with him was titled "Tolerance," *Moskovskiie Novosti* 36 (September 6, 1987): 10).

However, the thoughts of liberals went much further than the recognition of pluralism and diversity as desirable values. They also recognize the importance of civil society, a network of institutions independent of the state. With the experience of the degeneration of the party apparatus in the 70s and 80s they realized, perhaps the first party ideologues in Soviet history to do so, what a monopoly of political power means. Unlike their ideological opponents in the present and past, they already muse on the pluralistic political system and understand that the existence of rivalry between parties is not an absurd political game, the rational of which lies only in the deception of the masses. Underscoring the importance of public criticism, Gorbachev noted that it is so vitally important for the Soviet society because "We do not have opposition," clearly hinting to the absence of a political force that could correct the mistakes of Communists (*Novoe Russkoe Slovo*, November 16, 1987). In his interview with NBC (December 1, 1987) he was asked about the prospect of the multi-party system in the country. Gorbachev did not reject this issue as absurd, the typical reaction of all Soviet leaders and politicians in the past, but rather calmly responded that Soviet society and the people do not need it and the Communist party can successfully fill the role of self-critic, too.

What is more, the idea of autonomous political organizations gradually made its way into liberal publications. Boris Kurashvili, a legal expert, could publicly defend the idea of the "democratic alliance," which could take the part in the public life of society as a force protecting self-management, the democratization of the political system, and so on (*Moskovskiie Novosti*, March 6, 1988). Fedor Burlatskii wrote, in April 1988, that "state has to yield a considerable part of its power, functions, prerogatives to civil society and its institutions." Moreover, he even demanded "the submission of state to civil society" (Burlatskii 1988).

The importance of public opinion was recognized even by Brezhnev's conservative ideology and was not opposed by neo-Stalinists either. However, only liberals are determined to regard it as a serious element in political life. It is even more important that they extended the concept of pluralism to public opinion as well, rejecting the idea that "good public opinion" should be monolithic, and regarding diversity in opinions as a normal phenomenon (Iadov, Bozhkov et al. 1987, p. 5).

Still, rejecting the idea of a party that could compete with the Communist party, liberal ideologues, however, clearly understand the necessity of building up some elements of organizations that would enjoy some autonomy from the state and the party. They promote this idea very slowly and cautiously but with some persistence.

Gorbachev and his lieutenants, for instance, were active in instigating the idea that film and theater figures have their own organizations that could confront such powerful institutions as the Ministry of Cinematography and the Ministry of Culture. Appeals for autonomy were sounded very distinctly at the congresses of these people in 1986 and 1987 (see *Iskusstvo kino* 10 (1986); see also Ul'ianov 1987, p. 3).

Liberals are favorable toward the so-called informal associations, mostly created by the youth, which mushroomed in the country during the period of *perestroika*. Understanding the threat to the dominant political order, liberals rather greeted these associations, keeping however their distance from those unofficial organizations which took a critical stance against Gorbachev's policies (Gorbachev, 1988b).

In their revision of the fundamentals of Soviet society, liberals also moved to the reconsideration of paternalism as a main tenet of the Soviet system. The Soviet people have been indoctrinated over decades that the state was their benefactor to whom everybody was obliged for everything—from education to apartments and health service.

With their idea of democratization liberals gradually have moved from the idea of the state as a benefactor of the masses to the concept that the state itself gets all its resources from the people. As Iurii Kudriavtsev, a prominent Soviet law expert states, "The growth in the well-being of the Soviet people was perceived (and was treated) as a good deed of the leadership and not as the fulfillment of the ordinary constitutional obligations of the state" (Kudriavtsev 1987, p. 3). Nikolai Popov called the Soviet people to get rid of "the psychology of supplicants," and for the State to use their rights (Popov 1988).

Moving further, liberals required the rejection of the idea of the superiority of the state over the people, which was clearly revealed in the Soviet Constitution, according to which the state has to expand the participation of the people in government. Liberals demand at least that "the authorities and the people be considered to be equal social partners" (Kudriavtsev 1987, p. 2).

THE LIBERALS' ECONOMIC MODEL

As was told in Chapter 3, the major concern of both dynamic ideologies—administrative and liberal—was the state of the Soviet economy. With a prospering economy and fast technological progress none of the advocates of these ideologies could gain the support of apparatchiks who indulged themselves in their unforgettable years of Brezhnev's rule.

However much both these ideologies differ from each other on almost all issues, they have in common the same idea about the major direction of economic reforms: decentralization of management. However, in their evaluation of the central planning system and in their determination to change it, both ideologies differ strongly from each other.

Liberal ideology tends in general to be extremely critical of what it calls the Stalinist model of the economy. It recognized its inefficiency, and not only in the present times but even to some degree in the past. Liberal ideologues see the major flaw of this model in its commanding (or administrative) character.

Rejecting what they call the "commanding-administrative model of the economy," liberals demonstrate their support and even admiration of the economic reforms in Hungary, Yugoslavia, and even China, which only a few years ago was the symbol of all sorts of evils both for these same liberals as well as for conservatives. What is more, in order to find new arguments in their favor abroad, liberals tend to idealize the state of affairs of the countries that they choose as sources of inspiration for their economic *perestroika* (see, for instance, M. Maksimov's article "The Yugoslavian Lesson" in *Literaturnaia Gazeta*, August 12, 1987).

The Autonomy of Managers

Along with the general line of the critique of Stalinist society these ideologues are sure that it is impossible to have an efficiency economy without the great autonomy of producers, in the first place of managers (see Gorbachev 1987a, p. 212, 1987c, pp. 31, 33).

Regarding the enterprise to be a major economic unit, liberals deem it necessary to allow directors the freedom to set up salaries for their workers, to buy and sell equipment, to dispose of profit after the necessary payments to the state and even to make major investment decisions. Liberals envisage the introduction of "the four S's," in the terms of Abel Aganbegian, a leading architect of Gorbachev's economic reforms: self-government, self-management, self-financing, and self-repayment (Soviet TV, November 11, 1987; see also Burlatskii 1987b).

In accordance with their ideas about the role of the masses in public life, liberals suppose that the autonomy of management will be combined with the active role of the workers in the decision-making process—from the election of managers of all levels up to their influence on the elaboration of the enterprise's policies.

The High Role of the Market

However, unlike neo-Stalinists who are also inclined to enlarge the freedom of choice for the captains of industry and agriculture, liberal ideologues not only are more resolute in the expansion of the independence of producers but emphasize to a much greater degree the value of market control over the performance of producers. They see in profit, prices, and bank credit very important tools for the evaluation of producers' performance (Gorbachev 1987a, pp. 212–213; ibid. 1987d, pp. 86–87).

The Consumers

Liberal ideologues want to increase the role of consumers in the assessment of the performance of all branches of the economy and other sectors of society even if they are far from the recognition of the consumer as the major figure in the economy. They want to introduce the wholesale trade method of production (for machines, raw materials, and spare parts) and introduce consistently self-supporting principles, including investments of profits earned by an enterprise (self-financing) to make producers strongly dependent on the real sales of their goods and services (Gorbachev 1987c, p. 37).

Competition and Monopoly

Revealing an understanding (even if limited) of the role of consumers as the major evaluators of economic performance, liberals realize that competition among producers is of great importance for the economy. Unlike the advocates of other party ideologies, they show some understanding of the impact of monopolism on economic activity. In several materials liberals suggest the necessity of preventing the monopolization of the production of a good in one enterprise as well as insisting on the importance of parallel research in science, and so on (Gorbachev 1987c, p. 33; see also the *Pravda* editorial in *Pravda*, August 7, 1987).

However, as with consumers, liberals are very restrained in their focus on competition and monopoly. It is characteristic that in his ninety-minute TV interview (Soviet TV, November 11, 1987) Aganbegian, who touched almost every aspect of the economic reforms, started to stagger when he approached this issue, clearly trying to skirt this subject and even trying to avoid the use of the term—replacing it with such words as "emulation" or "contest," which do not carry such a capitalistic flavor as "competition."

The reluctance of liberals to take the final steps in their economic philosophy and recognize the vital significance of competition for economic efficiency is quite clear. To put competition with consumers in the center of the economic restructuring would mean the creation of a really automatic mechanism of self-regulation, an idea that is ultimately deeply alien to party liberal ideology, which with all its orientation to the Western economic model remains an ideology that has to serve the existing political order and the nomenclature, and therefore cannot advocate the release of the economy from state control.[3]

The Preservation of Administrative Control

In light of these considerations, it is not amazing that liberal ideologues are not advocates of a pure market economy. They want to preserve the commanding role of the state and central planning, limiting the activity of the planning bodies to the major decisions.

The program of economic reforms offered by liberals supposes that the state will control, through so-called "state orders" (a new term which replaced the old one—"planning indicators"), the bulk of the most important goods in the country. The state and the party continue to be the major evaluators of producers' performance, with much more influence on the promotion and reward of managers and workers than consumers. So, for instance, the performance of enterprises in honoring their contracts with other enterprises is again supposed to be evaluated not so much by the consumers of production goods but by planning bodies on the basis of the special indicator (Gorbachev 1987c, p. 33).

What is more, it will be the state that will set the norms that determine the size of the profit left at an enterprise's disposal (the percentage of profit taken by the state and the amount of profit the enterprise can use for various purposes—productive investment, social and cultural needs, and so on).

PRIVATE INITIATIVE AND THE PROPERTY ISSUE

Liberal ideology attacks not only the planning system and the command style of running the economy but also the backbone of the Soviet economy: state property, and advances radical changes in the attitudes toward private property and private initiative.

The Property Issue in Liberal Ideology

Assaulting the dogmas about socialist property, liberal ideologues have probably made the strongest attacks against the fundamentals not only of the Stalinist model of the economy but of the Soviet system as such. The official concept of property dating from the 30s was attacked from various directions.

First, liberals reject the idea that state property is the supreme form of socialist property which has to swallow such inferior forms as cooperative and all the more private property in economic activity. Liberals rehabilitated all forms of property as equally important and in this opened the way for the legalization of privatization in the economy (Iakovlev 1987, p. 13; Gorbachev, 1988a).

But this was not enough for them. They called for an open-eyed look at the property issue. They asked the party apparatus to recognize that the absolute majority of the Soviet people, including managers, regard socialist property as belonging to nobody (Gorbachev 1987a, pp. 218–219), that the average Soviet individual behaves at his or her enterprise as a tenant (Iakovlev 1987). The existence of mass pilfering from enterprises and collective farms along with the unbelievable waste of resources are eloquent proofs used by liberals to back this statement (Gorbachev 1987a, p. 219).

What is more, liberals went so far as to raise doubt about the real nature of property relations in the country, suggesting that in fact the Soviet people face not real socialist but state property, controlled by bureaucrats (Karpinskii 1987, pp. 40–42). As Anatolii Butenko put it, "state property in the USSR is in fact a phenomenon 'empty of real content' because there is no real human interest in controlling and using it as well as in its multiplication" (Butenko 1987, p. 8).

The Collective in Liberal Ideology

Rejecting old dogmas about socialist property, party liberals took a critical stance toward the concept of the socialist collective and the workers being the masters of their enterprises.

They have consented that the socialist collective as the owner of an enterprise is also a myth that served the private interests of managers who turned their subordinates into members of "mafias."

At the same time, liberal ideologues cannot abandon the idea of the socialist collective as a collective owner of an enterprise, because they do not see another solution to the issue of property.

The Attitudes Toward Private Business

In their sober analysis of Soviet economic performance liberals were not afraid to look objectively at the comparative efficiency of state and private businesses. They straightforwardly acknowledged that the productivity of people working in their own or partly own enterprise is much higher than in a state one.

In the publications of 1985–1987 liberals cited data that would have been regarded as counterrevolutionary in the past and that left no doubt about the superiority of private activity over work in state businesses. Alexander Iakovlev, a member of the Politburo, praised "the family business" in agriculture as being able to attain productivity two to three times higher than "in other forms of labor organization" (Iakovlev 1987, p. 13; see also Burlatskii, October 10, 1986).

The eulogy of NEP has been widely used by liberals for propping up their views on the partial privatization of the economy.

Fedor Burlatskii and L. Karpinskii refer to the miraculous resurgence of the Russian economy with NEP after the civil war (Burlatskii 1986a, p. 2; Karpinskii 1987).

The Expansion of Private and Semiprivate Enterprises

Having accepted the idea of the efficacy of private business, liberals became ardent advocates of its expansion in the economy as much as possible.

Certainly they did not have in mind the reprivatization of the Soviet economy, in particular, industry. As reformers, and revolutionaries (as they liked to present themselves), they envisioned the gradual introduction of private and semiprivate business on the condition that this process would not undermine the existing political order and would not undermine the directive role of the state in economics. Thus the liberals do not even raise the issue of the privatization of industry and some of them are explicitly against the dismantling of collective farms (see Zaslavskaia 1987a).

As could be expected, it was agriculture that became the first arena for the growth of private initiative. Here private plots, despite much persecution throughout Soviet history, produced before 1985 one-third of all agricultural produce. As was mentioned, Brezhnev's regime initiated the change in attitude toward private plots from hostile to benevolent.

Liberal ideologues demanded much more: not only the approval of private plots as an important source of food for the country, but also a policy of active state assistance to peasants and workers who privately produced meat, milk, vegetables, fruits, and other goods. Gorbachev's regime, in accordance with these ideas, sanctioned the use of the overall plan in helping the owners of private plots to expand the scope of their activity.

However, liberals considered active support of private plots only a first step in their program for the privatization of the Soviet economy. The next was much bolder because it encroached on the structure of state and collective farms. This was the idea of the "family farm" developed by Gorbachev at the Twenty-seventh Party Congress. It was supposed to provide a family of peasants with land and equipment on, as it were, a long-term lease and to allow the peasants to earn as much as they might by selling their products to the state at official prices and in farmer's markets at competitive prices (Gorbachev 1986a).

Along with family farms liberals also want support for the idea of a collective working under the same conditions as family farms, with the difference that they consist of people who are not related to one another (in kin relations) as a team working on the basis of one contract. As in the case of family farms it is supposed that the means of production will be attached to the small collective of peasants or workers for a long time and the team will dispose of its income on its own. These teams got the name of "tenants."

Liberals proposed to make the same team a leading production unit in industry and other sectors of the economy—particularly in industry but even in hospitals.

Not being satisfied with these ideas, which are deeply hostile to other party ideologies, liberals came out as fierce champions of so-called individual labor activity, or simply of private activity in service and industry. They speak for private activity in maintenance and repair services, in the restaurant business, in the production of clothing and toys, in tutoring and many other activities (Burlatskii 1986, p. 2).

In the beginning liberals figured private business to be based on the labor of only a single individual who could be assisted by the members of his family. Then, very soon after the legalization of "individual labor activity" (May 1, 1987) liberals realized that the family, in view of many reasons (the small size of families, the heterogeneity of a family with different interests of its members, and others), cannot be the fulcrum of private activity and they immediately endorsed private cooperatives as a leading form of privatization in the economy, able to gather people without kin connections for private activity.

However, again it took only a few months to understand that private cooperatives could hardly function effectively if they were to observe the rule imposed on them by the new law—to rely only on people who are not employed by the state (pensioners, housewives, students) and on people ready to work after five o'clock. To permit full or even part-time workers in cooperatives offers means to challenge the state economy, this time directly.

By the beginning of 1988, a new law on cooperation rescinded the obstacle for the development of private cooperatives, allowing them to hire people on a full-time basis without any limitations, and even encouraged the enrollment of people who were released from state enterprises, in the process of revamping the economy.

In his speech at the congress of collective farmers, Gorbachev went beyond himself, praising the new cooperatives (he certainly avoided labeling what the Soviet people did as private) which, in his own words, "foster the feeling of master, initiative and entrepreneurship" and which are really self-managed organizations. Gorbachev called for the spreading of free cooperatives in all spheres of Soviet life—from industry to services—and for the strong prohibition of the state to interfere in the activities of the new cooperatives. What is more, Gorbachev demanded the transformation of collective farms in the federations of the economically autonomous "units" (*Pravda*, March 23, 1988).

In their movement toward privatization, the liberals went so far as to support the idea of selling stocks by state enterprises, an idea which only a few years ago seemed to be anathema for Marxists. In 1988, Soviet newspapers began to support this idea as being the most progressive (see the articles "Workers buy stocks" in *Izvestiia*, January 21, 1988, and "Factory borrows money from workers" in *Nedelia*, January 21, 1988; see also Shmelev 1988 and *Moskovskiie Novosti*, January 31, 1988).

THE QUALITY OF LIFE

All party ideologies claimed their concern for a high standard of living in the country.* Stalin never missed this point in his reports to the party congresses and many other speeches. The same is true about any other Soviet leader, including Brezhnev and Andropov. There is no doubt that they all rejected the ideas of "barracks communism" and asceticism and sincerely wanted their people to prosper and hail their leaders for a happy life.[4]

What is more, the conservative Brezhnev ideology, after the Polish riots in the end of the 60s and the early 70s, even proclaimed that raising the standard of living is the major task of the government (Brezhnev 1971). Therefore, the pretensions of liberal ideologists to be the first, after Lenin, to declare this goal to be of primordial importance for the country is not at all substantiated.

What is more, liberal ideology does not differ from others in the justification of the necessity of the growth of prosperity in society. It also (if less explicitly) sees in it a condition for the growth of productivity and political stability.

The major difference between liberal and other ideologies lies however

---

*As I have mentioned, only the Russophilism has not, by 1988, reached the status of a party ideology and has started to challenge the liberal ideology in 1986–1988—to praise universal asceticism opposing economic growth to moral values (see Mikhail Antonov's article in *Moskwa* 3 [1988]).

in the ranking of the quality of life as a goal among other objectives. For Stalin and all his successors the standard of living was placed at the tail end of the real goals and they were ready to direct, using Gorbachev's words, only "residual resources" for an increase in people's well-being.

With their critique of other ideologies, liberals claim that in their plans the prosperity of the masses is ranked as a real primary goal.

Social Differentiation

Unlike the representatives of other ideologies, liberals are convicted foes of egalitarianism for the masses. Neo-Stalinists in the person of Andropov also raised the issue of distribution and vowed to make it more fair. However, their concept of "social justice" was directed mostly against wheeler-dealers of the second economy as well as slouchers and shirkers and the illegal privileges of apparatchiks. The concept bore an obvious egalitarian flavor and was aimed against high income and "high life."

However, in the evolution of Gorbachev's regime, this concept gradually began to serve a rather opposite goal—the justification of social differentiation through the vindication of high legal earning. If neo-Stalinists castigated high illegal income, liberals on the same concept praise high salaries and scolded those who resisted them (Gorbachev 1987a, p. 341).

In his book *Perestroika and a New Thinking* Gorbachev openly defended legal privileges for various kinds of people—from intellectuals to workers in special branches of the economy and regions to party officials (Gorbachev 1987d, p. 100).

Soviet liberals in 1986 and especially in 1987 ardently advocated the allowance of high income earned honestly and furiously rejected all egalitarian arguments. They also vindicated high earnings not only in the state economy but even in private business, as long as it is legal. Gennadii Lisichkin, a leading economist in this discussion, argues that low incomes make people dependent on the authorities for getting various goods and services, make them indifferent to their productivity, and turn them into people deprived of self-esteem (Lisichkin 1987a).

Party Privileges

Regarding the bureaucracy as the major foe of social progress, and the social antagonism between it and the masses as a serious threat to the stability of society, party liberals had to define their position toward the privileges of apparatchiks, one of the thorniest social issues in the country.

Using Marxist terminology, it is possible to say that in no other issue was the contradictory "class position" of party liberals manifested so clearly as in their attitudes toward this subject. Two opposite trends are clearly discernible in the liberal ideology, though their relative weight has changed in even such a short period as two years.

With their liberal orientations and with the willingness to restore Lenin's spirit in society—which is supposed to be hostile to any privileges for party members—and (and this is especially important to them) with a strong desire to gain the support of the masses for their reforms, liberals are inclined to eliminate all the advantages of apparatchiks, especially the closed stores, hospitals, resorts, and other benefits accrued only to them. What is more, to some degree even neo-Stalinists, as some of Andropov's actions in the first months of his rule showed, were also prone to curtail the bureaucrats' prerogatives in material life. Only conservatives of Brezhnev's ilk were committed advocates of all privileges, both legal and illegal.

As mentioned before, on the eve of the Twenty-seventh Party Congress Gorbachev was very much geared toward taking radical measures against privileges and the famous articles in *Pravda* (February 2, 1986) as well as Boris El'tsin's speech at this congress (*Pravda*, February 28, 1986) were landmarks in this crusade against the special status of apparatchiks.

At the same time, party liberals understand (in particular this became clearer to them when they were able to fathom the degree of bureaucratic resistance to the new course) that the removal of privileges would tremendously strengthen the opposition of the apparatchiks. They are also aware that the consistent elimination of privileges would hurt their own material status and also the status of the cultural elite.

To the end of 1987 the second trend was clearly stronger than the first. The retreat of liberals from their attacks against privilege became easier for them because they became very vocal in the defense of high legal income and in their sallies against egalitarianism. In this context, the refusal to recognize the right of high officials to special treatment does not sound as convincing as it could be if the struggle against social differentiation were a part of social policy (for more on this see below).

At the same time, liberals even in 1987 did not fully curtail rather casual onsets against the privileges of apparatchiks (see, for instance, *Sovietskaia Kul'tura*, September 29, 1987) but this theme clearly became lower than secondary in the liberal ideology. What is more, party liberals managed to elaborate a special theory that equaled apparatchiks to figures in science and the arts as well as people working in remote places of the country or in industries with difficult conditions and therefore to vindicate some privileges for all of them (see Gorbachev 1987e, p. 100).

However, liberal ideology remains irreconcilable to all semilegal and illegal privileges and does not accept them at all.

THE ETHNIC AND REGIONAL DIMENSION OF LIBERAL IDEOLOGY

As was mentioned above, the ethnic issue is one of the sharpest in Soviet society, which is in fact the last multinational empire in history. For this reason, it is only natural that nationalistic ideologies flourish in the USSR and play a significant role in Soviet life. Of these ideologies, of course, Russophilism is the most powerful because it reflects the feelings and the interests of the dominant ethnic group which makes up the majority in the highest echelons of power as well as in the intellectual community.

Russophilism as a more or less cohesive ideology with its focus on Russian tradition, orthodoxy, and the rejection of Western values including democracy and pluralism, and with its ideas of the messianic destiny of Russia, became a leading ideology among Russian intellectuals in the 70s, forcing the democratic ideology which was most popular in the 60s into retreat.

Russophilism in the 70s acquired strong support in the Kremlin and many actions of the advocates of this ideology would have been impossible if powerful people in the highest echelons of power had not encouraged them (see Yanov 1978). What is more, Russophilism became, as was shown above, an important part of the dominant party ideology and even public ideology as it was presented through movies, novels, and plays.

However, it would be wrong to assert that even in this period Russophilism could be considered to be a party ideology. In fact, none of the factions in the Kremlin looked at Russophilism as a serious program for the country. Just because of this, the most ardent and ungovernable representatives of Russophilism, such as the members of the Leningrad Russian Christian Alliance and a number of other Russophiles, were arrested and sentenced to long prison terms.

It is impossible to exclude the emergence of Russophilism as a party ideology but so far this has not happened. In this capacity (and not as an ideology of intellectuals and ordinary people) Russophilism would bring a radical new stage to Soviet society, changes much more significant than those which liberal party ideology want to implement in Soviet society today. As an ideology of the political elite, Russophilism would herald the transformation of the Soviet political order into a Nazi state with numberless consequences for the multinational Soviet empire. So far, none of the Soviet leaders has dared to attempt this.

With all this, the role of Russophilism is so great that in the post-Brezhnev era all politicians and ideologues have had to take a stance on it.

It would be only natural to suppose that repressive, neo-Stalinist ideology represented by Andropov had to be prone even to increase the elements of Russian chauvinism in its ideology, taking into account the place of Russian chauvinism in Stalinist ideology in the 40s and 50s.

However, this did not happen, perhaps because of the personality of Andropov himself. Whatever the explanations, even in the first months of his rule Andropov demonstrated his adversity toward Russian chauvinism. A number of publications made it very clear (see, for instance, Iulian Semenov's article in *Pravda*, January 4, 1983, which derides nationalism and even anti-Semitism; see also the sharp negative review in *Kommunist* 5 (1983) of Iurii Davydov's Russophile book *The Ethics of Love and the Metaphysics of Arbitrariness*, 1982; see as well the anti-Russophile articles in *Pravda*, January 23, 1983 and *Literaturnaia Gazeta*, January 5, 1983). This specific feature of Andropov's ideological policy can be regarded as rather a deviation, demonstrating the role of the leader in a system of the Soviet type. As further developments showed, repressive ideology in the Soviet historical context gravitates toward an alliance with Russophilism, even if not completely identifying with it. The members of the active chauvinistic society *Pamiat'* (Memory), which emerged in 1986, demanded not only the rejection of all non-Russians from the political, economic and cultural institutions of the country but also advocated harsh administrative measures for the solution of all the problems of society.

Liberal party ideology, as it came to shape itself in the mass media and speeches of Gorbachev and his people, avoided the ethnic issue in the beginning. It could be supposed that according to the known correlation between liberalism and internationalism (or the hostility toward ethnic discrimination) that Gorbachev's regime had to evolve in a direction inimical to Russophilism. Some rejuvenation of Russophile aggressiveness in *Nash Sovremennik* (see, for instance, Lubomudrov's article in issue 6, 1985) could be disregarded as an action that had nothing to do with developments in the Kremlin.

However, developments again, as was the case with Andropov, took a rather unexpected turn. The causes lay in the determination of the regime to eliminate corruption and to restore the authority of centralized political power with respect to regions and republics. Since corruption was especially rampant in Central Asia, the new regime with each of its steps in the struggle against corruption came into deeper and deeper conflict with the republics of this area. However, probably an even much deeper cause of the further developments was the seeking of a radical shift in the mentality of party apparatchiks and intellectuals in the last two decades when in general even liberal-thinking people gradually moved from genuine internationalism to various forms of Russian nationalism—from very harsh variants to relatively mild ones. The ideas that the well-being of Russians is lower than that of other peoples living in the country, that Russia while being accused of being the dominant nation is however exploited by the others, that Russian culture as well as Russian nature are neglected, all became widespread in the party apparatus and the intellectual community and are seemingly an important element in the minds of those who came to power in 1985.

Taking stock of Brezhnev's heritage, the immediate factor that the new regime seemingly could not escape was the conclusion that the traditional Soviet policy of supporting national cadres and national republics had failed, that national apparatchiks were deeply inimical to Moscow and wallowed in the most arrogant corruption, and that Russians should not delude themselves about the loyalty of the provinces.

These attitudes were clearly revealed in Egor Ligachev's speech at the Twenty-seventh Party Congress, in which he demanded "the interregional exchange of cadres," a statement that was obviously directed against national cadres (*Materialy XXVII S"ezda*, v. 1, 1986, p. 243).

The removal of Kuniaev from the post of first secretary of Kazakhstan and the appointment of Kolbin, an ethnic Russian, in his stead, ended in the riot of Kazakh students (December, 1986) and similar developments in Iakutiia, Frunze, and the northern Caucasus (on these events see *Komsomol'skaia Pravda*, April 16, 1987) and significantly changed the status of the national issue in the country and in ruling political circles.

The rise in the activity of *Pamiat'* with the clear support of the authorities (about *Pamiat'* see *Moskovskiie Novosti*, May 17 and November 24, 1987, February 14, 1988; *Komsomol'skaia Pravda*, May 22 and December 19, 1987; *Ogoniok* 2 and 22, 1987; *Nedelia*, 51, 1987; *Izvestiia*, June 8, 1987, and February 27, 1988), as well as the strong chauvinistic statements of a number of Russian writers (Viktor Astafiev, Iurii Bondarev, and others), came in the same period and are clearly correlated with the atmosphere in the Kremlin around the ethnic issue. The cancellation by the government of the project that was supposed to reroute Siberian rivers toward Central Asia, under the strong pressure from Russian writers (*Pravda*, August 14, 1986), could only encourage Russophiles and increase the hatred of Moscow among apparatchiks and intellectuals in Central Asia.

Regarding themselves in the first place to be Russians, Russian patriots and members of the political elite seemingly recognized their differences in their attitudes toward aggressive Russophilism represented by *Pamiat'*, *Nash Sovremennik* and other organizations. Whereas those who espoused the neo-Stalinist approach to reforms were inclined to support, if not too publicly, the activity of harsh Russophiles (Egor Ligachev is almost evidently the leader of this group), party liberals (Alexander Iakovlev is clearly the main theorist of them)[5], sharing many common ideas on the national issue, were however against Russophile extremism which endangers in their view even the survival of the country (as it was put by one author in *Sovietskaia Kul'tura*, September 8, 1987).

These differences were manifested clearly in the middle of 1987 when the central press obviously split on attitudes toward the non-Russian republics and especially toward *Pamiat'*. On the one hand, during the first half of 1987 *Pravda* published a series of articles with clear chauvinistic messages, humiliating non-Russians and indirectly supportive of *Pamiat'* (February 11 and 13, March 28, May 20 and 23).

Gradually, *Komsomol'skaia Pravda* (May 22, 1987), *Sovietskaia Kul'tura* (May 28), *Moskovskiie Novosti* (May 17, 1987), and *Ogoniok* (#21, (1987): 4–5) took the diametrically opposed stance, strongly criticizing *Pamiat'* and other extreme forms of Russian chauvinism.

Seemingly, toward the end of 1987, mostly influenced by the nationalistic demonstration in the Baltic Republics on August 23, 1987, some accommodation on the national issue took place in the Kremlin, rather in favor of the liberals, and the Soviet mass media apparently converged on the old official postulate about internationalism, the friendship of the Soviet people, and so on. Newspapers stopped publishing inflammatory articles against non-Russians and against respect for non-Russian languages and the traditions of non-Russian people. The *Pravda* articles in the second half of 1987 were much more favorable to national cultures and languages than in the first half of 1987 (see *Pravda*, August 25 and September 20, 1987).

Other Soviet newspapers increased the number of publications in support of non-Russian languages and cultures (see, for instance, *Komsomol'skaia Pravda*, October 7, 1987). Of no less significance is the fact that during this period the public attacks against *Pamiat'* became more intensive (*Komsomol'skaia Pravda*, December 19, 1987; *Moskovskiie Novosti*, November 15, 1987 and February 14, 1988; *Izvestiia*, February 27, 1988, and others).

Some decline in the activity of the supporters of extreme Russian chauvinism at the top to the power ladder and the apparent success of moderates cannot, however, adumbrate the Russophile element in liberal party ideology.

Even when *glasnost* reached its peak (in the middle of 1987) it was never extended to the ethnic issue. Restoring truth in the presentation of many spheres of Soviet life, including such sensitive topics as the activity of the courts and police, the Soviet mass media did not seriously touch ethnic relations in the country and at almost no time voiced a protest against Russian chauvinism. The national issue, emotionally the most important for almost a half of the Soviet population, even in 1986–1987 could not be discussed publicly as had been the case before. In other words, *glasnost* in its full scope was a boon for Russians who could speak out on almost all the issues that worried them but this was not so for non-Russians, especially non-Slavs, who had to keep silent publicly on the issue that burned most in their hearts.

The Soviet media continued to stick to the completely false interpretation of the events of 1940 which led to the incorporation of the Baltic republics into the USSR as if the Estonians, Latvians, and Lithuanians actually voluntarily voted in favor of the Soviet system and to join the USSR. Official propaganda also totally rejected that there might exist even a hint of Russification, supporting the idea that the Russian language is not studied enough in the republics.

Even if *glasnost* allowed some intellectuals of Jewish origin to play a more visible role in cultural life (Natan Eidel'man, Arkadii Vaksberg, Mikhail Shatrov, Boris Sarnov, and a few others), anti-Semitism as an issue remained taboo for discussions as it had been in the past. Even in the most critical article on *Pamiat'* the author again characterized Zionism and anti-Semitism as dangers to Soviet society (*Komsomol'skaia Pravda*, May 22, 1987). Having included in its agenda many of the flaws of Soviet society, liberal ideology avoided Russian chauvinism and anti-Semitism.

If Gorbachev's liberal ideology takes a stance on many other issues, by the Spring of 1988 the ethnic question clearly remained to not be settled. Opposite trends are in play here—the popularity of Russian chauvinism among Russians, the multinational character of the Soviet state, international relations—and it is still difficult to predict (at the beginning of 1988) what will be the ultimate position of Gorbachev's liberal ideology toward this question. It is very likely that some spontaneous developments will force the regime to define its position in an even more obvious way.

THE TSARIST AND GORBACHEVIAN REFORMS

The Alexandrian and Gorbachevian reforms were both directed against the dominant class which had ignored the higher interests of the country and suppressed human energy and initiative to pursue its own egotistical objectives. Both leaders represented those factions of the political elite who insisted that only liberalization of life in the country, and the restraint of the bureaucracy, could help them to accomplish their mission: the restoration of the might and prestige of the country in the international sphere. The program of reform in both cases clearly contained two main packages: one economic, the other political. Each economic package had one and the same orientation: toward the significant widening of individual activity and toward increasing the role of market forces in the functioning of the economy.

There are radical differences between the two regimes in the formulation of their economic policy. It is curious that the Russian Tsar's government, which ruled a country in which private property was already a fundamental institution, was much less articulate in the promotion of individual and private initiative than was the leader of a socialist society.

If the themes of the curtailment of the state's role in the economy, and the expansion of private business, were some of the leading issues in official speeches and documents of 1985–1987, the Tsarist officials raised the same issue much less often, and never as a formal goal of the reforms. In advancing his agricultural reforms, Gorbachev emphasizes the stimulation of peasants' production. Alexander II and the authors of the peasant reform mostly spoke about "the improvement of peasants' life" (Valuiev [1961], V. 2, p. 425).

However, as various sources show (in particular, Valuiev's diary, Valuiev 1961, see, for instance, p. 335), the authors of the reforms in the 1860s unequivocally expected that private initiative would increase considerably in the future.

However subordinate it may seem, and despite the fantastic technological and other changes in Russia, the agrarian issue is still as pivotal as it was 125 years ago. What is more, the content of this issue is practically the same: how to encourage the peasants to work efficiently. So, this goal was explicitly set only in the Soviet Union while in the pre-revolutionary Russia the Czarist government spoke about "the improvement of the living conditions of peasants." In both cases the proposed solution lay in their liberation from the bonds of external forces—then the landlord, and now the state and its bureaucracy. In Tsarist Russia this objective presupposed, in the first place, the curtailment of feudal power over the peasants, the abolition of serfdom per se, land reform. In Soviet Russia this objective requires the enfranchisement of collective farmers and abolition of the de facto serfdom that binds them to their native villages, where they are officially prevented from moving about as free labor; in addition it means the introduction of payment for their work in social production (under Stalin they received practically nothing), and finally the curtailment of arbitrary party control over managerial autonomy and the encouragement of private initiative by peasants.

In fact, the "peasant reform" in the USSR started soon after Stalin's death, and, as with Alexander's reforms, due to the slow pace of redemption of feudal lands by the peasants, dragged out for over three decades. The actual emancipation of collective farmers finally took place only in the early 70s, when all peasants at last received the same internal passports that "normal" Soviet citizens carry and so could legally change their place of residence in the same way as others. With Khrushchev, and even more with Brezhnev, serfdom on collective farms was attacked and peasants began to get a monetary return for their work. Gorbachev's intention is to move the Soviet "peasant reform" further still. His major contribution lies in affirming the autonomy of managers, and especially in a transition to "the family farm," that is, a production unit consisting of land and equipment operated by a family that exercises the right to dispose of surplus for its own profit. This system resembles the *obrok* that existed before Alexander's reforms, when the peasants' release from feudal obligations required payments in money or in produce, known as "*metayage*."

THE REFORMS IN INDUSTRY AND SERVICES

Alexander as well as Gorbachev wanted to pursue liberalization not only in agriculture, but also in the rest of the economy, especially in industry. Certainly, in Gorbachev's reform the roles of city, industry, commerce and service are greater than in Alexander's, the authors of the reforms of 1860s did not use the same language ("productivity"/"efficiency," "market regulation" and other) as the reformers one century later. But the differences should not be exaggerated; control over the economy also took different forms. Tsarist Russia did not know such an organization as the Party, with its network of units able to supervise minutely the activity of each enterprise. In general, the bureaucratic regulation of industry and other spheres of economic activity in Soviet Russia is immeasurably greater than in the Russia of Nikolas I. Nevertheless, despite all these specific factors, the thrust of the modifications undertaken in industry by these two potentates was essentially the same.

In fact, Alexander's peasant reform objectively sought the acceleration of industrial growth, by allowing millions of peasants, especially those without land, to engage in nonagricultural activities, even to set up their own businesses. This, and also the urban reform, helped private ventures in industry and commerce to overcome the inhibiting influence of the nobility and the local and central bureaucracies of the economy. Furthermore, the Alexander reforms were meant to reduce significantly the economic role of the state in favor of private enterprise. The case of railroad building is especially informative: in the first two decades of Alexander's reign private business laid fifteen times more track than did the state, whereas previously nearly all railroads were built by the state (Khromov 1950, pp. 208–09).

Gorbachev's reforms have the same vector of change: toward the curtailment of state regulation over economic activity. In separate historical contexts, with the state assuming a different character in each, both reformers planned to expand the rights of those who make economic decisions at the enterprise level, compelling them to follow the prescriptions of the marketplace.

Moreover, in essence moving from the distinctly separate starting points both reformers, with whatever realization of what they were bringing about, encouraged an increasing role for private ownership, trying to involve millions of people in economic activity either as full owners of the means of production—the case of Alexander—or as partial owners with some real control over economic activity.

Their predecessors, Nikolas I and Leonid Brezhnev, with their deep animosity toward any structural reform, also relied on foreign capital and technology as means of coping with economic problems. Alexander Herzen sold his Russian estates to Rothschild but Nikolas, who considered this Russian émigré to be his personal enemy, did not want to honor the bargain. However, as soon as the banker hinted that this posture could endanger Russia's foreign credit, the tsar had to defer to Herzen in spite of himself. Brezhnev, in turn, permitted Jewish emigration in the 70s only because he hoped thereby to attract American credit and technology for his ailing economy. Both Alexander and Gorbachev greatly exceeded the horizons of their predecessors in their willingness to exploit the West for the overhaul of Russia's economy and the acceleration of its technological progress. With their clear awareness of Russia's economic backwardness they allotted the West a crucial role in their plans, a circumstance that had a serious impact on Alexander's domestic policy as well.

So far it is too early to sum up the influence of the West on Gorbachev's economy, but we can do so with respect to Alexander. For twenty years the influx of foreign capital and new technology increased dramatically, stimulating a Russian economic boom now only reluctantly being acknowledged in Soviet official histories (Orlov and Georgiev 1984, pp. 234–35; Nosov 1978, p. 278).

THE RESEMBLANCE OF THE POLITICAL REFORMS

An attempt was made above to demonstrate that the economic programs of Alexander and Gorbachev have many common features and the same orientation toward economic liberalism, but these rulers are much closer to each other in the purely political domain. Having been reared, as typical members of their classes, in strong antidemocratic traditions (Miliukov 1969, pp. 6–8; Kornilov 1909, p. 8), both were compelled to understand that it is impossible to control bureaucracy by administrative methods, and that only relatively autonomous institutions can supply the effective antidote. For this reason, they both introduced *glasnost*—this term was very popular in the first years of Alexander's reign, being used in the same sense as currently under Gorbachev (Zhuk and Demchenko 1981, pp. 48, 182)—and significantly reduced the role of censorship. In Alexander's Russia a nearly free press existed for one decade.

Both rulers released hundreds of political prisoners of the previous regimes: Decembrists and members of the Petrashevtsev circle in one case, dissidents in the other. The late 1850s and the early 1860s constituted exactly the same period of "liberal reform spirit" (using the words of a Soviet historian), of passionate public discussion on subjects forbidden only yesterday, and of revelations about the past, as the times that the Soviet people now experience in 1985–1987.

Seeing in the liberal intellectuals their most consistent allies, both Alexander and Gorbachev (of course, the general secretary was much more active in the direct enrollment of intellectuals in return activities), invited them to struggle against the evils of a corrupt bureaucracy for the renovation of the country after decades of stagnation. If Gorbachev encouraged, in the first year of his rule, such critical writers as Evtushenko and Rasputin, Alexander likewise lent his majestic support to Mikhail Saltykov-Shchedrin, a writer exiled by the previous regime and the author of *Provincial Essays*, which caustically unmasked the Russian bureaucracy. In both cases the government, as a gift to the intellectuals, permitted the publication of books forbidden by censors for decades. The Alexandrian regime ingratiated the Russian public through bestowing permission to own the complete works of two major writers: Alexander Pushkin and Nikolai Gogol, while Gorbachev's authorities did the same with two writers harassed earlier: Boris Pasternak and Andrei Platonov. Alexander also markedly eased travel abroad for his subjects by cancelling the general prohibition against visiting foreign lands and the extremely high exit visa fees (Kornilov 1909, p. 19); by the beginning of 1988, Gorbachev was still far behind Alexander in this respect, however, even if some progress was made.

With such courtship of intellectuals, who were accustomed during the previous regimes to very different attitudes from above, it is not amazing that the cream of the educated stratum in both periods was absolutely delighted with the new ruler. As a prerevolutionary Russian historian said, "Each word uttered by Alexander was interpreted in this time as favoring social resurgence" (Kornilov 1909, p. 20). Literally the same took place in 1985, and particularly in 1986, when Gorbachev became the idol of the majority of the intellectuals. The atmosphere that emerged in Petersburg in 1855–1858 was amazingly similar to that in Moscow in 1985–1986, and the reaction of those who visited the capitals for the first time after the change in regimes was quite literally the same. The letter of Balabin, the Russian ambassador in Vienna, to his colleague in Paris, could have been written 130 years later by an American correspondent in Moscow after a five-year absence: "If you should come to Russia now, you would not recognize it. On appearance it seems to be the same, but you feel that a new era has begun. The most consistent skeptics . . . have to recognize that in these two years public opinion in Russia has made tremendous progress. Read our newspapers and magazines, listen to what is said in brilliant salons and modest homes, and you will be startled by the changes in minds" (Kornilov 1909, p. 47).

However, even more important than the flirtation with the intellectuals was the determination of both leaders to increase the number of people involved in the political process. They both were very far from the promotion of a consistent democratic system that presupposed the destruction of the society they commanded, but with all this, they were convinced that the creation of institutions able to check and balance the bureaucracy is indispensable for the modernization of Russian society.

Alexander's political reforms truly changed the structure of Russian society. The first of these reforms created the *Zemstvo*, a truly autonomous regional body; his second reform—municipal—led to the emergence of an independent city government; the third—educational—which, among other things, introduced a sort of autonomy for universities and decentralized control over elementary schools, significantly reduced the influence of official religion on education; and the fourth reform fostered the creation of a court structure based on the jury system.

The judicial reform was probably the most democratic. The real autonomy of the new court was manifested in instances of the acquittal of radicals like Vera Zasulich, as well as in the habit of acquitting writers charged with press offenses brought to trial by the government (Vilenkii 1969).

So far, Gorbachev's regime is very far from the tsar's achievements. Local governments in regions and cities are still in the hands of the party apparatus and do not play any autonomous role, even if Party liberals in 1988 demanded with fervor the separation of state bodies from the Party.

Demands for "judicial reform" were only raised in 1987, and so far the Soviet court is completely controlled by local bureaucrats (*Literaturnaia Gazeta*, January 7, 1987, March 30, 1988, *Pravda*, March 14, 1988). Soviet universities so far have no autonomy, and the people have no influence on elementary and secondary education.

Gorbachev's reforms are only beginning: What is their future? Those who consider them a serious attempt to change life in the USSR are divided into pessimists and optimists. Though it is impossible to predict the future, the history of Alexander's reforms can nevertheless shed some light on this subject.

NOTES

1. Gorbachev's hostility toward the bureaucracy as well as his populism is obviously revealed in the fact that the figures which he named overestimated by many times the real number of bosses because they included also the army of technical workers and clerks working in the party and state apparatus who do not perform an actual managerial role. His comparison of the resources spent on the bureaucracy and the increment of the national income is also meaningless because these figures are of a different nature. His deliberate statistical errors only disclosed how much Gorbachev was involved in 1987 in the attack on the apparatchiks.

2. The attitudes of liberals toward the Ministry of Education is a remarkable example. The staff of this Ministry was accused for all the evils in Soviet schools, in many cases clearly unfairly. In fact, the liberal mass media did not even allow the representatives of this Ministry to respond to criticism, which often took demagogical overtones (see, for instance, the materials of the discussion "School and the Future" in *Literaturnaia Gazeta*, September 9, 1987, p. 11).

3. It would be erroneous to declare that the representatives of other ideologies have not been aware of the deleterious impact of monopolization on the economy.

Being in the process of creating a consistent command model of economics (1934), Stalin also could come up against the monopoly on the consumer market and advocate competition in the trade of consumer goods (Stalin 1952, p. 500).

4. In his speech to the congress of collective farmers in 1933 Stalin set as a main task to make all peasants "wealthy" (Stalin 1952, pp. 452–53). Two years later, speaking to the Stakhanovites, when the country had the Terrible Hunger behind it, Stalin contended with evident satisfaction that "life has become better, more merry" (ibid., p. 536).

5. Alexander Iakovlev was fired in 1972 from his position as the first deputy of the Department of Propaganda of the Central Committee for his article in *Literaturnaia Gazeta* in which he criticized Russophiles. By all accounts, he held the same position in 1987, when in his article in *Kommunist*, he again, if only indirectly (it is remarkable that a member of the Politburo could not express himself more openly), reprimanded them as denigrators of the revolutionary past and principles (Iakovlev 1987, p. 20).

Conclusion

This book is about the subjective world of the Soviet people and not about their "objective" material life; it is a book about ideologies but not about *Realpolitik* in Soviet practice; it is a book about the intentions of the Soviet leaders but not about their political activity.

It is also self-evident that an ideology is implemented in practice only when its advocates have the strong possibility of doing so according to its prescriptions. Concrete circumstances always force the advocates of each ideology to alter their ideology, make concessions, and borrow some elements from others—even if they are hostile to the ideology in question.

However, even given all the distance that separates the subjective and objective worlds from each other, the influence of the first on the second is enormous. The author has tried to demonstrate that the fate of Russia in the next decades depends very much on the conflict between three major party ideologies, that is, on political and social programs espoused by various factions in the political establishment which all have their constituency in the party apparatus, the intelligentsia, and the masses—in the major actors of the Soviet political scene.

It would be erroneous to dismiss completely the chances of a conservative ideology winning the struggle of the two main rivals—two dynamic ideologies—neo-Stalinist and liberal. In the forthcoming years, we will witness the fierce battle between both ideologies, with many social, political, and economic consequences.

In favor of the liberal side, there is the all-embracing crisis of Soviet society, as well as other socialist countries, and the seemingly evident failure of the neo-Stalinist model to cope with the crisis, in particular with economic decline. The scientific and technological progress, the necessity to maintain military parity with the West, the fall of the prestige of socialism throughout the entire world, the pessimism and cynicism on the part of the average Soviet individual—all of these factors act to strengthen the historical chances for a liberal ideology.

At the same time, factors working against a liberal ideology are its inconsistency in all spheres of social life, as well as its orientation toward the "mixed strategy" in affairs of economics, politics, and culture. Meanwhile, historical experience goes against such a strategy, even if it is impossible to exclude some chance for its success—witness the reforms of the 1860s in Russia.

There are many odds against the economic reforms of liberals, who, fostering privatization and market regulation, want at the same time to keep many elements of the centralized planning system. In addition, the outcome of the reform is of vital significance for liberals, who, without serious improvement in their quality of life, can hardly hope to be victorious.

Even more dangers face a liberal ideology in the realm of politics. Here, the mixed strategy can turn out to be especially fatal. Liberal ideology does not intend to create a political system which will deprive the party of its political monopoly. But, without the pluralistic political mechanism, liberal ideology is always at the danger of being wiped out by totalitarian tendencies.

On the side of neo-Stalinists is its cohesive and consistent nature in its main elements, which functioned, even if very inefficiently, over five decades, and which managed to create the class of apparatchiks strongly devoted to it, as well as its own culture and mentality accepted by the majority of the population. Neo-Stalinists are supported by the entire political mechanism, which is compatible only with their ideology. They enjoy the devotion of the gigantic bureaucracy, and the many groups of the population directly linked to it. It cannot be denied that neo-Stalinists have some chance to improve their model, and to enhance discipline (and consequently, productivity in society) using harsh repressive measures.

The big advantage for neo-Stalinists is their readiness to use any means in their fight against their political opponents, while liberals are much more restrained by ethical considerations and by the convictions that, by definition, they should be morally better than their enemies. Neo-Stalinists are usually better organized than liberals, their solidarity is often much more solid than that of liberals, who very often lapse into internecine conflicts among themselves.

However, the major trump card of neo-Stalinists against liberals is related to the ethnic issue. The liberalization of Soviet multinational society leads, unavoidably, to the exacerbation of national conflicts, which by itself is a powerful argument against *glasnost* and other elements of liberal ideology.

But, an even more serious weapon in the hands of neo-Stalinists is Russian chauvinism. Neo-Stalinists, by the logic of internal political struggle, will probably move to a direct alliance with Russophiles. While liberals (even with their inner sympathy for Russian nationalism) cannot use nationalistic slogans which would be in strong contrast to the fundamentals of their ideology, neo-Stalinists can easily—it has already been done by Stalin—incorporate the most rabid form of chauvinism, thus becoming a form of Nazi ideology.

Meanwhile, chauvinism, openly buttressed by the official power and mass media, has a very high chance of gaining great popularity and of helping neo-Stalinists crush liberals as antipatriots, as the agents of the West and zionism.

It is impossible to predict just how the interaction of numerous factors can determine the outcome of the ideological and political struggle in Russia. It would seem that, for many years ahead, Russia will continue to oscillate between the outburst of neo-Stalinism and some movement toward a democratic society. We will witness many events in this drama, a drama which began in Russia at the end of the eighteenth century, when the first move toward a liberal society was made by Russian intellectuals.

Selected Bibliography

Abalkin, A. *Dialektika sotsialisticheskoi ekonomiki.* Moscow: Mysl', 1981.
Abramov, Fedor. *Bratia i sestry: Dve zimy i tri leta.* Leningrad: Russkii Sovetskii Pisatel', 1973.
Adamovich, A. "Posledniaia li Pastoral'." *Literaturnaia Gazeta,* September 30, 1987.
Afanasiev, Iu. "S pozitsii pravdy i realizma." *Sovietskaia Kul'tura,* March 21, 1987.
———. "Vospitanie istinoi." *Komsomol'skaia Pravda,* September 1, 1987.
———. "Nelepo boitsia samikh sebia." *Moskovskiie Novosti,* September 13, 1987.
Afanasiev, Iu. and Shatrov, M. "Chasy s boem." *Moskovskiie Novosti,* November 8, 1987.
Afanasiev, V. *Osnovy filosofskikh znanii.* Moscow: Mysl', 1976.
Agafonov, V. "Kul'turnyi imperializm," in *Bez grima.* Moscow: Moskovskii Rabochii, 1985.
Aganbegian, A. "Na novom etape sotsialisticheskogo stroitel'stva," *EKO* 8 (1985): 3–25.
Aganbegian, A. and Moskvin, D. *Povyshenie effektivnosti narodnogo khoziastva.* Moscow: Nauka, 1984.
Ageev, V. *Ekonomicheskie interesy i stimuly pri sotsializme.* Moscow: Sovetskaia Rossiia, 1984.
Aitov, N. *Rabochiie khoroshiie i plokhie.* Moscow: Sovietskaia Rossia, 1983.
———. *Sovetskii rabochii.* Moscow: Politizdat, 1981.
Alekseeva, L. and Chaldidze, V. *Mass rioting in the USSR.* Silver Springs, Maryland: Foundation for Soviet Studies, 1985.
Alekseeva, V. *Molodoi rabochii.* Moscow: Mysl', 1983.
Allivuieva, S. *Tol'ko odin god.* New York: Harper & Row, 1969.
Ananiev, A. "Chelovek na zemle." *Literaturnaia Gazeta,* September 2, 1987.

Anderson, F. "Concepts, Propositions and Schemata: What are the cognitive units?" *Nebraska Symposium on Motivation.* Lincoln: University of Nebraska Press, 1980.
Andreeva, N. "Ne mogu postupatsia prinzipami," *Sovietskaia Rossia,* March 13, 1988.
Andropov, Iu. *Izbrannye rechi i stat'i.* Moscow: Politizdat, 1983.
Antonov, Sergei. *Vas'ka. Iunost'* 3 (1987) and 4 (1987).
Arab-Ogly, E. "Ot konfrontatsii k vzaimodeistviu." *Moskovskiie Novosti,* September 13, 1987, p. 7.
Arutiunian, Iu. "Sotsial'no-kul'turnyi aspekty razvitiia i sbilneniia natsii." *Sovetskaia etnografiia* 3 (1972): 3–25.
———. "Natsional'no-regional'noe mnogoobrazie Sovetskoi derevni." *Sotsiologicheskie issledovaniia* 3 (1980): 73–81.
Ashin, G. and Midler, A. *V Tiskakh dukhovnogo gneta.* Moscow: Mysl', 1986.
Ashkenazy, V. *Beyond frontiers.* London: Collins, 1984.
Astafiev, V. *Rasskazy.* Moscow: Sovetskaia Rossiia, 1984.
———. *Tsar-Ryba. Povestvovanie v rasskazakh.* Moscow: Molodaia Gvardia, 1984.
Azol'skii, A. "Stepan Sergeevich." *Novyi Mir* 6 (1987), 7 (1987) and 8 (1987).
Babosov, E., ed. *Nravstvennaia kul'tura lichnosti.* Minsk: Nauka i Tekhnika, 1985.
Balagushkin, E. *Kritika sovremennykh netraditsioznykh religii.* Moscow: Moskovskii Universitet, 1984.
Bednyj, M. *Sem'ia, zdorov'e, obshchestvo.* Moscow: Mysl', 1986.
Bek, A. *Naznachenie.* Munich: Posev, 1971.
Belikova, G. and Shokhin, A. "Chernyi rynok: Liudi, veshchi, fakty," *Ogoniok* 36 (1987): 7.
Belov, V. *Kanuny. Khronika kontsa 20kh godov.* Moscow: Sovremennik, 1976.
———. "Vse vperedi." *Nash Sovremennik* 7 (1986): 29–106 and 8 (1986): 59–110.
Benn, S. and Gaus, G. *Public and private social life.* New York: St. Martin Press, 1983.
Bestuzhev-Lada, I. "Druzhba, liubov', sem'ia," in *Demografy dumaiut, sporiat, sovetuiut,* ed. G. Kisilieva. Moscow: Finansy i statistika, 1984, 124–32.
Bialer, S. *The Soviet paradox.* New York: Alfred A. Knopf, 1986.
Bigulov, E. et al. "Material'noe blagosostoianie i sotsial'noe blagopoluchie." *Sotsiologicheskie issledovaniia* 4 (1983): 88–93.
Bikkenin, N. *Sotsiologicheskaia ideologiia.* Moscow: Gospolitizdat, 1983.
Bliakhman, L. and Shkaratan, O. *NTR: Rabochii klass i intelligentsiia.* Moscow: Politizdat, 1973.
Blinov, N. *Trudovaia deiatel'nost' kak osnova sotsialisticheskogo obraza zhizni.* Moscow: Nauka, 1979.
Boiko, V. *Molodezhnaia sem'ia.* Moscow: Statistika, 1980.
Bokarev, N. *Rasshirenie uchastiia trudiashchikhsia v upravlenii proizvodstvom.* Moscow: Nauka, 1979.
Bondarev, Iu. *Vybor.* Moscow: Sovetskii pisatel', 1980.
———. *Igra.* Moscow: Sovetskii pisatel', 1985.
Bozhkov, O. and Golofast, V. "Otsenka naseleniem uslovii zhizni v krupnykh gorodakh." *Sotsiologicheskie issledovaniia* 3 (1985): 95–101.

Breslauer, G. *Khrushchev and Brezhnev and leader building authority in Soviet politics.* Boston: George Allen and Unwin, 1982.
Brezhnev, L. *Otchetnyi doklad Tsentral'nogo Komiteta KPSS XXVI S"ezdu Kommunisticheskoi Partii Sovietskogo Soiuza.* Moscow: Politizdat, 1971.
_____. *Otchet Tsentral'nogo Komiteta KPSS i ocherednye zadachi Partii v oblasti vnutrennei i vneshnei politiki.* Moscow: Politizdat, 1976.
Bulgakov, M. *Izbrannoe: Master i Margarita: roman, Rasskazy.* Moscow: Khudozhestvennaia literatura, 1983.
Bunich, P. *Glavnoe—zainteresovat'!* Moscow: Ekonomika, 1986.
Burlatskii, F. "Kakoi sotsialism narodu nuzhen," *Literaturnaia Gazeta,* April 20, 1988.
_____. "Lenin i strategiia krutogo pereloma." *Literaturnaia Gazeta.* April 16, 1986, p. 2.
_____. "Razgovor nachistotu." *Literaturnaia Gazeta,* October 10, 1986.
_____. "Uchitsia demokratii." *Pravda,* July 18, 1987, p. 2.
_____. "Politicheskoe zaveshchanie." *Literaturnaia Gazeta,* July 22, 1987.
Butenko, A. "Protivorechiia razvitiia sotsializma kak obshchestvennogo stroiia."*Voprosy filosofii* 10 (1982): 16–29.
_____. "Eshche o protivorechiiakh sotsializma." *Voprosy filosofii* 2 (1984): 124–29.
_____. *Moskovskiie Novosti* 43 (October 18, 1987): 8–9.
_____. "Mekhanizm tormozheniia: Chto eto takoe i kak s nim borotsia." *Moskovskiie Novosti,* October 25, 1987, p. 8.
Bykov, V. *Znak Bedy.* Moscow: Molodaia gvardia, 1984.
Byrnes, R., ed. *After Brezhnev. Sources of Soviet conduct in the 1980s.* Bloomington: Indiana University Press, 1983.
Chaikovskaia, O. "Chestnoe slovo." *Literaturnaia Gazeta,* April 16, 1986.
Chalmaiev, V. *Neizbezhnost.* Moscow Molodaia Gvardia, 1968.
Changli, I., ed. *Trud.* Moscow: Nauka, 1973.
_____. *Sotsiaisticheskoe sorevnovanie: Voprosy teorii i praktiki organizatsii.* Moscow: Nauka, 1978.
_____. "Trud kak osnova sotsialisticheskogo obraza zhizni," in *Trud kak osnova sotsialisticheskogo obraza zhizni,* ed. V. Staroverov. Moscow: Institut Sotsiologicheskikh Issledovanii, 1979.
Chernakova, N. "Informatsionnye potrebnosti auditorii gazet, radio i televideniia," in *Sotsiologicheskie problemy obshchestvennogo mneniia i deiatel'nosti sredstv massovoi informatsii,* ed. V. Korabeinikov. Moscow: Institut Sotsiologicheskikh Issledovanii, 1979.
Cherniavskii, V. *Voprosy effektivnosti i optimal'nosti planirovaniia v upravlenii.* Moscow: Nauka, 1985.
Chukovskaia,L. *Opustelyi dom.* Paris: Alagante, 1981.
Churbanov, E. *Kul'tura i sotsial'no-ekonomicheskii progress.* Moscow: Znanie, 1986.
Cohen, S. *S. Bukharin and the Bolshevik Revolution: A political biography, 1918–1938.* New York: 1973.
_____. "Bolshevism and Stalinism," in *Totalitarianism reconsidered,* ed. E. Menze. Port Washington, NY: National University Publications, 1981.
_____. *An end to silence.* New York: W. W. Norton and Co., 1982.

Colton, T. "Approaches to the politics of systematic economic reform in the Soviet Union." *Soviet Economy* 2 (1987): 145–70.
Conquest, R. *The harvest of sorrow.* New York: Oxford University Press, 1986.
Crankshaw, E. *Khrushchev: A career.* New York: Viking Press, 1966.
Davydov, Iu. *Etika liubvi i metafizika svoevoliia.* Moscow: Molodaia Gvardiia, 1982.
Demkin, S., ed. *Anatomiia prestuplenii: TsRU protiv molodezhi.* Moscow: Molodaia Gvardiia, 1985.
Der Spiegel 4 (1987): 112–113.
Djilas, M. *Razgovory so Stalinym.* Frankfurt: Posev, 1970.
Dolguchev, L. *Za Shchast'em na chuzhbinu.* Moscow: Mysl', 1986.
Dragunskii, D. and Sukharev, A., eds. *Belaia kniga.* Moscow: Iuridicheskaia Literatura, 1985.
Drozd, V. "Tak vernetsia li ikh vremia." *Literaturnaia Gazeta,* September 30, 1987, p. 13.
Dudintsev, V. "Liudi v belykh khalatakh." *Neva* 3 and 4, 1987.
Dumnov, D., et al. *Budzhet vremeni naseleniia.* Moscow: Finansy i statistika, 1984.
Efremov, Oleg. *Pravda* February 21, 1986.
Egorov, A. and Loginov, V. "Pravda istorii i literatura." *Literaturnaia Gazeta,* October 21, 1987, p. 3.
Ehrenburg, I. *Den' vtoroi.* Moscow, 1934.
Eidelman, N. *Agenty "Kolokola" v Rossii.* Moscow: Mysl', 1973.
Evenko, L., ed. *Gosudarstvo i upravlenie v SShA.* Moscow: Mysl', 1985.
Evladov, B., et al. "Chetyre tysiachi i odno interv'iu." *Zhurnalist* 10 (1969): 34–37.
Evtushenko, E. *Iagodnyie mesta.* Moscow: Sovietskii Pisatel, 1982.
Fainburg, Z., "Tsennostnye orientatsii lichnosti v nekotorykh sotsial'nykh gruppakh sotsialisticheskogo obshchestva," in *Lichnost' i ee tsennostnye orientatsii,* vol. 2, ed. V. Iadov and I. Kon. Moscow: Institut Konkretnykh Sotsiologicheskikh Issledovanii, 1969.
_____. ed. *Sotsiologiia sotsialisticheskgo proizvodstvennogo kollektiva.* Moscow: Profizdat, 1982.
Fall in Love at My Own Desire (film), 1982.
Fedoseev, P., ed. *Nauchnyi kommunizm. Uchebnik.* Moscow: Politizdat, 1985.
Field, D. *The End of serfdom: Nobility and bureaucracy in Russia, 1855–1861.* Cambridge: Cambridge University Press, 1976.
Firsov, B., ed. *Massovaia kommunikatsiia v usloviiakh nauchno-tekhnicheskoi revoliutsii.* Leningrad: Nauka, 1981.
Fitzpatrick, Sh., ed. *Cultural revolution in Russia, 1928–1931.* Bloomington: Indiana University Press, 1984.
Furman, D., et al. *Religiia v politicheskoi zhizni SShA.* Moscow: Nauka, 1986.
Geertz, C. *Interpretation of Culture.* New York: Basic Books, 1973.
Gelman, A. Vremia Sobiraniia Sil. *Sovietskaia kul'tura,* April 9, 1988.
_____. *We, the Undersigned* (*My, nizhe podpisavshiesia*) (film), 1979.
Gerasimov, A. *Obshchestvo potrebleniia.* Moscow: Znanie, 1984.
Ginzburg, E. *Krutoi marshrut* Vol. 1. New York: Posev, 1985.
Gladkov, F. *Cement.* Moscow: Khudozhestvennaia literatura, 1964.

Glezerman, G., et al., eds. *Sotsialisticheskii obraz zhizni.* Moscow: Politizdat, 1980.
Golub, P., Korablev, Iu., and Kuznetsov, M., eds., *Velikaia Oktiabrskaia revoliutsiia. Entsiklopediia.* Moscow: Sovetskaia Entsyklopediia, 1987.
Goncharov, I. *Obyknovennaia istoriia.* Oblomov, Moscow: Khudozhestvennaia Literatura, 1986.
Gorbachev, M. *Izbrannye rechi i stat'i.* Moscow: Gospolitizdat, 1985.
———. *Izbrannye rechi i stat'i.* Moscow: Politizdat, 1986.
———. *Izbrannyi rechi i stat'i.* V. 3. Moscow: Politizdat, 1987a.
———. "Oktibar' i perestroika: Revoliutsiia prodolzhaetsia." *Kommunist* 17 (1987f): 3–40.
———. "O Perestroike i kadrovoi politike Partii." *Kommunist* 3 (1987b): 5–52.
———. "O Zadachakh partii po korennoi perestroike upravleniia ekonomiki." *Kommunist* 10 (1987c): 5–46.
———. *Perestroika i novoe myshlenie.* Moscow: Politizdat, 1987d.
———. "Potentsii kooperatsii—delu perestroika," *Pravda,* March 24, 1988a.
———. "Rech' v Murmanske." *Pravda,* October 2, 1987e.
———. "The speech in Tashkent," *Pravda,* (April 10). About the image in Tashkent, 1988b.
Granin, D. *Zubr. Novyi Mir* 1 (1987) and 2 (1987).
———. "Kartina," *Novyi Mir,* 1 and 2, 1980.
Gregory, P. and Stewart, R. *Soviet Economic Structure and Performance.* New York: Harper & Row, 1974.
Grigorenko, P. *Memoirs.* New York, Norton, 1982.
Grossman, V. *Vse techet.* Frankfurt: Posev, 1971.
———. *Zhizn' i sud'ba.* Paris: L'âge d'homme, 1980.
Grushin, B. and Onikov, L., eds. *Massovaia informatsiia v Sovietskom promyshlennom gorode.* Moscow: Politizdat, 1980.
Gudilina, E. *Bor'ba s nravstvennymi porokami i pozitsiia lichnosti.* Moscow: Znanie, 1985.
Gvishiani, D., ed. *Osnovnye printsipy i obshchie problemy upravleniia naukoi.* Moscow: Nauka, 1973.
Gvozdev. N. *Stimuly sotsialisticheskoi ekonomiki.* Moscow: Ekonomika, 1985.
Hayek, F. *The road to socialism.* Chicago: University of Chicago Press, 1944.
Hill, J. *The Soviet Union: Politics, economics and society: From Lenin to Gorbachev.* London: Frances Pinter, 1985.
Hoffman, E. and Laird, R. *Technocratic socialism. The Soviet Union in the advanced industrial era.* Durham, NC: Duke University Press, 1985.
Iadov, V. "Otnoshenei k trudu: Kontseptual'naia model' i real'nye trudnosti." *Sotsiologicheskie issledovaniia* 3 (1983): 50–63.
Iadov, V., ed. *Sotsial'no-Psikhologicheskii portret inzhenera.* Moscow: Mysl', 1977.
———. *Samoregulatsiia i prognozirovanie sotsial'nogo povedeniia lichnosti.* Moscow: Nauka, 1979.
Iadov, V. and Bozhkov, O., et al. "Pravo na mnenie." *Sovietskaia Kul'tura,* August 4, 1987, p. 5.
Iadov, V., et al. *Chelovek i ego rabota.* Moscow: Mysl', 1967.

Iakovlev, A. I. *Effektivnost' ideologicheskoi raboty.* Moscow: Politizdat, 1984.
Iakovlev, A. N. "Perestroika i nravstvennost'." *Sovietskaia Kul'tura,* July 21, 1987.
Iakovlev, A. S. *Tsel' zhizni.* Moscow: Politizdat, 1966.
Iakovlev, Z. *Pravovaia statistika.* Moscow: Iuridicheskaia literatura, 1986.
Iakovleva, A. N. "Dostizhenie kachestvenno novogo sostoianiia novogo obshchestva i obshchestvennye nauki." *Kommunist* 8 (1987).
Iavorivskii, V. "Chto izvolite." *Literaturnaia Gazeta,* October 28, 1986, p. 3.
Ikonnikov, S. *Deiatel'nost' Organov Narodnogo Kontrolia Moskvy. 1965–1977 gg.* Moscow: Nauka, 1984.
Ikonnikova, S. and Lisovskii, V. *Na Poroge grazhdanskoi zrelosti. Ob Aktivnoi zhiznennoi pozitsii sovremennogo molodogo cheloveka.* Leningrad: Lenizdat, 1982.
Il'f, I. and Petrov, E. *The golden calf.* Moscow: Khudozhestvennaia Literatura, 1975.
———. *The twelve chairs.* Moscow: Khudozhestvennaia Literatura, 1975.
Il'ichev, L. et al., eds. *Filosofskii entsiklopedicheskii slovar'.* Moscow: Sovetskaia Entsiklopediia, 1983.
Inkeles, A. and Bauer, R. *The Soviet citizen: Daily life in a totalitarian society.* New York: Atheneum, 1968.
Iskusstvo kino 10 (1986).
Iskusstvo kino 8 (1987).
Iunost 3 (1987).
Ivanov, A. "Dvizhenie vremeni, dvizhenie literatury." *Ogoniok* 46 (1987): 6–7.
Ivanova, R. *Pererastanie sotsialisticheskogo truda v kommunisticheskii.* Moscow: Nauka, 1983.
Iziumov, Iu. *Neofitsial'noe puteshestvie.* Moscow: Moskovskii Rabochii, 1983.
Izvestiia, January 21, 1988.
———. February 27, 1988.
———. March 5, 1988.
Kamenetskii, B. and Aleksandrova, A. "Ispoved' zhenshchiny." *Kontinent* 38 (1983): 209–20.
Karpinskii, L. "Ne vredno posmotret' na sebia so storony." *Moskovskiie Novosti,* October 11, 1987, p. 12.
———. "Sotsialism—Eto prosto normal'naia zhizn'." *Vek i mir* 7 (1987): 36–43.
Kataiev, S. "Muzikal'nye vkusy molodezhi." *Sotsiologicheskie issledovaniia* 1 (1987):77–80.
Kataiev, V. *The Embezzlers* in *Sobranie sochinenii,* vol. 1. Moscow: Khudozhestvennaia literatura, 1956.
———. *Time Forward* in his *Sobranie sochinenii,* vol. 1. Moscow: Khudozhestvennaia literatura, 1956.
Katsenelinboigen, A. *Studies in Soviet Economic Planning.* White Plains: M. E. Sharpe, 1978.
Kelle, V. ed. *Sotsialisticheskie problemy nauchnoi deiatel'nosti.* Moscow: Nauka, 1978.
Kelley, D. *The Politics of developed socialism: The Soviet Union as a post-industrial state.* New York: Greenwood Press, 1986.
Kesel'man, E. "Sotsial'no-demograficheskie faktory professional'no-

proizvodstvennoi deiatel'nosti rabochikh," in *Rabochii klass SSSR na rubezhe 80kh godov*. Moscow: Nauka, 1981.

Kharchev, A., ed. *Sem'ia i obshchestvo*. Moscow: Nauka, 1982.

Khomiakov, A. *Stikhotvoreniia i dramy*. Moscow: Khudozhestvennaia Literatura, 1969.

Khromov, P. *Ekonomicheskoe razvitie Rossii v XIX–XX vekakh*. Moscow: Gospolitizdat, 1950.

Khromov S., ed. *Grazhndanskaia voina i voennaia interventsiia v SSSR. Entsiklopediia*. Moscow: Sovietskaia Entsiklopediia, 1987.

Khrushchev, N. *Sorok let Velikoi Oktiabr'skoi Revoliutsii*. Moscow: Pravda, 1957.

Kind People (Dobriaki) (film), 1979.

Kitaev, V. *Ot frondy k okhranitel'stvu*. Moscow: Mysl', 1972.

Klopov, E. *Rabochii klass SSSR (Tendentsii razvitiia v 60–70 gg)*. Moscow: Mysl', 1985.

Kluckhohn, C. "Values and Value Orientations in the Theory of Action," in *Toward A General Theory of Action*, ed. T. Parsons and E. Shills. Cambridge, MA: Harvard University Press, 1951.

Kochetov, V. *Bratiia Ershovy*. Moscow: Sovietskii Pisatel, 1958.

———. *Chego zhe ty khochesh*. Moscow: Sovietskii Pisatel, 1969.

———. *Sekretar obkoma*. Moscow: Sovietskii Pisatel, 1961.

Kolbanovskii, V., ed. *Kollektiv kolkhoznikov: Sotsial'no-psikhologicheskoe issledovaniie*. Moscow: Mysl', 1970.

Kommunist 5 (1983).

———. 16 (1985): 3–73.

———. 16 (1985): 33–42.

———. 5 (1988).

Komsomol'skaia Pravda, July 20, 1984.

———. January 18, 1987.

———. April 16, 1987.

———. May 22, 1987.

———. July 8, 1987.

———. September 5, 1987.

———. October 7, 1987.

———. October 23, 1987.

———. December 19, 1987.

———. January 15, 1988.

———. January 29, 1988.

———. February 21, 1988.

Kondrashov, S. "V Chuzhoi stikhii." *Novyi Mir* 11 (1985).

Kondratenko. *Pod maskoi ob"ektivnosti*. Moscow: Mysl', 1986.

Kondratiev, V. "*Na Stantsii Svobodnyi*," *Iunost'*, 1987.

Kopelev, L. *Sotvorim sebe kumira*. Ann Arbor, MI: Ardis, 1978.

Kornai, J. *Contradictions and dilemmas*. Cambridge, MA: MIT Press, 1986.

Kornilov, A. *Obshchestvennoe dvizhenie pri Aleksandre II*. Moscow: Mamontov, 1909.

Korotich, V. *Litso nenavisti*. Moscow: Sovetskii pisatel', 1985.

KPSS v Rezoliutsiiakh i resheniiakh S"ezdov, Konferentsii i Plenumov TsK, part 1. Moscow: Politizdat, 1953.

Kudriavtsev, Iu. "Perestroika i prava cheloveka." *Nedelia,* October 25, 1987, pp. 2–3.
Kukarkin, A. *Burzhuaznaia massovaia kul'tura.* Moscow: Politizdat, 1985.
Lane, D. *Soviet economy and society.* Oxford: Basil Blackwell, 1985.
Lenin, V. I. *Polnoie sobraniie sochinenii. V. 54,* Moscow: Politizdat, 1965.
Leontieva, T. *Likhachev,* Moscow: Molodaia Gwardia, 1987.
Levin, B. and Petrovich, M. *Ekonomicheskie funktsii sem'i.* Moscow: Finansy i Statistika, 1984.
Lewin, M. *Political undercurrents in Soviet economic debates: From Bukharin to the modern reformers.* Princeton, NJ: 1974.
Liang Heng and Shapiro, J. *After the nightmare.* New York: Knopf, 1986.
Liang Heng and Shapiro, J. *The son of the revolution.* New York: Knopf, 1983.
Liashchenko, P. *Istoriia narodnogo khoziastva SSSR.* Moscow: Politizdat, 1947.
Likhanov, D. "Klan." *Strana i mir* 4 (1987): 43–53.
Lincoln, B. *In vanguard of reform.* DeKalb, IL: Northern Illinois University Press, 1982.
_____. *Nicholas I, emperor and autocrat of all the Russians.* Bloomington: Indiana University Press, 1978.
Lipkov, A. *Proverka na dorogakh. Novyi Mir* 2 (1987): 202–25.
Lisychkin, G. "S toskoi o ravenstve," *Literaturnaia Gazeta,* June 24, 1987.
Literaturnaia Gazeta, January 5, 1983.
_____. December 18, 1985.
_____. December 25, 1985.
_____. January 15, 1986.
_____. April 16, 1986.
_____. June 25, 1986.
_____. July 16, 1986.
_____. November 5, 1986.
_____. December 3, 1986.
_____. January 7, 1987.
_____. January 21, 1987.
_____. April 8, 1987.
_____. May 27, 1987.
_____. June 8, 1987.
_____. July 29, 1987.
_____. August 5, 1987.
_____. August 12, 1987.
_____. September 2, 1987.
_____. September 9, 1987, p. 11.
_____. October 7, 1987.
_____. October 21, 1987.
_____. October 28, 1987.
_____. November 4, 1987.
_____. November 15, 1987.
_____. February 24, 1988.
Littlejohn, G. *A sociology of the Soviet Union.* New York: St. Martin's Press, 1984.

Litvinov, P. "O dvizhenii za prava cheloveka," in *Samosoznanie. Sbornik statei,* ed. P. Litvinov, M. Meerson-Aksenov, and B. Shragin. New York: Khronika, 1976.
Losenkov, V. *Sotsial'naia informatsiia v zhizni gorodskogo naseleniia.* Leningrad: Nauka, 1983.
Makarov, A. *Sovietskaia Kul'tura* July 28, 1987.
Malyshkin. *People from a remote place.* Moscow: Molodaia gvardia, 1957.
Mandelbaum and Talbot, S. *Russians and Reagan.* New York: Vintage Press, 1984.
Marushkin, B. *SShA: Strategiia interventionizma.* Moscow: Znanie, 1986.
Maslov, N. "Uchitsia u istorii, chtoby idti vpered." *Moskovskie novosti* 29 (1987): 10.
Materialy XXVII S"ezda KPSS. Moscow: Politizdat, 1986.
Medvedev. R. *K Sudu istorii.* New York: Knopf, 1974.
Meyer, A. *The Soviet political system: An interpretation.* New York: Random House, 1965.
Mikhalkov, N. *Relatives (Rodnye)* (film). 1982.
Miliukov, P., ed. *Reforms, Reaction, Revolutions (1855–1932).* New York: Funk and Wagnalls, 1969.
Mises, L. *Socialism.* London: Jonathan Cape, 1936.
Mitrokhin, L. *Religii "Novogo Veka".* Moscow: Sovetskaia Rossia, 1985.
Modzhorian, L. *Mezhdunarodnyi sionizm na sluzhbe imperialisticheskoi reaktsii.* Moscow: Mezhdunarodnye otnosheniia, 1984.
Momdzhian, A. *Pluralizm: Istoki i sushchnost'.* Moscow: Nauka, 1983.
Moore, B. *Privacy: Studies in Social and Cultural History.* Armonk, NY: M. E. Sharpe, 1984.
Moskalenko, A., et al. "Nekotorye sotsial'no-psikhologicheskie aspekty upravleniia nauchnym kollektivom," in *Nauka. Organizatsiia i upravlenie,* ed. D. Beliaev, et al. Moscow: Nauka, 1979, pp. 35–55.
Moskovskiie Novosti, May 17, 1987.
———. June 21, 1987.
———. August 16, 1987, p. 12.
———. September 6, 1987, p. 10.
———. September 20, 1987.
———. October 4, 1987, p. 8.
———. November 15, 1987.
———. January 31, 1988.
———. February 7, 1988.
———. February 14, 1988.
———. February 21, 1988.
———. March 6, 1988.
———. April 24, 1988.
Moskwa, #3, 1988.
Mozhaiev, B. *Dozhd' budet.* Moscow: Sovietskii pisatel', 1985.
My Dear Edison (Dorogoi Edison) (film), 1986.
Nash Sovremennik 1 (1987): 112–69.
Nedelia 32 (1987).
———. 35 (1987).

———. 5, 1988.
———. 8, 1988.
———. 51, 1988.
Neisser, U. *Cognition and reality: Principles and implications of cognitive psychology.* San Francisco: Freeman, 1976.
Neizvestnyi, E. *Govorit neizvestnyi.* Frankfurt: Posev, 1984.
The New York *Times,* January 12, 1982.
Nikolaev, V. "Amerikantsy vos'midesiatye gody." *Nash Sovremennik* 9 (1985).
Nosov, N., ed. *Kratkaia istoriia SSSR,* part 1. Leningrad: Nauka, 1978.
Nove, A. "Socialism, centralized planning and one-party state," in *Authority, power and policy in the USSR,* ed. T. Rigby, A. Brown, and P. Reddaway. London: Macmillan, 1980, 77–97.
Novoye Russkoe Slovo, November 16, 1987.
Novyi Mir 1 (1987): 3–18.
———. 7 (1987): 181–235.
Office Romance (*Sluzhebnyi roman*) (film), 1977.
Oganov, G. *Pautina.* Moscow: Politizdat, 1985.
Ogoniok 3 (1987).
———. 25 (1987).
———. 29 (1987).
———. 46 (1987).
———. 10 (1988).
———. 12 (1988).
Orlov, A. *The secret history of Stalin's crimes.* New York: Random House, 1953.
Orlov, A. and Georgiev, V. *Posobie po istorii SSSR,* vol. 1. Moscow: Vysshaia shkola, 1984.
Orlova, R. *Frida Vigdorova.* Vnutrenniie Protivorechiia, 1982: 3.
Orwell, G. *1984.* New York: Signet, 1974.
Osipov, G., et al. "Rabochii klass i inzhenerno-tekhnicheskaia intelligentsia." In *Sovietskaia sotsiologiia,* V. 2, T. Riabushkin and G. Osipov, eds. Moscow: Nauka, 1982.
Ovchinnikov. *Vetka Sokury.* Moscow: Sovetskii pisatel', 1975.
Panferov, A. *Bruski.* Kishinev: Kartia Moldoveniaske, 1986.
Panova, V. *Kruzhilikha.* Moscow: Sovetskii pisatel', 1985.
Perevedentsev, V. "Vosproizvodstvo naseleniia i sem'ia." *Sotsiologicheskie issledovaniia* 2 (1982): 80–87.
Pipes, R. *Survival is not enough.* New York: Simon and Schuster, 1983.
Plaskii, S. *Tvoi molodoi sovremennik.* Moscow: Molodaia gvardia, 1982.
Platonov, A. *The pit. Novyi Mir* 6 (1987).
Poliakov, Iu. "ChP raionogo mashtaba." *Iunost* 1 (1985): 12–52.
Ponomarev, B., ed. *Istoriia Kommunisticheskoi Partii Sovetskogo Soiuza.* Moscow: Gospolitizdat, 1982.
Ponomareva, I. *Stremlenie k vlasti nad narodami.* Moscow: Mezhdunarodnye Otnosheniia, 1983.
Popov, G. "Kak na Rusi otmeniali krepostnoie pravo, p. 1," *Znaniie-sila* 3, pp. 65–71; 4, 82–86; 5, 78–83, 1987b.
———. "Tochki zreniia ekonomista." *Nauka i zhizn'* 4 (1987a): 54–65.

Popov, N. *Amerika 80-kh g. Obshchestvennoe mnenie i sotsial'nye problemy.*
   Moscow: Mysl', 1986.
———. "Prava lichnosti," *Sovietskaia kul'tura,* January 28, 1988.
Pravda. May 9, 1965.
———. May 24, 1968.
———. January 4, 1983.
———. January 23, 1983.
———. September 21, 1985.
———. September 22, 1985.
———. February 12, 1986.
———. February 27, 1986.
———. February 28, 1986.
———. March 1, 1986.
———. March 2, 1986.
———. March 3, 1986.
———. March 5, 1986.
———. March 6, 1986.
———. June 19, 1986.
———. August 2, 1986.
———. August 14, 1986.
———. August 24, 1986.
———. September 20, 1986.
———. September 29, 1986.
———. December 19, 1986.
———. January 4, 1987.
———. January 8, 1987.
———. January 14, 1987.
———. January 21, 1987.
———. January 27, 1987.
———. January 28, 1987.
———. January 30, 1987.
———. January 31, 1987.
———. February 6, 1987.
———. February 8, 1987.
———. February 11, 1987.
———. February 12, 1987.
———. February 13, 1987.
———. February 15, 1987.
———. February 26, 1987.
———. March 13, 1987.
———. March 16, 1987.
———. May 16, 1987.
———. June 1, 1987.
———. June 25, 1987.
———. June 27, 1987.
———. July 6, 1987.
———. July 16, 1987.

———. July 30, 1987.
———. August 7, 1987.
———. August 21, 1987.
———. August 23, 1987.
———. September 7, 1987.
———. October 2, 1987.
———. October 12, 1987.
———. November 3, 1987.
———. November 21, 1987.
———. November 25, 1987.
———. December 10, 1987.
———. January 13, 1988.
———. March 23, 1988.
———. April 5, 1988.
———. April 10, 1988.
Prokhanov, A. "Afganskiie voprosy," *Literaturnaia Gazeta*, February 17, 1988.
Radaiev, V., ed. *Intensifikatsiia sotsilisticheskogo proizvodstva i khoziastvennyi mekhanizm*. Moscow: Moskovskii Universitet, 1984.
Rasputin, V. *Povesti*. Moscow: Molodaia Gvardiia, 1980.
———. "Pozhar." *Nash Sovremennik* 7 (1985): 1–50.
———. *Vek zhivi-vek liubi*. Moscow: Izvestiia, 1985.
Riasanov, E. *The Garage (Garazh)* (film), 1980.
———. *Railway Station for Two (Vokzal na dvoikh)* (film), 1982.
Rimashevskaia, N. and Karapetian, S. *Sem'ia i narodnoe blagosostoianie v razvitom sotsialisticheskom obshchestve*. Moscow: Mysl', 1985.
Rogovin, V. *Sotsial'naia politika v razvitom sotsialisticheskom obshchestve*. Moscow: Nauka, 1980.
Rokeach, M. *The nature of human values*. New York: Free Press, 1973.
Rothbart, M., et al. "Recall for confirming events: Memory processes and the maintenance of social stereotypes." *Journal of Experimental Social Psychology* 15 (1979): 343–55.
Rubenstein, A. and Smith, D., eds. *Anti-Americanism in the Third World: Implications for U.S. foreign policy*. New York: Praeger, 1985.
Rubin, T. "One to One: Understanding Personal Relationships." *U.S. News and World Report*, February 11, 1983.
Rumiantsev, A., ed. *Nauchnyi Kommunism. Slovar'*. Moscow: Politizdat, 1983.
Rybakov, A. *Children of the Arbat. Druzhba narodov* 4, 5, 6 (1987).
———. "Zarubki na serdtse." *Literaturnaia Gazeta*, August 19, 1987, p. 19.
Samsonov, A. and Kovalenko, D., eds. *Kratkaia istoriia SSSR*. Leningrad: Nauka, 1978.
Sbytov, V. *Upravleniie sotsial'nymi i ideologicheskimi prozessami v period razvitogo sotsialisma*. Moscow: Nauka, 1983.
Seleznev, Iu. *Glazami naroda*. Moscow: Sovremennik, 1986.
Seliunin V. and G. Khanin. "Lukavaia Zifra," *Novyi Mir* 2 (1987): 181–92.
Semeniuk, V. *Sovremennyi sionizm*. Minsk: Belarus, 1986.
Semenov, G. *Gorodskoi peizazh*. Moscow: Sovetskii pisatel', 1985.
———. *Zapakh sgorevshego porokha*. Moscow: Sovremennik, 1985.

Sennett, R. *The fall of public man.* New York: Knopf, 1977.
Shatrov, M. "Po Pravde i sovesti." *Sovietskaia Kul'tura,* July 3, 1986, p. 8.
Shcherbakov, A. *Sotsial'no-ekonomicheskie problemy effektivnosti nauchnogo truda.* Novosibirsk, 1975.
Shchekochikhin, Iu. "Pered zerkalom," *Literaturnaia Gazeta,* September 2, 1987, p. 13.
Shestakov. "Sud'ba 'Amerikanskoi mechty' v khudozhestvennoi literatury SShA," in *Amerikanskaia khudozhestvennaia kul'tura v sotsial'no-politicheskoi kontekste 70-kh godov XX veka,* ed. A. Muliarchik and V. Shestakov. Moscow: Nauka, 1982, pp. 43–77.
Shevtsov, I. *Tlia,* Moscow: Voenizat, 1969.
———. *Vo imia otsa i syna,* Moscow: Soviet Pisatel, 1968.
Shipler, D. *Russia: Broken idols, solemn dreams.* New York: Times Books, 1983.
Shkaratan, O. *Promyshlennoe predpriiatie.* Moscow: Mysl', 1978.
Shlapentokh, V. *Chitatel' i gazeta: chitateli Izvestii i Literaturnoi gazety.* Moscow: Institut Konkretnykh Issledovanii, 1969a.
———. *Chitatel' i gazeta: chitateli Truda.* Moscow: Institut Konkretnykh Issledovanii, 1969b.
———. "K voprosu ob izuchenii esteticheskikh vkusov chitatelei gazet," in *Problemy sotsiologii pechati,* ed. V. Shlapentokh. Novosibirsk: Nauka, pp. 57–74.
———. *Sotsiologiia dlia vsekh.* Moscow: Sovetskaia Rossiia, 1970.
———. "Metodicheskie problemy sopostavleniia pokazatelei v sotsiologicheskom issledovanii," in *Sotsial'nye issledovaniia: Postroenie i sravnenie pokazatelei,* ed. E. Andreev, N. Blinov and V. Shlapentokh. Moscow: Nauka, 1978.
———. "The sociologist: There and here." *American Sociologist,* August, 1982a.
———. "Moscow's war propaganda and Soviet public opinion." *Problems of communism* (September–October, 1984a): 88–94.
———. "The study of values as a social phenomenon: The Soviet case." *Social Forces* 61 (Spring, 1982b): 403–17.
———. and Kontorovich, V. *Motives and values of Soviet managers with regard to innovation.* Silver Springs, MD: The Foundation for Soviet Studies, 1984b.
———. *Soviet public opinion and ideology: Pragmatism in interaction.* New York, Praeger, 1986.
———. *Public and private life of the Soviet people.* New York: Oxford University Press, 1988.
Shmelev, N. "i Dolgi Avancy." *Novyi Mir* 6 (1987).
———. "Pochemu ia ne pessimist." *Literaturnaia Gazeta,* September 30, 1987, p. 13.
Shokhin, A. *Neprimirimost' k netrudovym dokhodam.* Moscow: Znanie, 1986.
Shtemler, I. *Univermag.* Moscow: Molodaia gvardiia, 1984.
Shukshin, V. *Zemliaki.* Moscow: Khudozhestvennaia Literatura, 1970.
———. *Ia prishel dat' vam volu.* Kishinev: Literatura artistika, 1982.
———. *Rasskazy.* Moscow: Khudozhestvennaia Literatura, 1984.
Simis, K. *USSR: The corrupt society.* New York: Simon and Schuster, 1982.
Sinel'nikov, A. "Statistika brachnosti i sluzhba znakomstv," in *Stabil'nost' sem'i*

kak sotsial'naia problema, ed. Z. Iankova. Moscow: Institut Sotsiologicheskikh Issledovanii, 1978, 146–60.

Slater, Philip. *The pursuit of loneliness: American culture at the breaking point.* Boston: Beacon, 1970.

Smirnov, V. *Sotsial'naia aktivnost' sovietskikh rabochikh.* Moscow: Politizdat, 1979.

Smith, H. *The Russians.* New York: Ballantine, 1976.

Smolianskii, V. *Tsennosti sotsialisticheskogo mira.* Moscow: Politizdat, 1977.

Sogrin, V. *Osnovateli SShA: Istoricheskie portrety.* Moscow: Nauka, 1983.

———. *Amerikanskaia iskliuchitel'nost': Mify i real'nost'.* Moscow: Znanie, 1986.

Sokolov, V. *Nravstvennyi mir sovietskogo cheloveka.* Moscow: Politizdat, 1981.

Solzhenitsyn, A. *The gulag archipelago, 1918–1956.* New York: Harper & Row, 1975.

———. *A world split apart. Commencement address delivered at Harvard University.* New York: Harper & Row, 1978.

Sonin, M. "Ne khochu zhenit'sia," in *Demografy dumaiut, sporiat, sovetuiut,* ed. G. Kisilieva. Moscow: Finansy i statistika, 1981, 189–94.

———. *Sotsialisticheskaia distsiplina truda.* Moscow: Profizdat, 1986.

Sotsiologicheskie issledovaniia 3 (1987).

Sovietskaia Kul'tura, May 23, 1985.

———. October 14, 1986.

———. January 10, 1987.

———. January 17, 1987.

———. June 23, 1987.

———. July 7, 1987.

———. September 8, 1987.

———. September 29, 1987.

———. November 24, 1987.

———. February 4, 1988.

Sovietskaia Novosti 24 (June 1987): 9.

Sovietskaia Rossia, March 13, 1988.

Stalin, J. *Voprosy Leninizma.* Moscow: Politizdat, 1952.

Starchenko, T. and Filippov, D., eds. *Gumanizm sotsialisticheskogo obraza zhizni.* L'vov: L'vovskii Universitet, 1984.

Stites, R. *The women's liberation movement in Russia.* Princeton, NJ: Princeton University Press, 1978.

Strana i mir 5 (1986).

Streliannyi, A. "Dva umozreniia." *Novyi Mir* 2 (1987): 234–49.

Svinninikov, V. *Sotsialism i svobodnoe vremia. Pravo na otdykh.* Moscow: Vyshaia shkola, 1985.

Tatu, M. *Le pouvoir en URSS.* Paris: Grassy, 1967.

Terz, A. *Spokoinoi nochi.* Paris: Syntaksis, 1984.

Tesser, A. "Self-generated attitude change." *Advances in Experimental Social Psychology,* vol. 2. New York: Academic Press, 1978.

Tesser, A. and Danheiser, P. "Anticipated relationship, salience of partner and attitude change." *Personal Social Psychology Bulletin* 4 (1978): 35–38.

Tesser, A. and Leonne, C. "Cognitive schemas and thought as determinants of attitude change." *Journal of Experimental Social Psychology* 13 (1977): 340–56.
Titma, M., ed. *Sotsial'no-professional'naia orientatsiia studenchestva.* Vil'nius: Institut filosofii i sotsiologii i prava AN Litovskoi SSR, 1981.
Toai, Doan Van and Chanoff, D. *The Vietnamese Gulag.* New York: Simon and Schuster, 1986.
Trifonov, Iu. *Vremia i mesto.* (NP): Postskriptum, 1982.
———. *Dom na naberezhnoii.* Ann Arbor: Ardis, 1983.
———. *Izbrannoe.* Minsk: Vysshaia shkola, 1983.
TsSU SSSR. *Narodnoie khoziaistvo SSSR v 1982 g.* Moscow: Finansy i statistika, 1982.
———. *Narodnoie khoziaistvo SSSR v 1984 g.* Moscow: Finansy i statistika, 1985.
———. *Narodnoie khoziaistvo SSSR v 1985 g.* Moscow: Finansy i statistika, 1986.
Tucker, R. *Stalin as revolutionary, 1879–1929: A study of history and personality.* New York: 1973.
Ugrinovich, D. *Vvedenie v religiovedenie.* Moscow: Mysl', 1985.
Ulanovskii, N. and Ulanovskii, M. *Istoriia odnoi sem'i.* New York: Chaldize Publishers, 1982.
Uledov, A. *Dukhovnaia zhizn obshchestva.* Moscow: Mysl', 1985.
Ul'ianov, M. "Teper' ili nikogda." *Sovietskaia Kul'tura,* February 7, 1987a.
———. "Trudnyi put' k samoupravleniiu." *Sovietskaia Kul'tura,* October 24, 1987b, p. 3.
Vaksberg, A. "Sud'ba prokurora," *Literaturnaia Gazeta,* October 28, 1987.
Val'tukh, K. and Lavrovskii, B. "Proizvodstvennyi apparat strany." *Eko* 2 (1986).
Valuiev, A. *Dnevnik ministra vnutrennikh Del,* V. 1, Moscow: izdatelstvo Akademii Nauk, 1961.
Vannikov L. 1988 "Zapiski narkoma," *Znamia* 1, pp. 130–60, 133–59.
Vasiliev, G. "Zavtra byla voina." *Iunost* 6 (1985): 8–56.
Venzher, V. *Kolkhoznyi stroi na sovremennom etape.* Moscow: Ekonomika, 1966.
Vernadskii, G. *A history of Russia.* New Haven: Yale University Press, 1966.
Vershinin, V. "Iskusstvo khoziastvovaniia." *Sovietskaia Kul'tura,* October 1, 1987.
Vilenkii, B. *Sudebnaia reforma i kontreforma.* Moscow: Iuridicheskaia literatura, 1969.
Vishnevskaia, G. *Galina.* New York: Random House, 1984.
Vlasov, Iu. *Sredstva massovoi informatsii i sovremennoe burzhuaznoe gosudarstvo.* Moscow: Moskovskii Universitet, 1985.
Voinova, V. and Chernakova, N. "Rol' sobranii obshchestvennykh organizatsii v protsesse formirovaniia obshchestvennogo mneniia trudovykh kollektivov," in *Voprosy sovershenstvovaniia deiatel'nosti obshchestvennyk organizatsii,* ed. N. Bokarev and A. Beliakov. Moscow: Znanie, 1979, 61–93.
Voinova, V. and Petrov, E. "Ob izuchenii roli i mesta sobranii v zhizni trudovykh kollektivov," in *Sotsiologicheskie problemy obshchestvennogo mneniia,* ed. V. Korabeinikov. Moscow: Institut Sotsiologicheskikh Issledovanii, 1975, 160–69.
Volkov, G. "Byt' li nam Mankurami." *Sovietskaia Kul'tura,* July 4, 1987.

Volkov, I. and Mukhachev, V. "Aktivnost' rabochykh v sisteme upravleniia obshchestvennom proizvodstvom," in *Aktivnost' lichnosti v sotsialisticheskom obshchestve,* ed. T. Iaroshevskii and N. Mansurov. Moscow: Nauka, 1976, 172–84.

Voskresenkii, L. "Smeshon li ded Shchukar." *Moskovskiie Novosti,* August 9, 1987.

Voslenskii, M. *La Nomenclature: Les Privilégiés en URSS.* Paris: Pierre Belfon, 1980.

Yanov, A. *The Russian new right: Right wing ideologues in the contemporary USSR.* Berkeley: Institut of International Studies, 1978.

Young, F., ed. *Privacy.* Chichester, England: John Wiley, 1978.

Zagladin, N. *V Pogone za nedostizhimym.* Moscow: Politizdat, 1984.

Zaionchkovskii, P. *Pravitel'stvennyi apparat samoderszhavnoi Rossii v XIX v.* Moscow: Mysl', 1978.

Zal'tsman, I. and G. Edel'gaus "Vspominaia urok tankograda." *Kommunist* 16 (1984): 76–87.

Zalygin, S. "A chto zhe dal'she", *Novyi Mir* 7 (1987): 201–10.

──────. *Tropy Altaia. Na Irtish. Rasskazy.* Moscow: Khudozhestvennaia literatura, 1966.

Zamoshkin, Iu. and Batalov, E., eds. *Sovremennoe politicheskoe soznanie v SShA.* Moscow: Nauka, 1980.

Zaslavskaia, T. "Paper to a Moscow Seminar." *Russia* 9 (1984), 27–42.

──────. "Chelovecheskii faktor razvitiia ekonomiki i sotsial'naia spravedlivost'." *Kommunist* 3 (1986).

──────. "Reshaushchie uslovie uskoreniia sotsial'no-ekonomicheskogo razvitiia." *Eko* 3 (1986): 3–25.

──────. "Perestroika i sotsiologiia." *Pravda,* February 6, 1987.

──────. "Interv'iu s akademikom Zaslavskoi." *Novoe Russkoe slovo,* October 9, 1987, p. 2.

Zaslavskaia, T. et al. "Problemy sotsial'nogo razvitiia Sibiri i puti ikh resheniia." *Izvestiia Sibirskogo Otdeleniia Akademii Nauk SSSR. Seriia Ekonomiki i Prikladnoi Sotsiologii* 1 (1986): 36–45.

Zheliagin, V. and Rutych. *Rossia v epokhu reform.* Frankfurt: Posev, 1981.

Zhuravlev, G. *Sotsialisticheskie issledovaniia v effektivnosti ideologicheskoi raboty.* Moscow: Mysl', 1980.

Zhuk, A. and Demchenko. *Svistok.* Moscow: Nauka, 1981.

Zhukov G. *Vospominaniia i razmyshleniia,* Moscow: Novosti, 1971.

Znamia, 1, 1988.

Zvorykin, A., ed. *Problemy sotsial'nogo planirovaniia v nauchnom kollektive.* Moscow: Institut Sotsiologicheskikh Issledovanii, 1976.

──────. *Problemy sotsial'nogo planirovaniia v nauchnom kollektive.* Moscow: Institut Sotsiologicheskikh Issledovanii, 1977.

Index

Academy of Sciences, 7, 80, 88
administrative control, failure of, 149–50, 156
Aganbegian, A., 164
alcoholism, 64–65
Alexander II, 69–74, 83–86, 179–89
Andropov, I.: and anti-democratism, 110, 113–14; and Brezhnev's ideology, 108, death of, 75; and economic reforms, 128; and egalitarianism, 171; and evaluation of performance, 12, 20; ideology of, 148, 174; and information dissemination, 67, 71; and intellectuals, 116, 117; and material stimulation, 111; and military retardation, 81; and misperceptions of Soviet economy, 118; and neo-Stalinism, 105; and political destabilization, 81; and preventive reforms, 77–78; and Russophilism, 174; and social justice, 78; and the standard of living, 170
antidemocratism, 109–14
anti-semitism, 177
Arkhangelsk [region], 48
Armenia, 44

Baibakov, N., 7

Baltic Republics, 176
Bolshevism, 126
Brezhnev, Leonid: ideology of: and anti-individualism, 95; and censorship, 73; and conservatism, 87–104, 90, 116, 146; and democratization, 150–51; depicted in fictional literature, 92, 96, 99–103; and economic reform, 132–33; and evaluation of performance, 16, 21, 41, 45–46, 94, 103–4; and information repression, 67, 103–4; literary commentaries about, 99–103; overview of, 95–97; and party glorification, 92–94; and propaganda, 103–4, 117–18, 155; and return to Stalinism, 91; and United States image, 97–103; on Western religion and political freedom, 99–103
Brezhnev, Leonid: regime of: and agriculture, 62, 71–72; and cadre selection policy, 107, 149; and central/regional power, 6, 20, 43, and conservatism, 71–72, 145; and consumerism, 42; and corruption, 20, 44, 60, 72, 93, 128–30; and criticism of Khrushchev's regime, 6; criticisms of, 7, 17; decision-making

mechanisms in, 15; depicted in fictional literature, 92, 96; and the dominant class, 107; and economic stagnation, 9; and the emigrant press, 74; and evaluation of performance, 21, 24–25; and industry and services reform, 179–80; and information availability, 68, and intellectuals, 63, 73, 75–76, 89, 107–8, 158; and liberalism, 88, 107; literary commentaries about, 71, 75, 107–8; and material stimulation, 45–46; mortality in, 72; movie commentaries about, 95–97; and passivity, 53; political ideology, 87–94; political stability, 78; and privatization, 41, 47, 149; reform, 84–85; Russophilism, 95–97, 97–103, 108; and stagnation, 75–76, 98; and Stalinist ideology, 106–7; system power and stability, 90–94; and technological retardation, 71, 72, 79–80; and working class glorification, 89

Brezhnev, Leonid, similarities to Nikolas I of, 69–74

Bukharin, Nikolai Ivanovich, 126

bureaucracy, 120–21

cadre selection policy: in Brezhnev's regime, 41, 94, 107; and Gorbachev's ideology, 127–28, 134–35; overview of, 24–25; reform under Gorbachev of, 81–82; and Stalin's regime, 120

Caucasus, 48

Central Asia, 44, 45, 62

central planning: and consumers, 4–5, 6, 7, 15, 17, 18–19; and corruption, 1, 7, 19–22, 27, 28, 31–60, 78; and decision making, 5–9; and evaluation of performance, 8, 9–10, 22, 27, 28, 33, 51; in fictional literature, 17, 20, 34–35, 50–51; and the film industry, 7; and labor ethics changes, 51–52; and liberal ideology, 164–69; literary commentaries about, 7–8, 17; and mistakes and punishments, 6–7, 8; opposition to, 5–6, 18; and outside control, 25–26; and privatization, 186; and productivity, 20

Central Planning Committee, 6–7, 68, 81, 82, 87–88, 98, 138, 146, 152; and *perestroika*, 132, 138, 139, 140

Central Statistical Board, 68

Chernenko, N., 75, 131

China, 164

civil society, definition of, 161

Committee of Control, 25

Committee of Standards, 12

Committee of Supply and Ministries, 132

Congress of Soviet Film Makers, 7–8

conservative ideology: and Brezhnev's regime, 69, 87–104, 145, 146; and bureaucracy, 120–21; definition of, 144; and evaluation of performance, 144; in Gorbachev's regime, 140; and political risk, 145; and propaganda, 118; in Stalin's regime, 145–46

Constitution (1936), in Stalin's regime, 112

Constitution (1977), in Brezhnev's regime, 90, 151

consumers: in the Brezhnev regime, 42; and central planning, 4–5, 6, 7, 15, 17, 18–19; and evaluation of performance, 3–5, 18–20, 28; fictional literature about, 13–14; general population as, 27, 29; in Gorbachev's regime, 29; literary commentaries about, 5, 13–14, 16–17, 18–19; and material stimulation, 9–10; as outside control, 25; political elite as, 27, 29; and privatization, 165; and productivity improvement, 19; in Soviet debates, 14–19; in Soviet society, 3–4, 18–19

corruption. *See* central planning; privatization

Crimean War, 85–86

Czechoslovakia, 70, 89, 90, 148

Decembrist rebellion, 69, 73, 180
decentralization, and liberal ideology, 164–69
democratization, 109–14, 150–55, 163
Department of Science and Higher Education [Central Committee], 89
dominant class, 27, 28

economy: and Brezhnev's regime, 71; and the commodity-money relationship, 29; efficiency and productivity of, 14–19, 15; opposition to, 17–18; stagnation of, 85; status of in early 1980s, 61–65
Einstein, A., 116
El'tsin, B., 133–34, 135, 140, 150, 172
England, 72
environment, pollution of, 62
evaluation of performance: in agriculture, 24; and Brezhnev's ideology, 16, 21, 94, 103–4; by central planning, 8, 9–10, 22, 27, 28, 33–36, 51; by class divisions, 28; and conservative ideology, 144; and consumers, 3, 5, 18–20; control of, 16; and corruption, 33, 43, 45–46; criteria and indicators, 22–25; definition of, 2–3; failure because of the bureaucracy, 148; fictional literature, 9, 10, 14, 24, 34–35, 45; and Gorbachev's regime, 16; and liberal ideology, 144; literary commentaries about, 14, 15; and managers, 36, 45–46; and material stimulation, 9–10; overview of, 2–5; and political elite, 27; and privatization, 31–60; and property as efficacy control, 11–13; and quality and technical progress, 14, 20–21; of science, 23; Soviet society, 3, 4, 9, 19–22, 27; and Stalin's regime, 28, 50–51; and Western culture, 4

family relationships, 64

general population: as consumers, 27, 29; fictional commentaries about, 48–49
General Procurator, 42
General Secretary, 152
Georgia, 43
Germany, 72
glasnost (openness): and bureaucratic opposition, 149; definition of, 156; and ethnic issues, 176–77, 186; and intellectuals, 158; and liberal ideologies, 119–20; and mass media, 155–56, 157, 161; and party glorification decline, 148; and pluralism, 161–62; and political activity/reforms, 57–58, 180–182; revelations because of, 25, 26, 43, 44, 45, 47, 53, 60, 117, 139
Gogol, N., 181
Gorbachev, Mikhail: ideology of: and bureaucracy, 138, 146–48; and cadre selection, 134, and central planning, 149–50; and conservativism, 146; and decentralization, 138, 139; and democratization 137–38, 139, 151, 152–53, 181; and the family farm, 133, 136, 169, 178; film commentaries about, 139; and government elections, 154–55; and intellectualism, 136–38, 157, 158; and literary commentaries, 139; and manager elections, 153–54; and neo-Leninism, 125–26; and party glorification, 138; and *perestroika*, 128, 137–38, 139, 181; and privatization, 139; and propaganda, 118; reaction to, 135–36. *See also* liberal ideology
Gorbachev, Mikhail: regime of: and agriculture reforms, 71–72, 169, 177–78; and consumers, 16, 29; and corruption, 71, 72; criticisms of Brezhnev's regime by, 6, 70; and economic indicators/reform, 61, 127–28, 138, 157, 158; and evaluation of performance, 20;

goals of, 127–28; and industry and services reforms, 179–89; and intellectuals, 76, 127–28, 138, 157, 158, 180–81; literary commentaries about, 140; and outside control, 25, 26; and passivity, 53; and peasant reform, 178; and political elite, 8, 18, 75–76; and privatization, 42; and property, 11, 12; reforms during, 71–72, 77–78, 81–82, 118, 169, 177–78; similarity to Alexander II of, 69, 83–86; and social justice, 78; and Stakhanov movement, 111, 114, 131, 133, 159; and technological retardation, 80; and Western culture, 99
Gromyko, Andrei, 79, 135
Gulag, 36, 91, 115

Harvard Study Group, 49
Hayek, F. von, 8
health, decline in early 1980s of, 63, 65
Helsinki Agreement, 76
history, Soviet: fictional literature about, 161; and liberal ideology, 158–61; literary commentaries, 160, 161; Stalin's regime and terror, 159–60
Hitler, Adolf, 112
Hungary, 11, 13, 70, 164

Iakovlev, A., 146
ideology: before 1985, 75–86; purpose of, 118–20. *See also name of specific ideology or regime*
information: accuracy of, 119; literary commentaries about, 118; repression of, 67, 68, 70–71, 75, 88, 103–4
Inspectorate of Quality of Ministry of Trade, 25
Institute of Foreign Relations, 42
intellectualism: during Brezhnev's regime, 63, 73, 75–76, 89; during Gorbachev's regime, 76, 127–28, 138, 157, 180–81
Irkutsk [region], 48

Jews, 36, 132, 177, 180

Karelia [region], 42, 105
Kazakhstan [region], 42, 45, 175
KGB [Komitet Gosudarstvennoye Bezopastnosti], 36, 44, 67, 68, 71, 75, 77, 93, 112, 118, 130
Khrushchev, Nikita, and iconoclasm, 94
Khrushchev, Nikita: regime of: and cadre selection policy, 24; and central/regional power, 43; criticism of, 69; criticism of Stalin's regime by, 6, 8, 105; and evaluation of performance, 23; and Gorbachev's liberal ideology, 127; and information dissemination, 118; and intellectuals, 158; literary commentaries about, 106; and privatization, 41, 47; and reforms, 77; and Russophilism, 95; and Stalinist ideology, 106; and voluntarism, 88
Khudenko, I., 45–46
Kirgizia [region], 42
Kirtbai, I., 45–46
Kornai, J., 3–4, 13
Kornilov., A., 85
Krasnodar [region], 42, 44, 72, 93, 118
Kronstadt rebellion, 77

Leningrad, 36, 42
Lenin, Nikolai, 125–26, 131
liberal authoritarianism. *See* neo-Stalinist ideology
liberal ideology: and Brezhnev's regime, 69–74, 88, 95, 159; and the bureaucracy, 120–21, 144, 146–50; and central planning, 166; and civil society, 161–63; and class separation, 148; and collectivism, 167; and competition and monopolization, 165–66, 186; dangers to, 186; and the Decembrist rebellion, 69; and decentralization, 164–69; definition of, 144; and democratization, 138, 139, 140, 150–53, 164–65; and economic

reform, 177–80, 186; and egalitarianism, 171, 172; and ethnic issues, 173–77, 186; and evaluation of performance, 144, 148; and the family farm, 169, 178; and the Gorbachev's regime, 127–28, 140, 144–87; and government elections, 154–55; history of, 125–43; and intellectuals, 156–58; and managers, 153–54, 164–65; and mass media, 155–56; and the party, 127, 152, 154, 171–72; and paternalism, 163; and pluralism, 161–62, 186; and privatization, 166–70; and property, 166–70; and public opinion, 163; and Russophilism, 173–77, 187; and Soviet economics, 164–69; and Soviet history, 158–61; and the standard of living, 170–71; and state vs. private business, 168; supporting factors of, 185–86; and Western political system, 156. *See also perestroika* (restructuring)

Literaturnaia Gazeta, 17–18, 45–46, 56, 71, 80, 118

managers, 33–41
Marxism, 83, 84, 99, 100, 156, 171–72
material stimulation, 4, 9–10, 14–19, 45–46, 111
military: in evaluation of performance, 27, 28; and retardation and reform, 78, 79–81, 85–86
Ministry of Cinematography, 163
Ministry of Culture, 163
Ministry of Finance, 25
Ministry of Internal Affairs, 25, 68
Ministry of Popular Control, 25
Ministry of Water Supply, 7
Mises, L. von, 8
Moldavia, 42, 62, 93
Moscow, 9, 25, 45, 46, 65, 69, 72
Moscow Party Committee on Propaganda, 89

Moscow University, 7

Nash Sovremennik [organization], 175
neo-Stalinist ideology (liberal authoritarianism): and antidemocratism, 109–14; and Brezhnev's ideology, 109–10; and the bureaucracy, 146; in the early 1980s, 108–9; failure of, 185–86; film commentaries, 110; and glorification of the state, 110; and information dissemination, 119; and the intelligentsia, 114–17; literary commentaries about, 113, 117; and material stimulation, 111; overview of, 105–24; and Russophilism, 110, 173–74, 187; solidarity of, 186
neo-Stalinist ideology (repressive authoritarianism), definition, 144
New Economic Policy (NEP), 48, 77, 125, 148, 168
Nikolas I, regime of, 69–74, 75, 84–85, 179–80
Nixon, Richard, 102
Novorsibirk memorandum (1984), 128

Ogarkov, M., 79
Onisimov, A., 37–39
Orwell, George, 20
outside control, 25–26

Pamiat [organization], 174, 175, 176, 177
Party Congress: Eighteenth, 114, 121; Tenth, 125; Twentieth, 108, 133, 157; Twenty-second, 95. *See also* Party Congress, Twenty-seventh
Party Congress, Twenty-seventh: and cadre selection, 134, 175; and corruption, 59; and economic reform, 130; and the family farm, 169; and *glasnost*, 156; and Gorbachev's ideology, 146; and information dissemination, 155; and intellectuals, 128, 136; and

perestroika, 138; political atmosphere prior to the, 131–33; and privatization, 172; and social justice, 78; and technical retardation, 80
Pasternak, B., 73, 181
Penza [region], 72
perestroika (restructuring): and democratization, 138, 139, 140, 150, 153; and Gorbachev's ideology, 84, 137–38; and intellectuals, 84, 117, 157, 158; and pluralism, 161–62; and Russophilism, 108; and working class revolution, 148
Platonov, A., 181
pluralism, 161–62, 163, 186
Poland, 76, 148, 170
Politburo, 6, 60, 71, 77, 87, 105, 106, 129, 152, 168
political atmosphere, status of in early 1980s, 65–67
political destabilization, 78–79, 85
political elite, 1, 27, 29, 60, 67, 75–78, 82, 89, 127
political ideology: and fictional literature, 89; and leader glorification, 91; and social justice, 78, 79; and working class glorification, 89. *See also name of specific regime or ideology*
political risk, 145–146
political stability, definition, 78
Popov, G., 17, 36, 69, 84, 163
power: central and regional, 42–45; and corruption, 43–45
Prague Spring, 89
Pravda [newspaper], 25, 43, 88, 98, 128, 133, 172, 176; Gorbachev's speech criticizing Soviet economy and politics [February 13, 1986], 129–30, 133, 134, 135, 137
private, definition of, 32, 47, 57
privatization: and agriculture, 56, 57, 72, 168–69; and Brezhnev's regime, 40–41, 149; and bureaucracy, 149; and central planning, 186; and consumers, 165; and culture, 57; damages to society of, 1, 31; and education and health, 57; and evaluation of performance, 31–60; and the family, 54–55; and Gorbachev's ideology/regime, 56, 57, 139; and illegal activities, 40–42, 52, 53–56, 58–60, 63, 78, 79; and industry, 168, 169; and liberal ideology, 166–70; literary commentaries about, 55–56, 79; and political activity, 57–58; and propaganda, 118; and services, 57, 169; in Soviet society, 33, 46–51; and the United States, 97–103
productivity, 14, 20, 168
propaganda, 103–4, 117–20, 146, 159
property, 11–14, 166–70
public, definition of, 31–32, 47
Pushkin, A., 181

Reagan, Ronald, 79, 85
reform: of agriculture, 178; and Alexander I, 177–78; in Brezhnev's regime, 84–85, 132–33; economic, 127–28, 130–33, 164–69, 186; during Gorbachev's regime, 127–28, 130–33, 134, 164–69, 177–78, 186; and industry and services, 179–80; influence of leader's personality on, 83–84; and intellectuals, 157; liberal, 83–86; and military retardation, 85; and Nikolas I, 84–85; political, 180–82; and political destabilization, 85; by political elite, 76–78; preventive and reactive, 77–79; technological, 134
repressive authoritative ideology [neo-Stalinist ideology], 144
Rostov [city], 42, 72
Russophilism: and Andropov's ideology, 174; and Brezhnev's ideology, 89, 95–103; and collectivism, 160; and criticism of Western culture, 98; and the intelligentsia, 117; and liberal

ideology, 173–77, 187; literary commentaries about, 174, 175; and neo-Stalinist ideology, 173–74, 187

Sakharov, A., 70, 73, 74, 107, 132, 157
Siberia, 46, 72
Solzhenitsyn, A., 43, 70
Soviet society: animosity toward political elite in, 78; and class antagonism, 148; in the early 1980s, 61–74, 75–86; fictional commentaries about, 32–33, 46–47; flaws in, 1–2, 3, 4, 7, 9; and human rights movement, 76; the ideal model, 32; literary commentaries about, 4, 5, 46–47, 65; obstacles to progress in, 17–18; post-Stalinist, 10, 29, 40, 46–47, 51–56, 77; stagnation of, 71, 80, 155; Stalinist model as basis of, 1; and validity of status reports in early 1980s, 67–69; work attitudes in, 52
Stakhanov movement, 131, 133, 159
Stalinist ideology, 105–8, 105–24; and Andropov, 108; in Brezhnev's regime, 106–7; and disregard for human life, 111; in the early 1980s, 107–8; and the Khrushchev regime, 106; and Stalin's deeds, 105. *See also* neo-Stalinist ideology
Stalin, Josef: regime of: Bolshevism in, 126; and censorship, 47; and central/regional control, 42–43; and conservative ideology, 145–46; and democratization, 150, 151; and evaluation of performance, 28, 50–51; and fictional literature, 17, 50, 111; friendship in, 55–56; and information dissemination, 119; Khrushchev's criticism of, 6; and leader's personality glorification, 160; managers during, 35–39, 43; movie commentaries about, 91; and political ideology, 91; and reform, 77; in Soviet society, 46–51; strengths of, 1; terror in, 159–60
standard of living, 61–64, 78–79, 170–72
State Bank, as outside control, 25
State Committee of Movie Production, 7
State Inspection of Quality, 150
State Planning Committee, 98
Surgutskii, V., 46

Tadzhikistan, 21
Trotsky, Leon, 126
Turkmenistan, 21, 44

Ukraine, 42, 48, 62
Urals, 62
Uzbekistan, 21, 42, 43, 44, 72, 93

Watergate, 102
Western culture: access by dominant class and political elite to, 28; attraction of, 40, 65; contrast between Russian and, 1, 4, 19, 55–56, 65, 72, 83; and evaluation of performance, 19, 23; fictional literature about, 98; image during Brezhnev's regime of, 97–103; imports from, 29; literary commentaries about, 65, 98; and propaganda, 119
Western economy, 61–62, 166, 180
Winter Palace, 74
World War II, 47, 77, 96–97, 98, 108, 111–12, 114–15, 120–21

Young Communist League, 47
Yugoslavia, 11, 164

Zaslavskaia, T., 16–17, 108, 128, 132

ABOUT THE AUTHOR

VLADIMIR SHLAPENTOKH is currently a Professor of Sociology at Michigan State University. Previously he was a Senior Fellow at Moscow's Institute of Sociology where he conducted the first nationwide surveys of public opinion in the Soviet Union. He has published numerous books and articles both in the Soviet Union, before his emigration in 1979, and in the United States. Among his most recent books are *Soviet Public Opinion and Ideology* (Praeger, 1986), *The Politics of Sociology in the Soviet Union* (1987) and *The Public and Private Life of the Soviet People* (1988).